ALIEN CONTACT:

THE DIFFICULT TRUTH

by Derek Tyler

Front cover logo is a unit patch believed to belong to the NRO. The
Latin roughly translates to "All your base are belong to us". The
group of five stars and a single star are used to denote that the units
associated with this patch are based out of Area 51. Notice the
stylized Reptilian which holds the entire world in its hands.

DEDICATION

In a world filled with disinformation and deception, it is often difficult to know who to trust. Nowhere is this truer than in the world of ufology. At some point, however, we find we must place our trust in others if we wish to continue to learn and move forward. Those whom we choose to trust must be selected with great care and attention. They must be individuals of high integrity and proven credibility, as well as possessing a deep knowledge of the subject matter. In a perfect world, they should be among the best at what they do.

Though I utilize a vast number of sources during the performance of my work, there is a short list of people whom I consider to among the very best at what they do and whose work I consider to be invaluable contributions to the field of ufology. While I do not automatically assume that everything they say is written in stone, when they speak I listen carefully and try to learn all I can from them. Some of these people I am proud to call my friends, others I have never spoken with at all. But each of them has, through their public and private statements and their personal commitment to honesty and integrity, earned my trust, respect and gratitude.

It is with all those things in mind that I wish to dedicate this manuscript, this product of a lifetime of research and experience, to the following individuals, whose contributions to the field of ufology are, I believe, unsurpassed and whose hard work and generosity have made it possible for all of us to increase our knowledge.

Whether we realize it or not, we owe each of these people a great debt and we stand gratefully in their shadows, the beneficiaries of their hard work and the risks they have taken by coming forward. Some of them have paid for doing so with their lives.

Those who are already gone include William "Bill" Cooper, Dr. Karla Turner, Phil Schneider, Col. Wendelle Stevens, USAF Col. Gordon Cooper, Col. Philip J. Corso, Thomas Castello, Budd Hopkins and Boyd Bushman.

Those who are thankfully still alive at the time of this writing: James Bartley, Dr. Stanton Friedman, Richard Hoagland, Robert Lazar, William White Crow, David Sereda, Paul Sinclair, Robert Dean and Dr. Barrie Trower.

I also wish to thank those individuals who chose to speak with me on an off-the-record basis with the condition that their names, ranks or positions never be divulged. You have educated me about many things I would otherwise have never had the opportunity to learn. Thank you for your courage and your trust.

TABLE OF CONTENTS

INTRODUCTION

Do what thou Wilt shall be the whole of the Law.
-- Aleister Crowley

Welcome to my nightmare
I think you're gonna like it...
-- Alice Cooper

We live in a world of illusion. Nothing is what it appears to be. All we see are the surface layers, which form an intricate, interlocking system of falsehood and deception. Nothing really works the way we think it does. Most of the things we have been taught to believe are true turn out to be lies.

No one is immune from this. If you are reading these words then you, too, have been a victim of this deception. Many people will not want to believe that and they surely won't. I tell you that it is true anyway. The fact that you are unaware of it does not mean that it has not occurred. Rather, it serves as a demonstration of the subtlety and efficiency of a methodical, meticulously planned combination of disinformation and propaganda which has been specifically designed to prevent us from being able to see the underlying truths.

These truths hold great power. They confer an enormous advantage to those who are aware of them. For this reason, they are revealed only to a carefully selected few. Those who are made aware of them operate covertly, standing unseen in the shadows and working behind the scenes. From there, they pull the strings of power which allow them to control the world.

Though I have studied the subject of alien contact for about a half century, most of you have probably never heard of me. That is alright—it is the way I wanted it. Flying below the radar has in many ways served me well as I conducted my investigations into this subject. It has allowed me the ability to meet and speak with people who would not have been willing to speak with anyone whose primary concern was selling books rather than finding the truth. Although my activities have not gone unnoticed by the government, I have for the most part been left alone because I kept to myself rather than making a big noise about the things I have learned along the way.

That is about to change. I have spent most of a lifetime acquiring the knowledge and the skills necessary to write a manuscript such as this and have determined that it is now time to do so. Along the way, I have interviewed over three thousand abductees and contactees.

I have been abducted repeatedly by both aliens and the United States military. In addition, I have had at least a half-dozen sightings of what I feel certain were alien spacecraft which were unrelated to my abduction experiences.

I have invested countless hours in researching the subject of alien contact in all its forms and made use of every resource which was available to me. I have spoken with wise men and with fools. I have found truth and learned that it is almost always surrounded by multiple layers of deception. I have met with—and, in some cases, befriended—people who work deep within the world of black ops, a place where access to secret knowledge always carries great risk and often costs people their lives. I owe these people a great debt. This manuscript is, in part, my way of thanking them.

It requires time for the brain to fully process and understand things which represent radical new concepts and the restructuring of our belief systems. It requires additional time for the brain to create the new synapses which are necessary to incorporate this information and these cutting-edge ideas into a picture of reality. This picture ultimately turns out to be very different from the things we have been so carefully manipulated into accepting as indisputable truths.

Because the process of integrating this information involves the physical construction of new synapses within the brain, and because this manuscript is information-dense, there is no way to avoid or shortcut the amount of time this will require. I do not recommend that you try to read this entire book in a day or two. When you begin to feel overloaded with information, stop reading. Give your subconscious some time to process the information, then start again.

There are many aspects of alien contact that I wish to address and there is much information that I wish to share with my readers. There is far more to be said than any single volume can contain. Because of this fact, the book you hold in your hand is not intended to stand alone, but rather to be the first volume of a series I intend to write. The title of each book in the series will begin with the words "Alien Contact", followed by a different subtitle for each volume.

As will be demonstrated, the topic of alien contact is one which has insinuated itself into our society in numerous ways, many of which are not immediately obvious. I do not believe it is possible to gain a true understanding of the realities and implications which face us without examining and carefully considering a multitude of factors relating to it, many of which are commonly overlooked despite their importance and relevance. I do not intend to take any shortcuts or to omit any information which I feel may be found useful by others.

It is my intention to provide the reader with sufficient information to allow them to gain an understanding of this complex issue on both a personal level and as part of the so-called "Big Picture" which affects us all equally. To be able to do this efficiently, it will be necessary to read the entire series of books rather than just a single volume. Anything less will necessarily result in only a partial understanding of the situation, something which in my view is both unacceptable and highly dangerous, all things considered. The second volume of the series will be entitled "Alien Contact: Paradigm Shift". Further volumes will be completed and published as soon as possible.

It is my sincere hope that those who read this manuscript will find it to be interesting and that it will also prove to be useful to them as they go about their own investigation. I have done a tremendous amount of research before undertaking this project and, if one chooses to take advantage of it, I can save them a lot of time by not having to research things I have already checked out carefully and vetted to the best of my ability.

All that remains now is to extend my thanks to you. I recommend that you strap yourself in nice and tight…because I am about to take you on a ride that will make your head spin and your jaw drop, one which will challenge your notions of reality and forever change the way you view the world.

CHAPTER 1: CONTACT CLASSIFICATION

*"You notice, by the way, that we never have a meeting with an alien.
It's always an ENCOUNTER."*
-- Jack McDevitt

*"Don't talk to strangers,
'Cuz they're only there to do you harm
Don't write in starlight,
'Cuz the words might come out real."*
-- Ronnie James Dio

The late Dr. J. Allen Hynek, who was employed as part of the original Project Blue Book operation to officially debunk or explain away reported sightings of UFO's—and who is perhaps best known for being the person who came up with the "swamp gas" pseudo-explanation for sightings—eventually concluded that there was far more credible evidence for alien spacecraft than it was possible to explain away. Originally a UFO skeptic, he eventually became convinced that alien contact was in fact taking place and that a large number of the reported sightings involved what could only be described as intelligently-guided craft of unknown origin.

Dr. Hynek developed a method of classifying sighting and contact reports based on the type of contact which was said to be involved. His classification system, which was later expanded upon, is still in use today.

While most of us are familiar with the phrase "Close Encounters of the Third Kind" from having seen the movie of the same name, most people have never had an opportunity to see the entire list of classifications devised by Dr. Hynek. They would have no way of knowing what is meant by the phrase "Close Encounter of the Fifth Kind", for example, nor would they be aware that it is even possible to have a Close Encounter of the Seventh Kind.

For that reason, I have decided to open this manuscript by describing the contact levels as they are defined by Dr. Hynek's system. Its brilliance lies in its simple, easy to understand format, the fact that it includes all of the different possible types of encounters between humans and non-human intelligent beings and its effectiveness as a tool which can be utilized by the entire UFO community.

Here, then, is the system of classification which can used to describe the entire range of alien encounters in a way everyone can easily understand

Nocturnal Lights: One or more unidentified lights which are observed in the night-time sky.

Daylight Disks: One or more unidentified objects which are observed during daylight hours and which have a disc or oval shape.

Visual-Radar Sightings: Unidentified objects which are observed and picked up by either civilian or military radar units. Though radar occasionally malfunctions, capturing a sighting on radar adds to its overall credibility and serves as a second source of information about it.

Close Encounter of the First Kind: Visual sighting of an unidentified flying object which is less than five hundred feet away and which is seen clearly or shows considerable visual detail.

Close Encounter of the Second Kind: A close encounter in which a physical effect is alleged to have occurred. This can be interference with electronic equipment or automobile engines, physical traces left on the ground from exhaust or landing pads, physical paralysis of those nearby or sensations of heat, an animal reacting to it, radioactivity associated with the sighting or other physical effects.

Close Encounter of the Third Kind: A sighting where a physical entity is present. This can be a living creature, a robot, an android, a human being or anything which appears to be piloting a spacecraft or associated with one.

Close Encounter of the Fourth Kind: This is the level of contact associated with being abducted by either a UFO or its occupants and taken aboard the craft involuntarily.

Close Encounter of the Fifth Kind: This type of Close Encounter involves direct communication between a human and an extra-terrestrial being. It is usually thought of as being friendly, proactive, human-initiated contact but it would logically include contact which is initiated by a non-human entity. This level of contact is also often used to describe what are said to be telepathic or mind-to-mind communications with extra-terrestrials which may not be physically present at the time.

Close Encounter of the Sixth Kind: This refers to a contact event which results in the death of an animal or a human. Though most have never heard of Close Encounters of the Sixth Kind, they have occurred on numerous occasions and have then been made to immediately and permanently disappear by agents of the government and/or military. This is not just something which has occurred within the borders of the United States, it has taken place all over the world.

Close Encounter of the Seventh Kind: An encounter which results in the creation of a human/alien hybrid, either through sexual reproduction or the use of artificial methods. This refers to the conception of a hybrid, not its physical birth. Since most abduction events involve the harvesting of human reproductive cells at some point, it is possible that many people have had an encounter which might qualify as a CE7, but in which the conception of the hybrid may have occurred later, when they were not physically present.

CHAPTER 2: PROPER METHODOLOGY

"To hell with theory. Follow the evidence!"
-- Boyd Bushman, senior research engineer for Lockheed-Martin

"Who can we get on the case?
We need Perry Mason!
Someone to put them in place
Calling Perry Mason again!"
-- Ozzy Osbourne

Over the course of a lifetime of research I have developed a system of principles and techniques which I've found to be invaluable as I navigated the always-treacherous terrain of this field we have determined to study. I will not say that we have "chosen" to study it. Though I suppose there are a few who have done so, it seems to me that most people who decide to immerse themselves seriously in the study of alien contact came to do so for reasons which were for the most part beyond their control. They are originally motivated because they are witnesses or contactees themselves and want to learn the truth about what happened to them. They are compelled to find out just who it is that is visiting our world and why they have decided to come here.

Many people have seen strange craft which clearly were not from this world. Some have memories of being abducted by extra-terrestrial beings, usually in the middle of the night and from the presumed safety of their own bedrooms. Others have had some type of positive contact experience with extra-terrestrials.

An encounter with something which is clearly either an alien spacecraft or an alien being results in an immediate and permanent change to one's worldview. It brings about an epiphany, it causes a paradigm shift the likes of which they have never experienced. What were once only opinions and best guesses are replaced with direct personal experience and certain knowledge. A close encounter with an alien spacecraft or an alien being is an event which has the potential to change one's life forever.

In my own case, I had what I would describe as a spectacular and extended sighting of something which was beyond question an alien spacecraft. It lasted for 42 minutes and eventually came to involve a pair of USAF F-16 fighters which were scrambled to intercept the craft. Though they did not fire on it, they clearly considered the intruder to be unfriendly, unwelcome and dangerous. Their actions left no doubt that they were willing to attempt to shoot it down if that was determined to be necessary (a full description of this incident will be found in a later chapter).

From that moment on, I never again had to guess or wonder about the possibility of an extra-terrestrial presence on and around Earth. I was now in possession of direct first-hand experience which allowed me to know with absolute certainty the correct answer to the question. Because of this, it also allowed me to know with absolute certainty what the *incorrect* answer was.

A great many people will spend their entire lives being stuck on the question of whether an extra-terrestrial presence is a fact or a fantasy. Because of this, they will be unable to move forward to the point of asking the questions which, when one understands that alien contact is a reality and that we have *never* truly been alone here on this world, are far more important and relevant than any well-intentioned debate about whether alien contact has already been established can ever be.

It should be pointed out that there are few things the Powers That Be—a designation which will be used throughout the book to represent a combination of various high-level members of the political, military, intelligence, financial and corporate hierarchies who exercise control over all information associated with the subject of alien contact and whom I will refer to from this point on as simply the "TPTB"--like better than having people debate the existence of intelligent alien beings and the reality of alien contact. They, too, fully understand that these are questions which can easily occupy the entire span of a person's life without ever being resolved to their satisfaction—and that suits the purposes of TPTB quite well.

Regardless of whether this book proves to be popular with the public or not, I know it will sell at least a few copies because there are without question going to be certain members of the military-intelligence community who will make a point of reading it. If you happen to be one of those people, I hope that you will at least have the courtesy to give my book a good review before deciding to have me terminated.

When it comes to the process of researching, investigating and analyzing matters related to alien contact a special methodology is called for, one which is unlike anything we need or make use of in any other area of investigation. The bottom line truths about alien contact are far-reaching, profound, often highly strange and at times almost unimaginably complex. In addition, they are also carefully concealed, distorted and kept securely out of reach of those who wish to learn about such things.

Because these factors are always in play it is necessary to construct a research methodology which is unique to the subject. It must be sufficiently flexible to accommodate the treacherous and difficult conditions which surround this topic and which will be encountered time after time by any person who makes a serious effort to study it. At the same time, it must be logical, coherent and fact-based. Our investigation must be conducted in a manner which allows us to methodically fit the data together like the pieces of a jigsaw puzzle until we are eventually able to assemble a picture of reality which, though perhaps not perfect in every detail, we can have a high degree of confidence is at least reasonably accurate.

We are forced to traverse terrain which is quite literally a battlefield. It is not something which becomes easier with practice. Rather, the more knowledge one acquires the more difficult it becomes to accept the apparent realities of the situation. We are required to completely revise our long-held and traditional ideas about who we are—a paradigm shift which proves to be more than many people are capable of.

The situation becomes infinitely more difficult when one is forced to contend with the implementation of the most intricately-planned psychological warfare operation in history. A subject which already represents the most complex and challenging field of study ever undertaken has been surrounded by layer upon layer of deceptions, each designed to prevent us from being able to find answers to even the most basic questions.

There is nothing relating to alien contact which has not been distorted, falsified or manipulated to serve the purposes of others.

Everything from movies and television to educational policies and scientific investigation has been targeted.

All those things and more have long been under the control of the people who control access to the unfiltered information. Those who occupy positions at or near the top of the food chain in this regard are able to operate completely without restriction or the need to work within any type of moral guidelines.

It is believed that there are less than twenty people in the world who are allowed such full access, and that the actual number may be closer to twelve than twenty. It requires a security clearance of a level so high that it does not even officially exist. The only people with the ability to accurately identify the members of this ultimate "short list" are those whose names are also on it, and their actions are protected by a black hole of secrecy so deep that nobody can penetrate it.

For all practical purposes, they are invisible and untouchable, above the law and accountable to no one. None of them have been elected to office or judged by the public as worthy to be entrusted with access to that level of knowledge and power. That fact represents a great danger to the rest of us.

You may rest assured that all the conventional methods of investigating the subject of alien contact have been identified long ago. Every one of them has been carefully analyzed. Multiple ways have been found to make sure that anyone who approaches a little too closely to the truth can be dealt with quickly by well-practiced professionals who are extremely good at what they do.

Nobody ever said that this was going to be easy, and it certainly isn't. In fact, it can be said that attempting to learn the truth about alien contact is the most difficult task a person could attempt. It can occupy a lifetime and still have no guarantee of success.

For those who are determined to do so anyway, there are a number of important concepts which must be kept in mind throughout the course of their research. My experience has taught me that if a person neglects or fails to pay attention to these things, they will be swiftly led into error and the result will be the waste of their precious time and an inaccurate view of the situation as it exists in objective reality.

It is because of this that I urge each of you to think carefully about the things I am about to suggest. Over time, I have developed a specific set of rules and guidelines which I feel are necessary to a proper investigation. When combined, these procedures and techniques will be found to work quite well and deliver results which you can be reasonably certain are not terribly far off the mark. They have worked for me and they will work for you, too, if you follow them consistently.

1. START FROM ZERO!

Forget everything you think you know about the subject and open your mind to new possibilities. Much of what you have been taught about this subject, even by those who are considered among the best in the field, is riddled with errors and shot through with misinformation and inflexibility. Do not assume you already know the answers—most people, if the truth were known, do not even ask the right questions. If one does not ask the right questions, it is all but impossible to come up with answers which will be of any practical use. Start from zero, thus allowing your brain to absorb the voluminous amount of information which will be coming your way in the most efficient and comprehensive way possible. You will find it to be quite helpful if you do.

2. ACCUMULATE AS MUCH DATA AS POSSIBLE!

Valid, credible data is the critical component of any legitimate investigation and you simply cannot have too much of it. There is a wide and diverse array of information which is available to those who are willing to make the effort to locate it. The success of our investigation will ultimately depend upon the quantity of data we accumulate and our ability to fit it together in a way that makes sense. It stands to reason, therefore, that the more data we have available, the higher the probability that it contains the valuable truths we are hoping to find.

Data comes in many forms and can be gathered from a wide variety of sources. It can take the form of witness statements, photographic evidence, radar or sonar records, testimony which comes from whistle blowers or insiders, relics or drawings from the ancient world or personal experiences. It can be obtained from books, magazine articles, personal interviews, radio or television broadcasts, historical records, diaries or in other ways.

One of the surest ways for an investigation to end in failure rather than success is to provide it with an insufficient amount of data from which to draw accurate conclusions. The more pieces of information we can bring to bear on the problem, the better our chances of having some of it provide the answers we are looking for or help to fill in the gaps in our personal knowledge.

The most important—as well as by far the most time-consuming—aspect of any researcher's job is that of data accumulation. It is quite literally a task that never ends. It is also a responsibility which cannot be neglected. There are no shortcuts when it comes to gathering the information on which the success of your investigation will depend. It will require dedicated time and effort from everyone involved, and additional data should be continually added throughout the course of the investigation. We must utilize every resource we can manage to find and our goal should be to eventually acquire a veritable mountain of data. It is this which will provide us with the means to discover the truths we seek, and nothing else can ever substitute for it.

3. ALL SOURCES ARE NOT CREATED EQUAL!

When one considers the number and types of available sources of information concerning the topic of UFO's and alien contact, it quickly becomes apparent that there is a wide disparity in terms of credibility and reliability from one source to the next. Some sources give every indication of being solid and dependable, while others give the appearance of being little more than frauds, con artists or lunatics.

There is no value whatsoever in collecting or utilizing information which comes from unreliable or dishonest sources, and we should make every effort to minimize the amount of time we spend in that manner. It can often be quite difficult, especially for the beginner, to correctly identify which sources are credible and which are not.

Differentiating between them is a major problem when one is first starting out on their research, because they have no readily-available means of comparing information coming from various sources and no experience to guide them in terms of being able to tell who is likely to be speaking the truth and who is likely to be engaged in disinformation or perpetrating a fraud. Even people with many years of experience sometimes make mistakes in this area, and when one is a beginner they will inevitably find that they are often mistaken and often misjudge the value and credibility of witnesses.

There is no avoiding this, unfortunately. The only solution to the problem is to continue moving forward, increasing your knowledge as you go. As you do, your ability to accurately judge which information is valid and useful and which is nothing but white noise that will slow you down will continually improve. There never comes a point where one is foolproof and never makes a mistake...but it does get significantly easier with time and you'll find that your batting average will eventually go way up compared to what it was at the beginning.

4. UTILIZE MULTIPLE SOURCES!

Collect information from as many sources as possible, the more varied the better. Combine witness statements with radar records, voice transmissions and photos or films. The more independent and unrelated sources you can come up with which agree with each other, the greater the possibility that they will prove to be correct and reliable.

Though it is certainly possible for a single source with sufficient access or experience to provide you with information which is both accurate and new to you, such sources must be vetted with great care before investing your belief in them. Anyone can lie and there are a variety of reasons they may be doing so, some of which may very well be unknown to you.

This is not to say you should dismiss such information out of hand, because sometimes the most unlikely-seeming people or the most trivial-appearing pieces of data can yield valuable clues which can assist you in your investigations. When they come your way, though, take them with a grain of salt and attempt to find other unrelated sources which corroborate and support them. You simply cannot have too much corroborating evidence or too much valid data. Evidence and data are, after all, the only reliable things you will have in the end from which to piece together an accurate picture of reality. And accuracy is what we seek here, to the best of our abilities.

5. QUESTION EVERYTHING!

Never be afraid to ask questions and examine closely any subject, idea or accepted truth. Some of the things we have been taught to believe are established scientific truths turn out to be nothing more than carefully-constructed fabrications. They have been sold to the public, incorporated into our educational systems and repeated constantly until for all practical purposes they "become" the truth...but they have never really been true at all. We are still very far from being able to claim that we possess the final answers and the ultimate truths. Until we do, everything is open to question!

6. IDENTIFY AND REJECT DISINFORMATION!

Disinformation is ever-present when dealing with these subjects, as will be discussed later in this manuscript. It is multi-layered, prevalent everywhere and undertaken by professionals who are subtle, intelligent, experienced and who work in teams. A serious researcher must always keep the awareness of disinformation in mind and must make the effort to study, understand and be able to identify it in its many forms whenever it is encountered. Because of the tremendous effort put forth to confuse, deceive and mislead the public on these matters it is very often difficult to tell the difference between disinformation and actual truth.

With experience this task becomes easier—but there will never be a time when one is immune to its pernicious influence and vast, well-financed tentacles. It is virtually certain that there are times any researcher will be taken in by one or another type of disinformation—accept it, it is part of the inevitable price of seeking the truth. When this happens and you eventually become aware of it, admit truthfully that you were fooled, resolve not to let it happen again and to be more careful in the future.

7. DISREGARD ALL GOVERNMENT STATEMENTS!

Never has there been a time when any official statement by the American government regarding the subject of UFO's and aliens has been truthful. Every such statement is in fact a carefully manufactured and vetted piece of disinformation which is designed to conceal as much as possible while revealing as little as possible. The purpose is never to inform the public of the truth, it is always to confuse, distract, deceive and misinform them instead. Every single official announcement regarding anything to do with extra-terrestrials is intentionally deceptive and is designed specifically to steer you away from the truth of the matter. No matter what any President or any agency of the government or military may say about the topic of alien contact, it will always be a lie. Never forget that.

8. NEVER MODIFY THE DATA!

Modifying data to suit one's own opinion or for the sake of convenience is nothing less than a form of propagating disinformation and it is something no serious researcher should ever consider doing. Modified data immediately becomes useless as a study tool or valid resource and must be discounted in importance or rejected in its entirety by any serious researcher.

The individual who is responsible for making the decision to modify the data in the first place loses credibility at the same time. In serious or important instances of intentional data modification, the person responsible for it may suffer the fate of never again being taken seriously by his peers. That is a price which is unacceptable; it is far too high to even consider paying.

Our personal credibility is one of the most valuable assets we will ever possess and something we must spend a lifetime to acquire and keep in good condition. It is far too important a thing to toss away carelessly or to waste.

Personal considerations aside, as researchers the data is really all we have. If it is arbitrarily modified by anyone for any reason its value immediately becomes suspect. The only way to produce accurate conclusions is to base our analyses on accurate, unaltered data. If we should choose for some reason to modify or intentionally falsify any of the data, we become part of the problem rather than part of the solution and lose all rights to describe ourselves as honest and unbiased researchers in search of truth. Engaging in such behavior is not only dishonest, it is foolish and harmful to the field of ufology in general. Never allow yourself to be tempted into making a mistake of that kind.

9. ALL DATA MUST BE ACCOUNTED FOR!

If data has been verified or can reasonably be presumed to be accurate, it then must be included in any factual analysis and must be accounted for in an honest and reasonable manner. The fact that certain data may be inconvenient or may point away from certain desired conclusions is irrelevant. We are not here on a mission of convenience; we are here to search for and try our best to understand the truth, whatever it may turn out to be. As far as there being "desired" conclusions, there are none. If you desire a certain outcome, you have already broken one of our rules and must either re-evaluate your analysis or disqualify yourself as an investigator due to personal bias. It could lead to a distortion of the facts or an unreasonable tendency to give one conclusion or another weight as evidence which it did not deserve.

10. CONSIDER THE WEIGHT OF THE EVIDENCE!

When studying the topics of UFO's and alien contact, it is crucial that we be willing and able to make use of the standards of reasonable doubt and preponderance of the evidence. These are the same standards used within our court system. We must carefully consider the combined weight of the testimony of individuals who are either known or can be presumed to be honest, credible, competent witnesses.

This is not to say that just because several people say the same thing it must automatically be true. That is clearly not the case at all. Just because a dozen people report that they saw a herd of pink cattle flying over their houses does not make it true. A statement like that violates logic and common sense, not to mention physics.

On the other hand, that is not the type of testimony we are going to get from credible, honest, competent people who have no apparent motivation to lie. When multiple witnesses come forward from the black ops world and tell the same story, there is far more reason to think they are probably speaking the truth. The likelihood that they have all independently invented the same lies, or that they have all decided to conspire together to deceive the public is extremely remote and cannot seriously be thought to represent the truth.

Even if the things they report sound bizarre to us—in fact, *especially* if they sound bizarre—we should by no means be quick to reject them. After all, these are people who were in a position to know—they had access to information and technology far beyond the reach of the average citizen and they most likely worked with it every day as part of their job.

An example of this would be when someone comes forward claiming to be a former military officer who was attached to a covert ops unit which worked with classified technology. He claims that the American government has access to technology which allows it to travel through time, both forward and backward. He does not know whether this is technology which was developed by the military itself or was obtained from extra-terrestrials. He also claims that the American government utilizes anti-gravity technology in some of its classified stealth aircraft projects.

As the only alleged witness who makes these claims, we cannot in good conscience presume that they represent the truth. This does not, however, imply that we think he is lying. We have no way of knowing one way or the other, therefore we can make no presumptions about that.

What he is telling us, bizarre as it sounds when we hear it, is something we are in no position to definitively say is impossible. It may sound to us as though it is highly unlikely...but "unlikely" and "impossible" are very different things.

Without additional confirmation from other independent sources, we cannot reasonably accept his statements as being true. We cannot make the presumption that the military can travel through time and utilize anti-gravity propulsion systems. Anti-gravity is, after all, a force which conventional science assures us does not actually exist.

But we must make note of his testimony anyway and set it aside as something which, though it is unconfirmed and we consider it to be unlikely, is not impossible and could even be true for all we know. After all, the military is known to have a lot of highly-advanced technology. We are hardly qualified to start an argument about the technical difficulties involved in constructing a time machine, nor does it seem advisable to insist that the fact that we have never heard of an anti-gravity engine proves that they do not exist.

If, on the other hand, a half dozen people who are unknown to each other come forward over the next few years, each claiming to have worked in black ops and each testifying that they have personal knowledge that our military has either built or been given a working time machine and that some of our stealth aircraft utilize anti-gravity propulsion systems, we have a very different situation.

Now we are faced with the choices of either assuming all these people just happened to invent the same set of lies attempting to get attention for themselves, or that we have multiple sources within the black ops community who tell the same story about time travel and anti-gravity engines because those things are real and they have personally seen and worked around them.

Are they all lying? We have no reason whatsoever to assume they are all lying about this, or that any of them would be motivated to do so. To reject their testimony without having a valid cause to do so would be a violation of proper investigative procedures. It might also do a great injustice to a group of men who have made the decision to risk their lives by coming forward and are speaking the truth, as well as cause us to arbitrarily disbelieve in technologies which exist and which we would like to learn everything we can about.

It turns out, as will be discussed later, that both anti-gravity and technology which allows time travel actually *do* exist, are in the possession of our military and are used daily. By the standards of conventional science, these things would be very difficult indeed to believe in, regardless of how many witnesses might come forward asserting otherwise.

This is an example of allowing our thinking to be constrained by the current level of our own civilian technology and scientific beliefs. Alien technology, of course, is not limited by those things at all. In this case, their advanced level of scientific understanding has revealed a force we were completely unaware of and their technology has given them the ability to do something which many people would believe is impossible.

By limiting ourselves to conventional knowledge, we would make the false assumption that it cannot be surpassed by things we have yet to discover. We would also have arbitrarily dismissed the testimony of a witness who risked his life to try to inform us that such discoveries have already been made by someone else.

11. AVOID USING THE WORD "IMPOSSIBLE"!

Following on from the previous point, we are not qualified to know what is or is not possible in this vast and infinitely complex multiverse we call home. We must never assume we are. Never assume that just because something is strange, unexpected, inconvenient or bizarre that it must be false. Be open to new ideas and consider them carefully before rejecting them.

Many things exist to be found which will be completely new to us. They will seem utterly strange and represent capabilities well beyond our own. That does not mean they are impossible, it only means they are impossible for *us*. That is a very important difference and one is wise to always keep it in mind. There is deep truth in that statement and the more one learns the more one realizes just how accurate it really is.

12. CORRECT YOUR MISTAKES!

All humans make mistakes from time to time. It is unavoidable and no one is immune. If you study this subject in depth you will occasionally be fooled by something. There may be photos you think are legitimate which are proven to be fakes, aspects about aliens or alien contact you believe to be true but which later information invalidates and falsifies, etc.

It may be helpful to keep in mind that people of genius make mistakes just like everyone else does. They may perhaps make less mistakes on average than others will, but there is no genius who will ever tell you they are incapable of making mistakes or that they never make one. The difference between a genius and a non-genius is not that one makes mistakes and the other doesn't, it is in what happens after a mistake is made. A genius will usually be able to recognize that a mistake has been made much sooner than others will. The genius will then locate the mistake, determine why it was made and then ensure that the same mistake is never made again for the same reason.

It is quite possible for people to never realize they have made a mistake at all. It is an unfortunate fact that some people will go through their entire lives believing, for example, that a commercial passenger jet can strike the Pentagon without leaving any trace of airplane wreckage or passenger's bodies in the debris. A genius would typically reject such a scenario immediately as being so unlikely as to be unworthy of serious consideration.

We must always be double and triple-checking the conclusions we draw and we must be willing to modify them as we go whenever we identify mistakes or uncover new evidence which invalidates them. The sheer volume of information which exists to be found combined with the inherently complex, multi-layered and difficult-to-understand nature of the topic in general will ultimately require us to re-asses and update our positions on many things.

It seems to me that if one has the same beliefs about alien contact now as they had two years ago, they have either failed to identify their mistakes or two years of research have been largely wasted. If, for example, one has accumulated sufficient evidence to prove to their satisfaction that an alien race known as the Reptilians does in fact exist, it is not particularly useful to continue to seek additional data which supports this belief. While it is true that we can never have too much corroborating evidence, it is also true that our time would have been better spent seeking out information which would allow us to have a clearer understanding of their motivations and agenda than in trying to expand a list of twenty items which serve to prove their existence to a list of thirty. The concept of accumulating data must be balanced by keeping in mind that life is short, there is much to be learned and wasted time is something none of us can afford.

This is a tricky and treacherous path we tread here—we are surrounded by traps and disinformation in every conceivable form. The important thing is not that we have made a mistake, but that we realize it and modify our beliefs accordingly.

It is not a crime to be mistaken sometimes. It happens to us all--it happened to me and it will happen to you, too. It is, however, a crime to *continue* to be mistaken after better information has become available to you.

13. FOLLOW THE EVIDENCE!

Don't be afraid of encountering new concepts or surprising destinations. Facts are facts, logic is logic and they should be followed to their reasonable conclusions. We have no choice but to let them guide us without regard to any personal beliefs we may have about the directions they take us in. Facts must always over-rule opinions or hopes.

14. THE TRUTH IS ALL THAT MATTERS!

It makes no difference what our opinions about certain things may be when the goal of an investigation is to uncover and illuminate the pure, unvarnished truth. It doesn't matter whether we like it, agree with it, think it's inconvenient and best ignored or find ourselves unable to come to grips with it rationally or emotionally. Those things have nothing whatsoever to do with facts or truth—and those are the only things we are interested in dealing with here. Facts and truth are all we are seeking and all we should properly care about considering if we are to have any hopes of reaching valid conclusions based on solid knowledge.

Try to never be personally invested in the answer to a question— if you are, if you favor one answer more than another, it will make it tempting to either ignore the data or skew it somehow until it is more in line with what you think it "ought to be". Nobody cares what you or I think it *ought to* be. Nobody *should* care. This isn't an opinion poll; it is an objective investigation. Opinions are subjective--we are concerned only with the facts here.

Don't ever let emotions, vanity, stubborn resistance or denial cloud your judgment. The truth is all that matters. If we are able to find it, we will then be able to make our best assessments and know better what—if anything—we should be doing about it.

15. THINK OUT-OF-THE-BOX!

Out of the box is what this stuff is all about. We are dealing with technologies which are literally beyond science fiction here. We are dealing with races which are so much more advanced than we are that we cannot even begin to comprehend the magnitude and scope of their achievements and abilities. On Earth, we went from the horse and buggy to landing on the moon, sending probes to the stars and connecting the entire world together via the internet in about a hundred years. We went from the Wright Brothers to the SR-71 Blackbird. People who literally rode a horse and buggy to school were still alive to watch men orbit the Earth, something they could never have imagined would be possible when they were younger.

Some of the extra-terrestrial civilizations which are known to our government are believed to have had interstellar travel technology for millions of years. Not only that, they are quite a bit more intelligent than we are.

This puts us at a severe disadvantage in terms of our ability to estimate the capabilities of these civilizations or the limits and constraints they may be operating under. We have no way of speculating about such things with any reasonable hope of accuracy--we don't have the tools to even know where to begin. Human civilization is measured in thousands of years. We can't even comprehend the scale of a number like a million, much less project forward to what an alien race could do with millions of years of interstellar travel under its belt. The truth is not only stranger than we imagine, it is stranger than we *can* imagine. The only thing we can be certain of is that these hyper-advanced civilizations will understand and utilize principles of science which are completely unknown to us. Because of this, they will surely routinely do many things which we currently believe to be impossible.

It is for this reason that we must be willing and able to step back from the ordinary, to think outside the box. That box is useless to us here. All it contains is what we already think we know—and no matter who we are, much of what we think we know is surely wrong. If one is unable to launch their mind out of "the box", they will never be able to comprehend these truths, many of which bend or shatter our commonly-held views of reality.

16. SIGHTINGS CAN BE EXPLAINED IN FIVE WAYS!

Every UFO sighting has a cause—there is something there which is responsible for it. There are only five possibilities which could account for it and all five must therefore be considered honestly by any reasonable person who seeks the truth.

The first possible explanation is a report by a psychotic or delusional witness. Of the five possibilities, this one is the least likely to be correct--but it does occasionally happen. When it does, it is usually not too difficult to identify it as such.

The second possibility is that it is a misinterpretation of a natural object or event. This includes things such as meteors, stars, airglow, planetary bodies such as Venus and any other natural processes or objects which might result in a sighting. This is often determined to be the source of sighting reports, despite the best efforts and intentions of the witnesses. There are natural objects which can manifest as strange lights in the sky. They can sometimes be—or appear to be—in motion and are quite capable on occasion of fooling even experienced and competent observers.

The third possibility to consider are man-made objects. These include all types of ordinary and exotic aircraft, satellites, balloons, flares and anything else produced by humans which can reasonably be thought to be responsible for a sighting. This category has become more common with the passage of time because our military has become increasingly capable over the years of producing and operating vehicles of exotic design and flight characteristics. It has never been easier than it is today to misidentify a craft of human military origin as an alien spacecraft.

This is made even more problematic because the black ops programs have increasingly had the ability to utilize alien-based technology which has been reverse-engineered and incorporated into a variety of military aircraft. It is also the case that there are alien spacecraft which have been recovered from crash sites and eventually returned to flying condition as well as a number which have been given to the United States government either as gifts or as part of a technology transfer that was included in the terms of a secret diplomatic agreement.

There is no question that many UFO sightings can be accounted for by invoking this possibility. It is also true, however, that any UFO sighting which involves a military aircraft which is making use of technologies or capabilities which originated with non-human beings can correctly be described as a sighting of an alien craft. Though not manufactured by an alien race, it displays performance characteristics which are far beyond anything human technology can produce. In terms of providing some type of proof of alien contact, a sighting of this kind should be considered a "hit" even though the craft may belong to the military and be piloted by humans.

The fourth category is that of an intentional hoax. This includes false statements, altered films or photographs, constructing objects which appear to be UFO's when photographed but are not and the creation or manipulation of images or events using computer graphics. As the capabilities of personal computers have increased, it has become more and more difficult to tell the difference between legitimate films and those showing objects which were designed with advanced software and editing techniques. Indeed, some people now create such film clips as a hobby.

While hoaxes have always been present, they have never accounted for more than a small percentage of sighting reports. That percentage is probably higher now than in past years due to the widespread availability of programs such as Photoshop. Even so, it by no means can account for most sighting reports and often such hoaxes are not particularly difficult for a careful observer to spot.

Mainstream science has at its disposal all the world's top experts and equipment when it comes to identifying natural or man-made objects or debunking hoaxes. If a sighting can be compellingly explained as belonging to one of these three categories, mainstream science has the tools necessary for the job. Many times, that is precisely what happens. A good ufologist will support the exposure of hoaxes and the explanation by conventional means of sightings to which such explanations apply. We are not interested in hoaxes or sightings of conventional aircraft other than for purposes of identifying them as such and keeping them separated from reports which cannot be explained in conventional terms.

This brings us to the fifth and final possible explanation for a sighting report. It is often the case that a sighting occurs which cannot be accounted for by any reasonable conventional explanation. An example of this might be an unidentified object operating outside of the atmosphere which is seen and filmed by the astronauts aboard one of our spacecraft. It is observed to change speed and direction in ways which cannot be explained by gravitational effects or other natural processes.

It cannot be identified as a craft belonging to another nation, nor is there any reasonable cause to presume that a man-made object is present in that location. It is clearly not a natural object, since no natural process we are aware of could allow for the observed behavior to occur to a piece of space junk or an incoming meteor. There is no reason to believe that the film has been modified or that the astronaut's observations are inaccurate. There is also no reason to presume that we have suddenly gone into the business of putting delusional psychotics or compulsive liars aboard our spacecraft and sending them into orbit.

In this situation, the only explanation which remains is that the object is an intelligently guided spacecraft of unknown—and presumably non-human—origin. To simply classify it as "unknown" is a cop out and a violation of proper scientific methodology. When there are exactly five possible explanations and four of them cannot be correct, the fifth possibility is all that remains.

In the absence of a better explanation which fits the data, it must be presumed to be an alien spacecraft and classified as such. There is no other choice, if accuracy and intellectual honesty are applied to a proper method of scientific inquiry. To attempt to identify it as anything else at this point is nothing more than obfuscation, a refusal to accept the evidence as it exists. It is an arbitrary departure from both logic and a legitimate search for the truth. It *must* be classified as a spacecraft of non-human origin, because no other explanation can account for it. By following proper investigative procedures, the data itself has led us to the correct answer.

17. THIS INVESTIGATION IS NOT ABOUT YOU!

All of us have egos, and ego is among the most damaging and least helpful aspects one can bring to bear in this matter. Always make sure you keep firmly in mind the fact that this is NOT about you, it is about the search for truth and understanding on behalf of the entire human race. None of us individually can ever have a monopoly on truth. All of us make mistakes, all of us have gaps in our knowledge and others will have a better understanding of certain things than we do.

Keep ego out of it, keep the search for unbiased and valid truth always the top priority. Personal ego gratification must be dead last on the list of things you need, want or can afford to carry along with you as you go. If defending your opinion or promoting your latest project becomes more important than spreading the truth, you are almost certainly doing more harm than good.

18. KEEP AN OPEN MIND!

As the quantity of information available to us increases, it becomes easy and natural to analyze it in a piecemeal fashion and to draw conclusions after doing so. This is a dangerous habit and one which can easily lead us astray. No matter which aspect of alien contact we may happen to be researching at any given time, it is almost always the case that multiple possibilities exist in terms of the ultimate objective answers we seek. By investing our confidence or belief in a specific solution, we risk closing ourselves off to the possibility that it may in fact be another answer which is correct.

Our goal is to eventually arrive at a position which allows us to draw accurate conclusions. The ability to do so requires us to first accumulate a prodigious amount of knowledge and experience. Attempting to draw conclusions which are based on insufficient evidence defeats the purpose of the investigation and leaves us with answers which do not jibe with reality. Clearly that is not something we can afford to allow.

How will we be able to know with certainty when we have reached the point that we can properly analyze the data and then draw conclusions we can have a high degree of confidence in? That is a difficult question to answer in a meaningful way, since the answer will vary from person to person.

Based upon my personal experience, I can tell you this: at some point, when enough pieces to this massively complex puzzle have been correctly assembled, you will find that many others seem to quickly fall into place on their own.

Data you add will be seen to fit in neatly with data you had before, in effect becoming much like a puzzle piece that fits into place in a way which is in harmony with the pieces you have already assembled together.

When you find that you are at this point, do not take it to mean that your learning is now at an end—it's not. But it is at this point that you have earned the right to feel confident about your ability to correctly analyze the situation and to draw conclusions which have a high probability of being accurate.

19. NEVER STOP LEARNING!

No matter how much we may learn about alien races and cultures we will never be able to know more than a small portion of all there is to be known about the subject. There will always be far more which is unknown to us than there is which is known. There will never be a time when we have learned all a person can about it, or are so well-informed that we don't need to keep current anymore and can rest on our laurels. Nobody is so good that they can't get better, nobody is so smart that they have it all figured out. We should never stop trying to increase our knowledge and improve our understanding.

It is a vast and complex tapestry which makes up the fabric of reality. The full array of possibilities regarding extra-terrestrial contacts and its implications reach far into our past and will in large part determine our future as a species. The more we can learn, the better able we will be to understand and effectively deal with the situation.

We stand on the shoulders of those who have come before us. Those who come after us will stand on ours. Let us do our very best, then, to make certain that the legacy we leave to them is one of careful study, accurate descriptions, flawless logic and penetrating analysis of whatever it may be that we learn. Let us always remember that no matter how much we accomplish, much will be left undone and it will be the job of those who follow in our footsteps to advance the knowledge and expand the scope of what is known. There is no time for vanity or egotism, no excuse for disseminating or promoting false ideas or disinformation and no limit to what may be possible for beings of sufficiently-advanced technology and intelligence.

We are small fish in an infinitely large pond and we are surrounded by alien intelligences whose capabilities and achievements are well beyond anything we can imagine. It is no exaggeration to say that the existence of our entire species is dependent upon our relationships with extra-terrestrials. It may ultimately be out of our hands entirely, something which is based on an arbitrary—and possibly capricious—decision on the part of extra-terrestrial visitors whose patience for human folly has reached an end and whose agenda has absolutely nothing to do with our best interests.

The way we conduct ourselves when interacting with hyper-advanced extra-terrestrials will very likely decide our fate in the end. It is likely to take place under similar conditions to those which apply when a primitive tribe is discovered in the jungle and is suddenly forced to deal with a superpower: if they do everything right, we might allow them to continue to exist. Maybe we would even offer them assistance in some ways. If, however, they make us angry or happen to be living on land that contains resources we covet, we can make their village disappear in a matter of minutes—and we might just do so.

Any interactions between ourselves and non-human visitors, whether as individuals or nations, may reflect upon all of humanity for all we know. Our decisions must be considered with extreme care and carried out only after a great deal of reflection and diligent thought. We cannot afford to make mistakes when our survival depends upon the choices we make. We must not allow individuals who are unconcerned with our safety and welfare—people who are literally willing to kill us for speaking our minds--to make decisions which will determine our fate.

As researchers, it is our responsibility to break new ground, to fearlessly venture into new territory without any way of being certain what we will find there, to show dedication and courage in the face of ridicule, intimidation and all manner of threats and to never allow personal interests or monetary concerns to limit the free flow of information or to distort the truth if we can avoid it.

Despite any disagreements that we may have with each other, it is an indisputable fact that we are ultimately all in this together and that all our fates are inextricably linked. With that in mind, I urge each of you to be thorough, accurate, logical and unwavering in your dedication to something which is far larger and more important than any of us can ever hope to be. I believe that by working together we can prove that we are up to the challenges we face. It is a goal which is well worth taking risks for and which will ensure a life of unending fascination filled with possibilities which are profound beyond anything I can imagine.

CHAPTER 3: SIGHTINGS CHECKLIST

*"Every day in the U.S.A., our radar instruments capture objects of
form and composition unknown to us."*
-- Astronaut Gordon Cooper, speaking at the United Nations

*"I wear my sunglasses at night
So I can, so I can look on
The light that blinded my eyes."*
-- Corey Hart

Under normal conditions, one has no way of knowing in advance
when and where a sighting will occur or what form it will take. When
a sighting takes place, it is almost always a surprise to those who
happen to witness it. Sightings are unpredictable by nature and
involve a wide variety of possible manifestations.

The first thing to keep in mind is that seeing something unusual in
the sky does not necessarily mean you are looking at an alien
spacecraft—in most instances that will not be the case. Statistics are
unreliable: considering that the source which generates them is often
the United States Air Force, they can safely be presumed to have been
intentionally falsified, just as virtually everything which is in any way
related to the subject of alien spacecraft and which is touched by the
USAF (or any other official agency of the government) is.

No matter what numbers may be released to the public, they will
not represent the truth on the ground. Instead they will represent what
the government wants people to believe is the truth, but which is
really nothing but a carefully-manicured piece of fiction which is
designed to mislead anyone who sees it and prevent them from ever
having knowledge of what the actual data shows.

In this case, the military/industrial/intelligence complex holds a
virtual monopoly on the accurate data and the inside information—
they are the only group which knows the bottom-line truths about the
situation. They don't talk about it much…and when they do, they
almost always lie. That may seem unfair and frustrating, but from
another point of view it can be said that this behavior on their part is
not a bad thing.

If they decided one day to take you into a small conference room, hand you a stack of folders to go through which were full of information about aliens but first decided to give you a military-style briefing on the topic to help bring you up to speed quickly, you would probably be inclined to consider it to be a great stroke of luck. It probably would not occur to you that your remaining lifespan could now very likely be measured in weeks or months but not in years.

Often a sighting of an alien craft or extra-terrestrial being will include what has become known as "high strangeness". This refers to exposure to technologies or capabilities which are so far beyond the normal human experience that we are unable to fully understand what is taking place because we have nothing to compare it to and no way to explain it in terms of currently-accepted scientific principles.

When a sighting of a craft of unknown origin or an extra-terrestrial being takes place, it is critically important that one does not panic or lose their cool. There are potentially few times in life when it will be more important to maintain your composure and think quickly and clearly.

Let there be no question about it: though it is not always the case, legitimate sightings can sometimes be tremendously frightening and extremely hazardous. It can be quite a challenge to remain calm and act in a logical manner in the presence of high strangeness, especially on those occasions where one finds they are being targeted or pursued by craft or beings of unknown origin and intent.

The more intense the situation, the more important it becomes to think and act rationally. There are certain times in life when one can ill-afford to make a mistake. Finding yourself in the presence of extra-terrestrials is one of those times.

If there is one thing you can be quite certain about when you see an alien spacecraft or an alien being, it is this: they did not travel here from some distant star or jump through into our reality from another dimension hoping they might have an opportunity to meet and speak with you personally. You may therefore safely assume that, whatever it is that they may be interested in doing right then, if you attempt to interact with them in any way you will be interrupting it or getting in their way. No matter which type of alien may be involved, that is not a position that anyone with even a small amount of common sense should wish to find themselves in.

The most important rule one must always and without exception be aware of and follow is this:

NEVER APPROACH, TOUCH, THREATEN OR INTERFERE WITH AN ALIEN SPACECRAFT OR AN EXTRA-TERRESTRIAL BEING!

It is foolish and highly dangerous to make yourself into a target of opportunity when there is no good reason to do so.

If you happen to see an alien spacecraft which has landed or is nearby and at a low altitude, stay well away from it! Though they may have no hostile intentions, it is known that some are distinctly unfriendly. Some are openly hostile toward humans and represent an extreme hazard to those they contact. There are some of them which are not only quite willing but are in fact eager to utilize humans as a food item—if they have a chance to turn you into a meal, they will do so. Since in most circumstances it is difficult or impossible to be sure exactly which race or group you happen to be encountering, the imperative of self-preservation requires that one take absolutely no chances during such encounters. If it is possible to vacate the area, do so with all possible speed.

If the craft is a good distance from you—and particularly if you happen to be with a group of other people, the need for escape is not nearly as important, as it is unlikely that you will make yourself into a target or that the occupants of the craft will have a reason to divert their attention to you personally.

The great majority of sightings last only a short time—it could be as little as a few seconds or perhaps a couple minutes in most cases. For this reason, you will want to keep several things in mind and do them as quickly as you can. If you can alert others to the presence of the spacecraft, you should do so immediately. This will help greatly in terms of confirming the sighting and additional witnesses may be able to pick up details about it that you miss. If you happen to have a camera of any kind nearby, use it!

Take as many photographs of the object as possible or film it if you have that option, being careful in both cases to hold the camera as steady as possible. This is especially important because many of these craft appear to be unstable in flight at low speeds or when hovering. They may wobble or appear to almost bounce in the air.

They may jerk rapidly side-to-side, appearing in the air as a streak or blur rather than as a solid object. If possible, include other objects in the picture too, for purposes of scale. It will help greatly later in determining the size, altitude and distance of the object. Telephone or light poles, houses or roofs, trees or other natural terrain features—whatever happens to be available at the time is what you must use.

Take care to make note of the exact time, if possible. Also, make note of the time the sighting ends. It is far better to know this for certain than to be forced to guess about it later.

In all cases, you will want to observe the object as closely as possible and remember as many details about it as you can. Size, color, any movements it makes, any exterior details you can make out if conditions permit that—anything about it that you can see and remember, you will be thankful for later. Watch it closely and do not take your eyes off it, if you are a safe distance away. You may not have long to observe it before it is gone.

It is not common to see an alien spacecraft land or take off, though such things do occasionally take place. If you happen to see an alien craft come down for a landing, again it must be stressed that approaching it is the last thing a rational person would want to attempt. It is neither wise nor polite to approach an extra-terrestrial spacecraft without being specifically invited to do so.

There is no reason to attempt to interfere with their business in any way or to cause them any type of concern when it is not necessary to do so. It is, of course, highly unlikely that you would pose any sort of a threat by the occupants of an extra-terrestrial spacecraft or that you would be able to cause them any harm no matter what weapons you happened to have nearby. On the other hand, it is extremely likely that if you get in their way or cause them any kind of problem they will neutralize you in short order, perhaps on a permanent basis.

In a contact event with an alien craft or alien being, humans should always presume themselves to be massively outgunned and extremely vulnerable. To approach the situation in any other frame of mind is unsafe, unwise and completely unwarranted. If you can travel across interstellar space to visit their home world, then perhaps you have earned the right to think of yourself on equal terms with the visitors. Until and unless that becomes the case, you are not equal. You are not even close to being equal—never forget that.

Once the sighting event has concluded, it is very important that you write down all you can remember about it as soon as it is possible to do so. Human memory is unreliable and it is a simple fact that as time passes the precision of the memories and the fine details attached to them tend to gradually fade away. It is therefore in your best interest not to neglect this step and not to delay it in any way.

If there were other witnesses, each witness should write down their own recollection of the event without conferring with each other or comparing stories first. It is important that everyone's individual memory of what occurred and what was seen is written down in their own words and in their own way. This too will greatly add to the credibility and believability of the sighting in question should you decide to go public with it. Otherwise people will be quick to charge the witnesses with getting together to make up a story they could all stick to. It makes no difference that such is not the case—someone somewhere will make the accusation anyway. They always do.

Do not transfer possession of your camera, films or photographs to any other person—keep them yourself. Make multiple copies of them if they are of high quality or particularly interesting for some reason. If you happen to have access to a safety deposit box or a fireproof safe of another type, it would certainly be advisable to keep the original photos and any photographic negatives which may be part of the package locked safely away and to make every effort to get them into that storage at the earliest possible time you can. Photographs and films tend to disappear or be stolen...and the higher quality the photos, the higher the chance that you will someday go look for those photos only to find that they have vanished, never to be seen again. Do everything within your power to prevent that from happening to you.

It is highly important that you never attempt to alter or manipulate the original copies of the photos/films, the negatives or the camera which was used during the sighting! Both cameras and film can be examined in detail by experts if it is found to be necessary to validate the reality of the event—tampering with the product in any manner whatsoever will cost both you and your photos or films a lot of credibility and might even ultimately result in the entire sighting event being written off as a prank or hoax. It is simply not worth tampering with the evidence in any way or for any reason. We are, after all, serious and straight-shooting researchers--we have no part in hoaxes or pranks and no tolerance for those who engage in such things!

It is rare indeed that a sighting will result in a friendly invitation to board an alien spacecraft...but it is a possibility and has on certain occasions been known to happen. Should you be present when such an event takes place, let your best judgment be your guide. As mentioned above, many races appear to be friendly toward humans in general and some seem to sincerely enjoy contact with us. It has happened in the past that humans have been invited aboard a spacecraft by the visitors and received a warm welcome—and occasionally a pleasant ride in craft itself with the extra-terrestrials acting as tour guide.

Having said this, it is also wise to keep in mind that, like humans, many aliens are well known for their habit of deceiving and manipulating humans whenever the opportunity presents itself. Certain alien races and groups have long experience when it comes to dealing with humans—thousands of years, in some cases even more—and they know much more about us than we can possibly know about them. They know our weaknesses and what makes us tick, both as individuals and societies. They are quick to take advantage of that when the chance comes along and see nothing wrong at all about lying to humans if it somehow furthers their goals.

Though it is certainly possible to find yourself in a situation in which friendly contact with an alien race takes place, it is also the sad fact that most UFO sightings which represent alien spacecraft are sightings of beings with profoundly negative characteristics and hostile intent. This because a certain group of ET's has had the opportunity to plan, extend and then consolidate their position. They are the predominant power as far as their influence over our planet is concerned and they have been and are being assisted by the United States government and possibly others in doing so, as will be demonstrated later in the manuscript.

If one has the least reason to suspect that the motives of an ET are questionable and escape from the situation is possible...do it. Leave. If it turns out that a group of benevolent Space Brothers are looking specifically for you, they will surely know how to locate you again and can be expected to resume their contact with you at some point.

If you happen to irritate a nine-foot-tall Reptilian, on the other hand, your journey through this life may be about to end the hard way.

The percentage of alien spacecraft on and above Earth which represents the activities of Greys is estimated by military sources to be around 25% of the total. As will be made clear as we proceed through the pages of this book, this is an alien race which no sensible human should want any part of meeting. That alone, to my way of thinking, is more than reason enough to never be tempted to approach or interfere with any type of strange or unknown aerial vehicle or any life form which you suspect may be of intelligent extra-terrestrial origin.

Depending upon the circumstances, a UFO sighting can sometimes be a frantic, powerful and emotionally-overwhelming experience. Try to remain as calm as possible, keep a level head and do your best to remember and follow the guidelines listed here. There will surely come a time later, when things are all over, that you will thank yourself for it.

CHAPTER 4: ANONYMOUS SOURCES

"I could tell you, but then I'd have to kill you."
-- Dr. No

"Break the silence!
Damn the dark, damn the light!"
--Fleetwood Mac

Whether you happen to be in the position of having to utilize anonymous sources yourself or not, they are a topic you will run up against again and again as you research the subject of alien contact. Because of this, I want to briefly touch on some of the realities about both these sources and the people who use them which may perhaps help you to understand the difficulties and dangers which are inherent in either becoming or using a source who for some reason does not wish to be publicly identified.

The first thing to understand is that nobody uses an anonymous source by choice. We would all like nothing more than to be able to list the name, rank and serial number of our sources, so to speak. Doing so adds credibility to our words if the sources are themselves credible and we can demonstrate that we know or knew them. Failure to do so gives people reasonable cause to doubt anything we say which we claim came from a source we cannot or will not name.

Nobody wants to go to the trouble of coming forward with information which it is forbidden and possibly even illegal to speak about publicly only to have their words casually dismissed because they didn't tell where the information came from. Researchers are sometimes accused of inventing material themselves and then attributing it to an anonymous source, attempting to increase its perceived importance.

While it is of course possible that this sometimes happens, I think it is safe to presume that if it does it is a rare occurrence rather than a common one. By now, sufficient information has been made available to the public that the prospect of inventing sources which do not really exist involves more risk than it is worth.

If an invented source adds nothing new to the database, there was no reason to invent it in the first place. If, on the other hand, an invented source says something which has never been heard before, there is a very good chance that someone who has access to the real information about whatever it may be will debunk the person who invented the non-existent source in short order. Most likely there will be people who are willing and able to do so. The result in that case will be that the author is left in a considerably worse position than if he had chosen not to make up a fictional source for the sake of adding a little drama to whatever he happens to be writing.

It is one of those situations in which the reward is quite limited and the risk is high enough that it's just not worth doing. The presence of an anonymous source will probably not have a significant effect on the total number of copies sold in the long run. Accusations of fraud and a reputation for questionable reliability, however, can instantly and forever kill the sales of a book. As a practical matter, not many people will think it's a clever idea to invent sources which do not exist at the risk of having their reputation ruined and their career brought to an untimely end. It is better to say nothing at all than to do that.

As for legitimate anonymous sources, I dislike using them because it's my credibility and reputation which are put on the line every time I do.

If I utilize them, some people are very likely going to think I'm lying, boasting, desperate for attention or just plain crazy. I know this in advance—it's part of the territory. But when I feel it is necessary, I go ahead anyway because that's my job and my responsibility. It is what I do...so I do it and hope for the best, despite the drawbacks and risks associated with it

I would ask that you notice I have never claimed to be an expert or an authority on the subject. I do not claim to have worked in black ops or the intelligence community. I do not claim to hold an above top secret security clearance. What I claim to be is a hard-working, dedicated, reasonably bright person with a lifetime of personal experience dealing with many different aspects of the subject. I have utilized a wide array of sources while doing so and it so happens that along the way I have accumulated quite a bit of knowledge about the subject, probably more than most are likely to be able to. That is the only claim I make and I fully stand behind it. It is not my intention here to attempt to impress anyone by making claims about myself that I am unable to support. It is my intent to share things, some of which have never been published before, and to provide original analysis and commentaries about them. I hope to provide the reader with some of the missing pieces of the puzzle in a way which is logical, coherent and impossible to debunk.

Within our military there are individuals who strongly disagree with the way our government hides the information from the public. They detest the way our own special forces are enabled to abduct, harass, defame and sometimes eliminate people who in good faith come forward to speak about their experiences. They think we are making huge mistakes as far as our dealings with ET races, our agreements and interactions with them. They find themselves in disagreement with the activities which are taking place and the agenda which is being advanced while working secretly with non-human beings. They believe that these things all too often conflict with the best interests of the public and should not be allowed to continue.

Many people are not aware, for instance, that in addition to hidden underground bases we also build and utilize secret bases located on the ocean floor at various points around the world. There is one a short distance off the coast of California and one underneath a lagoon in Puerto Rico. There is another located a short way off the coast of South Africa, and many others as well. Some of these bases do not belong to us alone--they are jointly occupied by ourselves and ET visitors of various types as part of the terms of the secret agreement which will be discussed in a later chapter. Others are designed and intended only for occupation by aliens. These secret bases were constructed by the Bechtel Corporation, the largest privately-owned construction and engineering company in the United States. The Bechtel family, including those who have acted as President of the corporation, are known to be supporters of the New World Order and are widely presumed to be members of the Illuminati.

These dis-satisfied individuals within the military think we are in a lot of trouble. They think that our government presents an enormous threat to us, one we are blissfully unaware of because we are unable to get the information that would prove or demonstrate it in a concrete manner. They consider our own government and the military/industrial complex to be a clear and present danger to the safety and security of our own people, if only we knew it. They want people to know. They want to step forward and tell people these things themselves, in their own voices and with the authority of their rank backing them up. But they are unable to do so for several reasons.

One is that their careers would end the same day they did such a thing--and everybody needs their job. They may very well have invested their entire adult lives into attaining the rank they hold and the benefits it carries, including their retirement benefits. The best thing that could happen is that they will lose all future access to secret matters and have their security clearances revoked. The worst is that they could be stripped of their rank, imprisoned for breaking their oath of secrecy, charged with treason and possibly executed or terminated in an apparent accident of some kind.

Actually, that isn't the worst. The worst is that the government might carry out the threat it holds over their head the whole time: talk about this to anybody and we will kill everyone you love. We will kill your spouse, your children and your parents...ALL of them. And THEN we will come for you.

At the same time, they are patriots who have sworn to uphold the Constitution and protect the best interests of the public. They do not lack courage by any means--many are highly decorated combat veterans. But nobody is going to risk the lives of their wife and children by coming forward to talk about ANYTHING. Put yourselves in their position for a minute. They feel an obligation to get this information out to the public but it is impossible for them to put it out there themselves.

To get the information out, they must trust someone. They must find someone they can share that information with whose willingness to maintain silence about their identities is the only thing the lives of their children depend on. If that person reveals their name, maybe their kids will be harmed or even killed. The government is very willing and able to take steps like that to keep the lid on.

Who can they trust? "Almost nobody" is the answer. There is almost nobody who can understand the information itself, which is often highly complex and detailed, explain it to others in a way which will be believed, attract a large enough audience that it will matter when they do and who can also be relied on to keep their word, forever, about maintaining the secrecy of the source. Failure at any of those steps either makes the whole thing not worth doing or risks the lives of innocent people whom they love with all their hearts.

Reveal the name of a confidential source and suddenly you will find that you no longer HAVE any. They will vanish like fog in the night, because you have demonstrated that you cannot be trusted, that you are willing to put their lives and the lives of their family at risk just to gain yourself a little fame and fortune. One name slips out of your mouth by accident and you are toast as far as ever getting any more inside information is concerned. That's just how it is. It's the price of getting into the game. You pay it or you don't get the information. You keep your word to these sources or people are going to get hurt. Not to mention the fact that they often have the power to hurt YOU--and they will, if you cross them.

I hope you will please try to understand my position when I talk about anonymous sources. I'd love to be able to tell you all about them...but I can't do that. You are under no obligation to believe a single word I say and some of you probably won't--I already know that. I don't care. In all the years I have spent researching these things, through all the nights I sat, hoping that by staying awake all night I could stop them from stealing me away, I have never attempted to make even a small amount of money from it for myself. I have gained nothing from this but a lot of stress, countless hours of my life being sucked away and probably an early grave from driving myself too hard for too long without enough rest.

I do it swimming against the tide the whole way. There is always someone around who doesn't know me at all but who is more than happy to inform people that I am a liar, I am delusional, etc. I put up with it because that, too, is part of the price of doing this thing I do.

It's part of the admission fee--you accept it or you go home and keep it all locked away inside you until the ulcers eventually come.

We all make our choices. This has been mine. I don't regret it one bit, not for a second, but I want you to realize that the price of doing what I do is not insignificant and that it is a difficult and risky business to want to be a part of.

It is my hope that you will give me the benefit of the doubt as I go about trying to share information with you—some of which it just so happens that I have, you do not have, and you probably have no other way of getting. That's what I do. I consider it my job and although I will eventually be paid for writing this book, the truth is that you'll have surely paid far less for it than the information it contains is worth.

An example of what I mean by that statement is this: if you should decide to make use of the methodology I laid out during your own study of the subject, the value that those rules of investigation will provide to you over time is far higher than the price you paid for this book. And that is just the first chapter.

The same could be said of the second chapter: if you happen to see an alien spacecraft and the information found there helps you to do something right or to avoid making a mistake, you may well end up thinking that the second chapter alone was worth more than the total price you paid for the book.

These are just the first two chapters. It does not even take into consideration the many additional things which are to be found in the rest of the book and which may prove to be valuable to the reader.

It would be no exaggeration to point out that I am risking both my credibility and my life by choosing to make this volume available to the public. Regardless of how much I may receive from it in terms of monetary compensation I will, realistically speaking, be underpaid for doing so. So please consider what I say before deciding to arbitrarily toss it out. That's all I am asking for. I am laying it all down for you, friends, whether you believe a word I say or not...and I am not doing it for my own benefit, I'm doing it for yours.

CHAPTER 5: HIGH STRANGENESS

"Even the bravest men are frightened by sudden terrors."
-- Tacitus

"Fell on black days,
Fell on black days
How would I know
That this could be my fate?"
-- Soundgarden

I had not intended to speak much about my own experiences in this manuscript. The manuscript, after all, is intended to deal with these topics on a macro level rather than a personal one. It is natural, though, that those who read this book will wonder who I am and where I attained my knowledge of the subject.

That is a rather long story, one which extends over about a half century and which I see no reason to spend an inordinate amount of time on here—from my point of view, it is the information itself which is important, not my personal story. For the most part, the information which is to be found here should in my opinion be able to stand on its own.

Though I have included descriptions of some of my personal experiences, this book is not intended to be about me. It is, rather, my attempt to share the knowledge I have been able to acquire over the years, along with my opinions on certain matters, with those who may be able to benefit from them in some way.

To dedicate one's lifetime to learning all they can about topics which are protected by the highest levels of security in human history, and then to die without ever having shared it with those whom it might help would seem to be a shame and a great waste. Sharing it is my intention. It is the reason I wrote this book. Even so, it is reasonable to ask about my experience and credibility, therefore it seems only fair that I describe them at least briefly for those who may be interested.

My interest in the subject began when I was a small boy—I had my first sighting in 1966. It was just a light-in-the-sky type of sighting, but it was a light which followed my family's vehicle for around a half hour up a twisting mountain road. That is the only memory I have of it, but it was enough to ignite my curiosity (a curiosity which remains to this day) and motivate me to learn as much about the subject as I possibly could (a motivation which also remains to this day).

The craft itself did not carry out any maneuvers which could not have been easily accomplished by a helicopter. All it did was follow us up this mountain road, matching the vehicle turn for turn. There is no reason for a helicopter to do something like that, since they are not constrained by the winding nature of a road which runs through a mountain pass—they could simply fly right over the tops of the mountains and be done it. If it was indeed a helicopter with a human pilot, it did something I have never again seen or heard of one doing…and it did so for no apparent reason. It is therefore my opinion that this sighting was most likely of an alien spacecraft rather than a conventional helicopter, but I have no way to be certain about it one way or the other.

I have had several other sightings which I consider to have been possible alien spacecraft and one spectacular and extended sighting which involved military aircraft and was without question a sighting of an extra-terrestrial spacecraft. One of the sightings involved three objects which appeared as lights in the night-time sky flying in formation and which, as I watched, appeared to merge together into a single object, which then flew away. Another involved a bright white light traveling at high speed at a fairly low altitude which performed an instantaneous 90-degree turn and then faded to black. One second it was headed west and then suddenly it was heading south.

Both the apparent merging together of multiple airborne vehicles and the instant 90-degree change of direction are characteristics which have been reported numerous times by witnesses who claim to have seen alien spacecraft. Although I am not aware of any human-designed vehicle which can accomplish such a merging of craft, I'm told that we now have vehicles capable of pulling an instant 90-degree turn and that these vehicles utilize alien technology to make this possible without having the G-forces crush the pilot. Both sightings, then, must in my opinion be considered either extra-terrestrial spacecraft or craft which make use of ET technology but are piloted by humans. For the record, the sighting which involved the 90-degree turn occurred around 1990 and the sighting which involved the three objects merging together occurred around 1998.

Another sighting I had involved military aircraft—there were two sightings total where this was the case—and took place at very close range. The sighting itself lasted only a matter of a few seconds but was highly interesting. I happened to be awake at around 3:30 AM— not an unusual time for me since I have always been a "night person". I heard helicopter engines approaching, obviously at high speed—the engines were revved up higher than I have ever heard a chopper engine rev before or since. I stepped out onto my deck to have a look and try to see what was going on. I didn't have long to wait.

Just across my next-door neighbor's yard, barely clearing the tops of a row of small trees he had planted in a row along the edge of his property, two helicopters moving very rapidly came into view. They flew past within about 40 feet of me, surely traveling as fast as they could. It was quite dark outside, so I couldn't be sure whether they were military choppers with standard insignia and decals on them or the fabled black choppers many have reported seeing. In between them, clearly being escorted by the choppers, was a small ball of light which appeared to be moving in a rapid but unstable and eccentric manner. It wobbled and jerked slightly from side to side as well as bouncing up and down a short distance like a basketball would. It was quite small—at the time I estimated it to be around 3-4 feet across. It changed color rapidly, white to green to blue to red. Then, as it passed directly in front of my location, it faded to black just as rapidly.

The helicopters (and, presumably, the ball of light-turned-black) rose slightly in altitude, just enough to clear the top of a nearby hill which was in their path. They went just over the top of it and out of sight. The total time of the sighting was no more than ten seconds.

Was the ball of light an alien spacecraft? I have no way of knowing for sure what it was...but it occurs to me that if it were a secret military vehicle of some kind there would have been no reason to escort it in such a fashion—they could have simply loaded it into one of the choppers and flown it to wherever its intended destination was. For the record, this sighting occurred in central Washington State a few miles west of the Yakima Training Center, which is a large Army facility comprising over 400,000 acres of mostly open semi-arid land.

The choppers and the ball of light were heading directly west, as though on a course from the training center to Fort Lewis Army base or McChord AFB, both of which are located just south of Tacoma.

It so happened that my next-door neighbors were a married couple who were both in the Army and were both stationed at Yakima Training Center. I asked them the next day if they had seen or heard about any unusual flying objects at the Training Center within the past few days. They told me that "something" had flown into the base and been quickly hidden, secured in a hangar nobody was allowed access to, but they had not personally seen it and nobody would tell them what the object was.

I can see no logical reason for such a small military vehicle of what would obviously be a secret nature to require a high-speed escort in the dead of night. Because that unstable, wobbly-bouncy motion is widely reported as being a characteristic which is present on what appear to be extra-terrestrial spacecraft, I presume that it may have been some type of intelligently-controlled ET probe or remotely-guided craft. If it contained aliens, they would have had to be very small ones. If it was a secret military craft, it would seem it was one which incorporated alien technology in its propulsion system.

I will never know for certain what it was or where it was going. I will never know why it required an escort of two Huey-style helicopters at maximum speed at the time of night when the least possible number of people would have any chance of sighting the group as it screamed westward.

This brings us, in a slightly roundabout fashion, to what was easily the most spectacular sighting of my life to date. It took place during the summer of the year 1984.

I was living at the time in Selah, Washington, which is a smallish bedroom community of the city of Yakima. I had recently returned from San Diego, where I had lived for several years, and was staying at my parent's house until I could find a place to live. I had seen an article in the newspaper that day which stated that, due to some unusual atmospheric conditions, it might be possible to see the Northern Lights in the sky above our local area that night. That is a very rare occurrence since that area is normally too far south to get any glimpse of them at all—I had never heard of it happening before, though it's possible there may have been other times that it did.

Being curious and hopeful of catching sight of them for the first time, I was outside in their yard shortly after sunset, looking up into the sky to see what I might see. As it turned out, it *was* possible to see the Northern Lights that evening, but I must say that they were quite unimpressive from my location, consisting of a barely-visible green color that slightly shimmered across most of the sky. Little did I know at the time that I was about to experience two of the strangest and most unexpected occurrences of my life.

There was a good-sized, multi-story medical facility located on a hill just north of Selah. It had originally been constructed as a tuberculosis hospital. During my lifetime, it had always been used as a facility which housed severely retarded children and adults, people who required round-the-clock care from a medical staff. It sat alone on top of this hill, with some small residential units which had recently been built sitting alongside the long, curving driveway which led up the hill to the parking lot and the hospital. The name of the facility, which still exists today, is Yakima Valley School.

Slightly behind and a few yards to the west of the hospital building lies the crown of another hill, slightly higher in elevation than the base of Yakima Valley School. As I stood in my parent's yard, much to my utter shock and amazement, I saw a large object which could only be an alien spacecraft rise up from behind the crown of this hill, barely enough to clear it, then float silently forward and take up a position right beside the hospital, no more than a few feet west of it and barely above the ground.

It was quite large. It was shaped like a classic disk, convex on both top and bottom, the same sort of shape you might see in the lens of a magnifying glass. Around the centerline of the craft there was a narrow belt of small multi-colored lights: red, blue, green and yellow. There were three lights all the same color, then three of another color, alternating in a similar fashion through all four colors and then repeating the pattern. Though it was surely just the lights themselves changing color in sequence, the belt itself appeared to be rotating around the centerline of the craft. It was not actually doing so—it was just the lights changing color in a coordinated fashion which gave this appearance.

Over the rest of the craft, which appeared in the growing darkness to be of a metallic silver color, small white lights like flashbulbs popped rapidly in an apparently random sequence from apparently random locations on the body of the craft. The best way I know of to describe the frequency and rhythm of the small lights is to imagine the sound of popcorn popping, with every pop being a point on the spacecraft which would flash briefly, looking like a flashbulb on a camera had just gone off.

For the first time in my life, I could immediately feel all the hair on my head and body stand on end. I was experiencing what is known as "High Strangeness". If you ever happen to find yourself wondering during a UFO sighting whether you are experiencing "High Strangeness", let me provide the answer for you right here: you are not. If you are, it will not be necessary to ask the question. You will *know*.

I realized instantly that I was in the process of having what would surely be the most singularly amazing and incredible sighting of my life. I was overcome with surprise and shock—of all the places I would have ever expected to see an alien spacecraft, hovering beside a constant care facility for the developmentally disabled, just above the ground, was surely one of the least likely locations I could have come up with.

Mostly, though, what I felt was a sense of awe and wonderment. Every cell in my body informed me with complete authority, a certainty beyond any possibility of question or doubt: "That is not from this world."

When you see something like this, the last thing you want to do is look away from it. Most sightings, after all, last for only a few seconds—a minute or two at most—and you do not want to miss any part of it. Your eyes become glued to the craft and tearing them away to look at something else is simply not an option.

The top of a tree line prevented me from seeing underneath the craft itself. The entire spacecraft was clearly visible: it was a summer evening with a cloudless sky and perfect visibility. It was not possible, however, for me to be sure whether the craft was simply hovering just above the ground or had extended some type of landing gear and set down. It has always been my strong impression however that it did not land, that it hovered no more than about three feet above ground level. Because of the tree line which blocked the view directly below the spacecraft, I was unable to see what—if anything—came out of the craft, what actions it may have performed or what if anything re-entered or was taken aboard the craft. I have some thoughts about that which I will discuss below...but from my position there was just no way to know for certain.

As I said, the very last thing one wants to do in a situation like this is look away from the object. I studied it as closely as I could. Though it was several blocks away from me I had an excellent and (other than the area underneath the spacecraft, as mentioned) unobstructed view. I was sure that it would certainly move away and out of sight momentarily, probably at high speed as many UFO's are reported to do.

Much to my surprise this did not happen. The alien craft—and there could be no doubt that an alien craft is what it was—remained beside the hospital, motionless, the belt of multi-colored lights still appearing to rotate around the vehicle as the individual bulbs changed color, the white flashbulb-like effect still apparent, popping off at seemingly random spots all over the rest of the hull. Still I did not move or look away from it. I stood there, staring, transfixed. The hair on my head, my arms, the fine hair on the back of my hands and all the other hair on my body remained standing on end the entire time.

How could I be sure as a practical matter that what I was looking at was an extra-terrestrial spacecraft and not an ATS craft built by our own government or even something belonging to another nation?

A chain of logic flowed quickly through my mind: If it belonged to Russia, it had just penetrated and passed through all of our coastal defenses without being detected and made its way well over a hundred miles inland over the state of Washington. To do this, it would have had to pass within easy range of Fort Lewis Army Base, McChord Air Force Base, Bremerton Naval Station, Bangor Submarine Base or some combination of those facilities. After somehow passing undetected through this rather massive array of highly-secure military bases and making its way inland, it would then have proceeded to carry out its primary mission. Which was, apparently, to turn on all of its exterior lights in a manner which made it impossible to miss and then hover just above the ground beside a large building full of retarded people in full view. It did this, for reasons known only to the inscrutable Russian rascals themselves, within two miles or so of the Yakima Firing Center, a large army base which included an enormous radar dish with at least a half-dozen underground levels that was known to belong to the National Security Agency.

Whatever it was, the craft I was looking at did not belong to the USSR or any other foreign nation.

As for the possibility that it was "one of ours", that also did not compute. I could think of no conditions under which an Above Top Secret saucer-shaped craft covered with colored lights and flashbulbs would hover beside the Yakima Valley School for what was becoming an extended period. There was no apparent reason for that to happen. It would immediately blow any possibility of secrecy. To the contrary, it was effectively boldly announcing its presence to anyone who happened to be looking its way. No--this was no domestic military aircraft of any kind, nor was it any type of hallucination or mistaken observation on my part.

I am human and, just like anyone else, I sometimes get things wrong. But mistaking the planet Venus or a reflected headlight beam for an alien spacecraft is not a mistake I would ever make. For all my human faults and weaknesses, I am far too competent to even vaguely approach that type of an error. What I was looking at, then, had to be the only other possibility which was left: an extra-terrestrial spacecraft of unknown origin which displayed advanced design parameters and performance capabilities.

I naturally anticipated that at any moment the spacecraft would depart in some fashion and the sighting would come to an end. Knowing as I did that this was the way most sightings usually played out there was no reason to think this one would be any different. Much to my surprise, this was not the case. Rather than making a short appearance followed by some type of swift exit, the alien spacecraft continued to hover beside the hospital wall—silent, motionless and ominous. Its commander was obviously not the least bit concerned about stealth, as the craft continued to provide a rather spectacular light show for anyone who happened to see it.

The shape of the craft itself did not appear to be anything I would have considered particularly unusual or unique—it was simply a large, perfectly-proportioned disk which was convex on both top and bottom. I presumed it would be easy to find other examples of identical craft somewhere within the voluminous archives of photographs and films which have been assembled by various individuals and groups.

Much to my surprise, this has not been the case. I have looked through thousands upon thousands of purported alien spacecraft photos searching for one which had the same appearance but come up short in every case. Occasionally I will find a photo which shows a craft which is similar to the one I saw that evening...but none of them has ever been an exact match.

I do not know the reason for this—surely, it seems, I would not have by chance been present the one and only time an alien spacecraft of this description was ever seen. Surely at some point someone somewhere would have had the opportunity to photograph another which was just like it. The idea that only one alien spacecraft like this exists, and that it had come here to hover beside the Yakima Valley School and then vanish forever doesn't make sense no matter how one chooses to look at it.

As this book was being prepared for publication, a friend of mine sent me a photograph of some ancient hieroglyphs which had been carved on a tomb. As I looked down at the photo, I got a shock. For the first and only time in over thirty years, during which time I have viewed countless thousands of photographs of UFO's, I was looking at a visual representation of craft I had seen in 1984.

The row of lights around the centerline of the craft, though the carved hieroglyph was not painted and appeared all in a single color, was exactly in the right position and was the correct size. The shape of the craft was identical. Whoever was responsible for building the craft I had watched for 42 minutes on a hot summer night in 1984 had also been present in ancient Egypt. They had been present, they had been seen and they had been recorded for posterity by an unknown artist on the wall of a king's tomb, becoming part of the history of the Egyptian civilization for all time.

That was not all. Slightly below the level of the spacecraft, to each side of it, was the artist's rendition of some of its crew members. It was nicely done. It was clear, it was accurate and there could be no doubt about who the occupants of the spacecraft had been.

I was looking at a depiction of an event which was considered of such importance that it was literally carved in stone. It had been given a spot on the tomb of the King to make sure that a record of the event would be passed along to future generations. As I stared at it, I felt the strangest sensation pass through my body. I couldn't escape the feeling that, against all odds, these alien beings had somehow managed to pass through thousands of years of time…and now they were standing there looking at me.

They had large heads. Their arms and legs were bone-thin. They had large, almond-shaped eyes.

A knot instantly formed in my stomach. I felt my hair rise up and stand on end, just as it had so long ago, as realization dawned and I understood what I was looking at.

They were Greys.

Later, after you have been made aware of my subsequent experiences with the alien race known as the Greys, you will understand both the knot in my stomach and my hair rising up once again, as if because of some automatic reaction. As if looking at this photograph of an event which had occurred thousands of years in the past was about to compel me to make a choice: fight or flight.

Though it might seem to make no sense to those who have not been in the presence of the Greys, those who have will surely understand. Deep in my mind, I thought I could hear something which sounded much like a voice. At first it was very faint, barely audible, as if it was coming from far away. Muffled and indistinct, as though obscured by a great wind that was blowing through my mind. And yet at the same time there was something about it that seemed almost familiar to me in a way, something that I couldn't quite put my finger on.

It was locked away, buried deeply beneath layers of false screen memories, forced injections of Versed--an anesthetic which also induces amnesia--and hypnotic commands which had ordered me to forget, forget, forget all that had happened. Through all these barriers to conscious memory, there came a sound that was haunting and yet at the same time somehow strangely familiar. It seemed to be slowly rising in volume until at last it was able to penetrate even the sound of the wind, as though it insisted on being heard.

Yes. I recognized that sound now.

It was the sound of my own voice. And it was screaming.

I had no way of knowing at the time—and there was no reason to think, as far as I knew--that I would have subsequent encounters with the race commonly called Greys. The idea of comparing the spacecraft later to the photographs taken by others did not even go through my mind as I stood there staring at it. I also had no way of knowing that a circumstance which might simply have been thought of as unfortunate was about to morph into one which has been a matter of endless frustration to me personally.

The events of the evening, as it turned out, were only beginning. They were about to become even more fascinating and compelling. What began as the most incredible and unexpected sight of my entire life was about to double down in ways I had no way of predicting. One of them, as you will soon see, would forever defy my ability to understand or explain in a fashion which is satisfactory to me and has certainly turned out to be one of the things in life which has caused me the most regret.

Ironically, this was not to be anything which was done by either the spacecraft or whoever it was who sat at its controls. It was a human thing—a shocking, incomprehensible, entirely unnecessary and easily avoidable display of what can only be called apathy. It would completely and forever change the way this sighting is viewed by others who hear it described. It was to my way of thinking so dreadfully unfortunate that I hesitate to even relate it. I find I cannot do so even here without shaking my head sadly as I do, knowing that I did everything right that evening to the best of my ability but was in the end short-circuited by something which turned out to be the second most unexpected and shocking occurrence of my life.

I hesitate to even put what happened next into words...but this is a matter of truth and accuracy, a time to give a complete description of all that happened that evening. Even though I would much prefer to not have to live with the memory of what came next, I will now tell the most unfortunate and--from my point of view--heartbreaking part of this story here, for what I earnestly hope will be the last time.

As I said previously, the spacecraft remained in its position beside the hospital, unmoving, and I remained in mine, staring at it, for what seemed like quite a while. After ten minutes, had passed and the craft showed no sign of being about to vacate the area, I decided that the time for action had arrived. The thought briefly flashed through my mind that I could easily drive up closer to it. In only a minute or so I could be in the parking lot of the Yakima Valley School itself, which in front of and slightly downhill from the main entrance to the facility.

I quickly vetoed the idea, being somehow aware even then that approaching an alien spacecraft without being invited to do so was a highly dangerous and completely foolish thing to do and could easily turn me from an unseen observer into a target of opportunity or perhaps even a perceived threat in some way to the occupants of the vehicle.

But as it continued to hover unmoving beside the wall of the hospital, I knew I had to do something. I had to try to do something which would validate the sighting when it was described later.

I decided I would run into the house and get my parents to look at it. It would surely be the most amazing sight of their lives, as it was mine. I turned and dashed inside. My parents were seated in their living room. My father was reading the newspaper; my mom was reading a book. "Look outside!" I shouted. "There's a huge spacecraft hovering right beside Yakima Valley School! You've got to see this!"

That was when the second-most unexpected thing ever to happen in my life occurred.

"Saw one when I was in the Navy," my father replied, not glancing up from the newspaper. "Don't care."

I couldn't believe it. "Mom! Look outside! Quick!" I repeated urgently.

"If your dad doesn't care, I don't care," my mother replied, barely glancing up from her book. Neither of them moved. Literally all they would have had to do is turn around in their swivel chairs and pull back the curtain and they would have seen the most spectacular sight of their entire lives. They refused to move. They weren't in the least interested. They truly didn't care.

I was almost in shock at what I considered to be their almost unbelievable lack of curiosity—it boggled my mind and to this day I do not understand it. It was such a simple thing to do, basically just turn around and look through their window. I had neve tried to get them to look at any type of a UFO sighting—none had ever occurred where I had the chance to do so. I knew full well that without additional witnesses to corroborate the sighting its credibility was probably shot. Why would anyone believe a story like this from a single witness, especially when the alien spacecraft itself was brightly lit up and in clear view of anyone in the area—impossible to miss for anyone who happened to be looking in that direction?

But there was no time to argue about it. I had to get back outside as quickly as I could! Fortunately, I knew my parents had a real nice camera, a Canon with a telephoto lens attached to it. I grabbed it out of the nearby closet, intending to shoot the entire roll of film and capture what would surely be some of the clearest and most unmistakable photographs of an alien spacecraft anyone had ever produced.

There was no film in the camera.

"Where's your film??" I hollered urgently, desperate to get back outside before the craft was gone.

"We don't have any," my mom replied casually. "We weren't planning to take any pictures until Christmas."

Oh my god, I thought. Are you kidding me? The one time in my life when I desperately need to take some photos in a hurry, a fine camera in my hands...and not a single frame of film anywhere to be found?

Can you feel my frustration by this point? But there was nothing to be done about it. My parents had absolutely no interest in turning around and looking out their window at an alien spacecraft...and not a frame of film in the house for their high-quality camera with the telephoto lens that had just been a single press of the shutter from making history.

Again, there was no time to be lost crying over spilled milk—I had to get back outside to what I already knew would be the most significant and mind-boggling sighting of my lifetime!

I decided to stop for a moment on the way out and dial 911, which would connect me with the county sheriff's department. "Nine-one-one, what is your emergency?" the lady who answered the call asked.

"You've got to get someone out to the Yakima Valley School as fast as possible!" I informed her urgently. "There's a large UFO hover--" (CLICK!)

She had hung up on me.

My frustration, disbelief and desperation increasing by the second, I decided to take the time to make one more phone call, to the local newspaper. I looked up their number as quickly as I could and dialed it. "Yakima Herald-Republic, how may I direct your call?" the operator at the newspaper said.

"You've got to get a photographer up to the Yakima Valley School as fast as you can!" I said quickly. "There's a large UFO hover—" (CLICK!)

She had hung up on me too. Oh my god. Could I not even get a single tiny break of any kind tonight? Apparently not.

At a loss for what else to try, I ran back outside. The whole series of events in the house had probably taken no more than three minutes or so. The alien spacecraft was still there, hovering serenely beside the hospital, acting as if it had all the time in the world.

I once again stared at it closely, taking in as many details as possible, having no way of knowing that things were about to become even more intense.

Only a short time after I had returned outside, I heard the blast of fighter engines with afterburners on coming from the East. I looked in that direction and immediately saw a pair of F-16's streaking westward toward the location of the spacecraft. I had the presence of mind to check my watch. Exactly 20 minutes had elapsed since the spacecraft had risen over the hill and settled beside the hospital.

A friend of mine had a brother who was an Air Force veteran and had at one time been assigned to fly F-16's out of Fairchild AFB, which is near Spokane, WA. He had once mentioned that it takes almost exactly 18 minutes on full afterburner to travel from Fairchild to Yakima Training Center, a 400,000-plus acre Army base which was located perhaps three miles west of Yakima Valley School.

The Yakima Firing Center, which has since been renamed to Yakima Training Center, was not equipped with a runway. Occasional military helicopters were the only air traffic which took off from and landed at the base. That meant the fighters, which had come from the east, had to have come from Fairchild AFB, a good 180 miles to the east of us.

It had taken them eighteen minutes to arrive at maximum thrust. That meant that Fairchild AFB had somehow become aware of the presence of this alien spacecraft and had scrambled a pair of F-16's to intercept it within two minutes of it appearing over the ridge! I suppose I will never learn how they knew the craft was there. Someone had apparently picked it up on radar from somewhere nearby and alerted the base instantly. The base had ordered the scramble almost immediately: no more than two minutes could have passed between the time the spacecraft came into view and the time the fighters were airborne. All other considerations aside, that was one hell of an impressive reaction time!

I thought briefly about running across the street to the neighbor's house, to try to get some additional witnesses from the elderly couple that lived there. But their windows were dark—they had obviously already gone to bed.

Considering the absolute lack of response on the part of my parents and the two telephone calls I'd made which had quickly resulted in the person at the other end of the line hanging up on me, I decided it was probably pointless to try and alert the neighbors. If my parents, the Sheriff's department and the newspaper were all completely uninterested in seeing a large, brightly-lit alien spacecraft hovering beside a local hospital, I would just watch the thing by myself. There seemed to be nothing else to do but that. Out of ideas, that is exactly what I did. I stood there alone, my hair still standing on end all over my body, and watched as closely as I could.

The F-16's tipped their noses skyward at about a 45-degree angle as they approached the craft. This is the attitude they must adopt for low-speed flight. If they remained in a level attitude there would not be enough air traveling over the surface of the jets to keep them airborne—they would literally fall right out of the sky. But by angling the nose of their planes upward it allows additional air to be caught by the surface of the wings, which were now angled upward too rather than remaining in the sleek and aerodynamic attitude they display in level flight.

Sure enough, the fighters slowed their speed, came over the top of the Yakima Valley School at low altitude and began to buzz this alien spacecraft one at a time. As one would pass close above the craft and then gain altitude to begin its turn for a repeat pass, the other would swoop downward and buzz the craft in its turn, passing a scant few feet above the top of it. As it gained altitude to begin its turn for another pass, the first plane swooped down on the spacecraft, gaining altitude afterward on the opposite side of the craft and again turning for another pass. It was clearly a well-rehearsed precision set of maneuvers and the pilots executed them flawlessly time after time after time.

The alien spacecraft to all appearances completely ignored them, as though they were nothing but a couple of insignificant insects which could do them no harm and which caused them no concern whatsoever.

Now able to compare it to the F-16's, I was finally able to get a better idea of the exact size of the spacecraft. It appeared to be about three times as tall as the F-16's, including their tail and canopy, and its circumference—the distance from one edge of the spacecraft to the opposite edge—was about twice the length of one of the fighters.

The length of an F-15 is 49 feet 5 inches, making the distance from one of the rounded edges of the spacecraft to the opposite edge about 100 feet. The height of the spacecraft in my estimation was about 30 feet. There have been sighting reports of spacecraft of far larger size than this...but as you can imagine it certainly seemed quite large and impressive to me at the time, as I stood there looking at it in awe and wonderment.

The fighters buzzed it repeatedly, one after another, back and forth, clearly making their presence known to it and just as clearly letting it know that they were not there for on a mission of friendship. They were fully armed with a 20mm Gatling cannon which has 500 rounds available to it and what I presumed were six air-to-air missiles each.

The pilots of the two F-16's did not fire on the spacecraft, but the encounter was distinctly hostile. From their actions and by passing within just a few feet of the spacecraft each time they buzzed it, their message seemed indisputable from my point of view: We see you, we consider you to be hostile, your presence here is unacceptable and we have our weapons locked on you.

A message like that from United States Air Force fighters changes the situation quite a bit. Naturally we would all greatly prefer to believe that any visitors who arrive here from an unknown point of origin have friendly intentions and act in a non-hostile manner toward humans. It was clear now that this was most decidedly not the case. The U.S. Air Force appeared to know who was in control of that craft and considered them to be hostile, intrusive, and dangerous.

The fighters continued to buzz the alien spacecraft, back and forth, over and over, for over twenty minutes. At no point during this time did the spacecraft appear to acknowledge their presence or display any type of concern or alarm related to it. Finally, the craft slowly gained a little altitude, just enough to clear the top of the hill it had flown over when it first appeared, and slowly and deliberately moved north away from the Yakima Valley School. It floated serenely over the top of the hill, clearing it by only a small distance, then sunk behind the hill and out of sight after passing over it, the fighters continuing to buzz and harass it as before while it moved away.

I checked my watch again: forty-two minutes had passed since the craft had first come into view! That was a tremendously long sighting, far longer and far more spectacular than anything I had ever dreamed might come my way. There could be little doubt that this would be the clearest and lengthiest sighting of my life, as well as the most exciting and informative. To this day that remains the case. I could feel my hair slowly relax and return to its normal position after the alien spacecraft—and there can be no question whatsoever that an alien spacecraft is exactly what it was—disappeared.

There is no way to anticipate or predict a sighting like the one I had that evening. It was pure luck, an accident—I just happened to be in the right place at the right time. Had I decided to go to a movie that evening, or to do anything at all rather than stand outside to try to get a glimpse of the Northern Lights, my life would be very different today.

I now had direct personal knowledge of several critically-important pieces of information:

1) I now had certain knowledge that non-human intelligences exist. The question of whether intelligent extra-terrestrial life exists is treated as a theoretical exercise by those who have never had a personal sighting. Because they have no direct proof one way or another, they often spend their entire lives stuck on this question. Unable to determine with certainty whether such beings actually exist or not, they typically will not make the effort to progress beyond that question and begin to ask the questions which come naturally to one who is able to answer the question.

2) Some of these alien beings have developed a method of traveling from their point of origin to our world.
3) The fact that they are here proves definitively that their technological capabilities are vastly superior to our own and strongly infers that their scientific principles and understanding of universal laws are also far more developed and advanced than anything ever produced by humans
4) The United States military—and therefore presumably the militaries of allied nations as well as other major nations which may not be considered friendly to us—is fully aware of the presence of these extra-terrestrials and almost certainly has been for many years.
5) Official denials of the existence of extra-terrestrial visitors and alien contact have always been direct, intentional lies which are part of a long-term program of disinformation and deception.
6) At least some of these extra-terrestrial visitors are considered by the United States military and government to be intrusive, unwelcome and dangerous.
7) Because warplanes were dispatched virtually instantaneously when this spacecraft made its appearance, it must be taken as a matter of certainty that these extra-terrestrials are viewed by the military as something which constitutes a clear and present danger to the safety and security of the citizens of the United States.
8) The distinctly unfriendly tone of the encounter combined with the decision not to attack a hostile target which is in proximity to our civilian infrastructure indicates that our military does not feel its weapons are capable of destroying or repelling these alien spacecraft. If they were, they presumably would have done so. Since that did not happen, it was most likely believed that the intrusive aliens and their spacecraft possess the ability to destroy our top-of-the-line aircraft without suffering damage to their own vehicles.

Considering the number of questions which exist regarding extra-terrestrials and the government's interactions with them, that is not a whole lot of answers. It does, on the other hand, provide answers to several of the most important questions on the list, questions which could easily consume the whole of one's lifetime otherwise.

By vehemently and consistently denying of the existence of alien spacecraft in our vicinity, the government has placed what amounts to the perfect obstacle to finding the truth. Almost nobody is going to invest the amount of time and energy necessary to find the deeply hidden answers when they have been made to doubt that alien spacecraft even exist. Any research they do will necessarily be focused on trying to ascertain whether extra-terrestrials are really here, rather than probing into the matter more deeply. After all, there is no reason to spend your time trying to learn about a government conspiracy or anything else if you're not even sure alien spacecraft exist in the first place.

Being in the right place at the right time resulted in several of the most important questions about the subject being answered definitively in less than an hour's time. I was given a gift of knowledge that night, and all I had to do to receive it was stand still and watch the events play out.

Though I had no way of knowing it as I stood there watching on that summer evening so long ago, the things I saw that night would ultimately shape my destiny. There is virtually nothing about the life I find myself living which would be even remotely the same were it not for that one sighting. I would live in a different city and have a different job. I'd have spent the last several decades doing completely different things than I have done and would undoubtedly be moving in very different social circles than I do now.

My journey has been difficult, dangerous and frustrating in many ways. There is almost nothing about it which could be called easy or convenient. But it has provided me with the most interesting life I could ever imagine having and I would not change a thing.

We all have our destinies. This has been mine.

CHAPTER 6: PSYCHOLOGICAL WARFARE

*"We'll know our disinformation program is complete when
everything the American public believes is false."
-- William Casey, Director of the Central Intelligence Agency*

*"Haven't you heard? It's a battle of words!"
The poster bearer cried
"Listen, son," said the man with the gun
"There's room for you inside"
--Pink Floyd*

If we are to have any realistic hope of making our way through the clutter and arriving at a reasonable facsimile of the truth, we must become familiar with the battlefield. If we seek a view of reality and our place within it which we can be confident reflects the situation accurately, it is necessary that we must first understand the forces arrayed against us.

Those forces are formidable indeed and they operate silently behind the scenes, unnoticed. The fact that they operate invisibly, employ a staff of experts, make use of exotic technologies which the public is not even aware exist and possess an unlimited budget makes them the most efficient and dangerous enemy we have ever faced.

The insidious and omnipresent nature of the operations they undertake ensures that their plans will be rewarded with success and that the nature and scope of those plans will remain invisible to the public. They are concealed and obfuscated behind multiple layers of deception. Each works in synch with the others, combining seamlessly into an overall plan which, if one is a member of the target group, can only be described as monstrous. If you are a member of the American public, you are a member of the target group and you are being attacked by this monster.

You will not notice the attacks coming, nor will you be aware that they have occurred. You will have no idea how effective they are, nor can you pinpoint the sources from which the attacks come or from which they are directed. If it were possible for you to do so, the attacks would not succeed, for secrecy and subtlety is the key component of their existence.

Whether you realize it or not—and most people do not—you are a victim of what is easily the most pervasive, well-financed and long-term psychological warfare operation in history. A great many of your attitudes, opinions and even your thoughts themselves are not your own. They are instead things which have been carefully and intentionally inserted into your consciousness to manipulate you into thinking, behaving and speaking in precisely the manner your enemy wishes you to think, behave and speak.

Without your knowledge or consent, unnoticed and unsuspected, you have been attacked from all sides throughout the entire course of your life. Much of what you believe to be real and true is neither of those things. Whether you realize it or not, you *have* been brainwashed. The result is that you have been co-opted, you have become an unwitting participant in a war against yourself and your own best interests…and you have been fighting for the wrong side without realizing it.

The perfect target is the person who does not believe themselves to be a target. The most effective psychological warfare operation, similarly, is one which the target does not believe exists. Combine those two elements and what you have is, from the point of view of a psychological warfare professional, a "perfect storm" of opportunity.

Let me demonstrate what I mean by that.

As you were reading the preceding paragraphs, the following thoughts flashed through your mind:

"That may be true about *most* people, but it is not true about *me!*"

"I am too intelligent to be manipulated like that!"

"Nobody tells *me* how to think! My thoughts are my own!"

There is no point in denying that those thoughts went through your mind—I already know they did. That is an important point upon which you will reflect if you are wise: the fact that I—without ever having a single second of training in the art and science of psychological warfare--could know the thoughts that just went through your head.

Not only that, I could cause those exact thoughts to occur to you, precisely when I wanted them to, simply through the act of typing a few sentences. I controlled your innermost thoughts. You believed those thoughts to be your own. They were not: I put them there intentionally. They were *my* thoughts, in *your* head. I put them there with a minimum of effort, no training whatsoever and with an absolute certainty that I would be successful *even after I had just finished warning you about it!*

As I was doing this--as I was manipulating your very thoughts themselves--you had absolutely no idea what was being done. You had no reason whatsoever to think that you might be the target of a psychological warfare exercise. You were firmly convinced that every thought in your head was completely your own. Because of that, I just controlled your thoughts in much the same way that a marionette controls a puppet on strings. I made you think the exact thing I wanted you to think.

You have no reason to assume that my reason for doing so had anything to do with your best interests. In fact, it is far safer to presume that the reason I did so was for personal gain and had *nothing* to do with them.

But I am not here to trick you. I have nothing to gain by manipulating your thoughts. My purpose was purely educational: it was intended only to demonstrate how easily such things can and are done to us without our conscious awareness.

I recommend that the reader give some serious thought to the manipulation that just occurred. After doing so, try to imagine the effect that psychological warfare professionals, armed with an unlimited budget and access to hyper-advanced technologies which you are probably not even aware exist, are capable of over a period of years and decades.

If you do not feel a cold knot of fear forming in your belly at this point, you have not understood the warning I bring and may wish to give it some additional thought.

No one is so intelligent or so clever that they are immune to the effects of large-scale psychological warfare. If you are reading these words, your thoughts and opinions have without question been modified in many ways by the constant barrage of propaganda and disinformation which is present in all sectors of our society. The fact that many people will refuse to believe that is true does not in any way negate its reality—rather it identifies them as precisely the type of target the disinformation was intended to affect and is a testament to its effectiveness.

I am certainly no exception to the rule. As an example, I was forced to watch a television show called "Hee Haw" when I was growing up and I can still easily recall the phone number of the car lot on the show which was run by Junior Samples: BR 549. I have difficulty, however, remembering my own. I am aware that the Navy is more than just a job (it's an adventure!), I know that Pepsi beats the others cold and that poor old Mr. Whipple doesn't want me to squeeze the Charmin. I am, however, unable to name the Libertarian candidate for President or the current Director of either the CIA or the NSA.

Information which has no possible use to me has been swapped in for information that might very well come in handy to me at some point. It has been imprinted on my memory and will stay there for a lifetime no matter what I do.

I should probably mention that none of those advertisements have been aired since the 1970's, but they still pop instantly into my mind. I should probably also mention that I have not watched television at all for over fourteen years at the time I am writing these words and that I consider it to be one of the best things I have ever done for myself.

Make no mistake about this, brothers and sisters. There are elements of the United States military and intelligence services which are completely out of control. They operate from a position above the law, immune to capture or prosecution and they have access to far more money than most people would imagine. The CIA, for instance, maintains a choke hold on the world's supply of heroin and all other opium-related products, 90% of which originate in the country of Afghanistan.

When the Taliban took control of that nation, one of the first actions it took was to ban the growth of opium poppies. Though many people have been fooled into believing that the United States attacked Afghanistan to pursue the terrorists responsible for 9/11 that is very far from the truth. The terrorists who were responsible for 9/11 were not located in Afghanistan—a fact that our government knew very well indeed. The primary motivation for that war was to oust the Taliban and re-establish the opium poppy as that country's primary cash crop and export.

The CIA had lost a tremendous amount of revenue when the growing of opium was outlawed there, since they had long controlled and distributed it worldwide, including making sure a plentiful supply was always available on the streets of America. Opium is considered the most profitable commodity in history: it is purchased for mere pennies from poverty-stricken Third World farmers in Afghanistan. It is then refined and sold for top dollar to the citizens of rich industrialized nations.

The profit produced in this manner is enormous, amounting to hundreds of billions of dollars per year…and it is all in cash. It is non-taxable, untraceable and available for the world's most dangerous intelligence agency to use as it sees fit. The President himself does not possess a high enough security clearance to be informed about their most important and secretive activities. This means that for all practical purposes the CIA operates as an independent agency which is financed through the national budget and by maintaining a monopoly on the world's drug markets. It also controls numerous "front" companies including banks such as BCCI, which it has established to launder money and which generates a tidy profit along the way.

The bottom line is that there are parts of the CIA which ultimately take orders from nobody and it is staffed by people who are, among other things, professional liars. Nothing they say can be believed and everything they do should rightly be suspect. There is nobody holding them to account for any of it. Nobody is forcing them to operate within any type of moral or legal guidelines or with restraint.

It has gotten to the point that, despite the fact I am legally guaranteed a right of free speech by the United States Constitution and have been an American citizen all my life, there is someone sitting in an office in Langley, Virginia—the location of CIA headquarters—who will read these words and decide whether to have me killed for publishing them.

It is not a question of whether that will happen, it's just a matter of when. At some point, that decision will be made--and whether I am to be allowed to live a while longer or destined to die prematurely from an artificially-induced heart attack will depend on what it turns out to be.

That would be a terrifying prospect under the best of conditions— and the best of conditions have never existed as far as this situation is concerned. This out-of-control group of spies, assassins and drug dealers which was designed and intended to work for the best interests of America and her citizens has instead declared war against us.

The CIA, the NSA and other groups are using money which ultimately comes out of our pockets to finance operations against their own people. There is no nice way to say it, just as there is no nice way of saying that even the fact that I dared to mention such a thing is enough to put my life in jeopardy. It is enough to cause people who are being paid to protect me to decide whether to have me killed for speaking my mind.

This is the reality of the America we live in today. Whether you realize it or not, we are at this moment only one emergency away from permanent nationwide martial law and a fascist state where freedom and justice will be nothing more than relics of the past.

Do you disagree with that assessment? Do you believe that something like that could never happen in the United States of America?

If so, it is because that is precisely what you were *intended* to believe by the very people who have the power to make those things happen and to impose such a system of government on you and I and everyone else. You believe it because a series of long-running psychological warfare operations have been carried out against you and they were successful. Otherwise you would not disagree with the statements I made—you would instead take a good look around you and conclude that what I said is not only true, it is obvious.

If you do not already realize it, groups like the CIA, NSA, DHS, Council on Foreign Relations and others of the same ilk represent the greatest threat and the most dangerous enemy this nation has ever had. They are currently well on their way to bringing America to her knees. Anyone who tries to stop that from happening--or who even says something which makes them nervous or uncomfortable--runs the risk of being terminated.

This is what a nation that was intended to be a shining example to the world of freedom, hope and opportunity has come to.

Never make the mistake of believing that you live in a free society or that our government operates under a system of democracy. We are very far from being free. We live in a military state operating under a soft form of martial law, one which could be turned into a fascist dictatorship very easily at any time. Indeed, that is the plan and we are moving rapidly toward the day when that is exactly what will take place.

You cannot give someone $10 trillion to build the most powerful military machine the world has ever known and then expect them to do what you tell them to do. They will tell *you* what to do…and you will do it, if you want to stay alive. Killing is, after all, their business—and nobody does it better.

Do not kid yourselves about that and never buy into the notion that you still reside in a place which is "the land of the free". Your freedom, such as it is, exists only by benefit of the sufferance of those who hold the power. It can be rescinded at any time, permanently, and you do not have the resources available to you to fight the federal government and have any hope of winning.

Remember what was said at the beginning: truth is what we seek…and we follow it wherever it leads, whether we like it or not. Truth matters.

Opinions are just opinions. One can have any opinion they like. Someone could be utterly convinced, for example, that UFO's are nothing but the detritus of delusional minds and careless exaggeration by mistake-prone individuals. Such an opinion will in no way affect the truth of the situation. If aliens are present within our solar system even as we speak—and they are—the aliens will still be here tomorrow regardless of what anyone's opinion about the reality of their existence may be.

Opinions matter greatly, on the other hand, when it comes to manipulating and managing the thoughts and actions of the public at large. An opinion espoused by an eminent authority, for example, can sometimes sway the perceptions of literally tens of millions of people simply by the perceived weight of his or her expertise and experience. An opinion which is based on false propositions or inaccurate data can be used to greatly influence both individual citizens and society in a way which is all but imperceptible.

This is a fact which is well-known to those in the intelligence community who are tasked with the responsibility of ensuring that the opinions and beliefs of the public conform to the opinions and beliefs that those in power wish them to have. Never for a moment should you believe that the news you see and hear on the conventional media represents the truth. Do not think that it will contain any information which those who control the media corporations do not wish us to have.

One very effective method of manipulating public opinion is to have the "news" media keep silent about some issues while emphasizing others far more than it is reasonable to do. This is being done every day.

Behind the scenes of the duly-elected or appointed leaders that the public sees and believes to be responsible for making the major decisions which determine the course of nations lies a small group of extremely wealthy and influential power brokers whose tentacles reach virtually everywhere and whose finances are for all practical purposes unlimited.

It is this elite group of super-wealthy and impeccably-connected financiers and influence peddlers who truly decide upon and initiate the actions which, when manifested, will ultimately determine the prosperity (or lack of prosperity) of the public and whose agenda will eventually control the course of history itself. Political leaders will come and go, but extreme wealth and the highest of high-level contacts remain in place long after the figureheads the public believe to be in charge have faded into irrelevance.

Every organization and every online discussion group which deals with the subject of UFO's or alien contact is monitored and infiltrated by intelligence groups. Agents sign up as members of forums for the express purposes of spreading disinformation, sowing confusion and derailing discussions which come too close to the truth for comfort.

There are many techniques which are used to subvert and discourage conversation and the sharing of information among members. Though it will appear that comments are made by innocent members of the public, the fact is that very often they will be posted by disinformation professionals.

Even though it is widely known that disinformation is utilized against those who seek to learn the truth about alien contact, the average person is not familiar enough with the techniques which are utilized to be able to identify them when they are present. Even people who know of the techniques have a difficult time accomplishing this, because by design it is extremely hard to differentiate between intentional disinformation and innocent or ignorant comments coming from members of the public who don't know any better.

It is sadly the case that, unknown to themselves, members of the public inadvertently assist them with their own comments and attitudes—all of which, it should be noted, are encouraged and promoted by the disinformation professionals who lurk around every corner.

Rather than allowing a discussion to focus on legitimate questions or issues, for example, a disinformation technique which is often used very effectively is to instead attack the credentials or credibility of the person who asked the question or presented certain information. By casting aspersions on that person's reputation, qualifications, mental stability, honesty, etc. it is often possible to either turn the conversation to a discussion of those things rather than the original points or to kill it entirely by causing others to be unwilling to discuss it further for fear of also being labeled foolish, unqualified, gullible or mentally incompetent. By attacking the messenger rather than addressing the actual message, countless discussions have been sidetracked or have completely ground to a halt because of personal attacks without ever actually being allowed to focus on the subjects which were originally raised.

Disinformation agents working in teams--or sometimes a single agent who registers multiple times in a forum and therefore appears to be several people who are in agreement--often team up against anyone who comes too close to truths they wish to conceal. It should be remembered that these people carry out these functions as a full-time job. It is their role to sit at a desk for eight hours a day and do nothing else but damage and discredit any legitimate discussion of the topics as quickly as possible. It will often be the case that when an original post has been made to a discussion group or internet forum, comments will begin to appear within minutes which question the author's experience, qualifications or integrity.

People will call the original poster a gullible fool and remark that anyone who agrees with or even takes that person seriously must similarly be soft-minded. They will imply that such people will believe anything they are told because they are not smart enough to know better. Laughter, scorn, eye-rolling, unfounded accusations and the like will surround the original poster like a swarm of flies. This will discourage others from taking his side or even from posting comments on the issue at all for fear of being judged in the same manner. This technique alone is enough to effectively curtail or permanently derail conversations which may have ultimately approached information the government wishes to remain hidden.

All things can be accomplished by a single disinformation professional at a computer keyboard who is assigned to monitor and disrupt the activities of, say, 30 internet discussion forums simultaneously. It is a very effective technique and one which has a high cost-to-benefit ratio in favor of the intelligence service which mounts it.

A half dozen such agents working in tandem can virtually paralyze an enormous number of otherwise credible discussions. They can turn sincere and honorable contributors into pariahs by staging attacks upon them which are neither warranted by the facts nor supported by any reasonable assumptions. Fear of guilt by association is enough, all on its own, to cause most people to avoid taking part in such discussions. Often, they will abandon the original informant or even switch sides and join in the snickering and name-calling, becoming unwitting disinformation assets themselves the second they do.

Any perusal of YouTube clips which purport to show videos of alien spacecraft, for example, will show that every one of them includes comments denigrating not only the original poster but also anyone else who happens to find it believable. They will be called idiots, gullible retards, mental basket cases and all other manner of things by apparently random members of the public. This is not the case for *most* videos of this type which appear on YouTube. It is the case for *all* of them!

Let's think about that for a moment. Let's imagine that there was a group of people who had somehow been convinced to believe that elephants could fly and that they had posted a million video clips to YouTube which they claimed showed elephants flying. Let's imagine that the average clip takes five minutes to watch and that it would require another five minutes to write and post a comment on it, for a total of ten minutes per clip.

You know that these video clips cannot possibly be legitimate. How much of your precious time would you invest in locating and watching them? How much additional time would you invest in going to the trouble of writing a comment on each of them, informing those who watched them that they were either gullible idiots, delusional or had been tricked by Photoshop?

Hopefully your answer was "none", because doing those things would be a complete waste of your time.

Now imagine that every one of those clips was followed by at least one such comment. At ten minutes per clip, it would require over fifty-seven years for someone to do this, assuming they spent eight hours a day at it and never took a day off. With a team of three people, each working an eight-hour shift per day, it could be accomplished in a little over nineteen years. If instead of a million clips there were ten million, it would take this three-person team one hundred ninety years—without taking a day off--to view the clips and add a single comment to each one.

Are we to imagine that people who are certain in advance that the clips of flying elephants are not legitimate would spend what amounts to a total of fifty-seven years watching them anyway and writing comments about how fake they are?

I'm sure you will agree that such an idea is ludicrous and that the possibility it would happen is, to say the least, extremely remote.

Even so, this is precisely what has occurred with the YouTube clips which purport to show alien spacecraft. If there are a million such clips which have been posted, we are either dealing with people who are collectively foolish enough to waste fifty-seven years on something they know in advance can't be true…or we are dealing with disinformation agents working in teams.

With a team of two hundred such agents, the job could be accomplished in around three months and a million conversations could potentially be permanently derailed, discouraged or killed outright. At the same time, the YouTube user ID's of every person who had left a supportive comment after the video could be collected and potentially added to watch lists. There are not many methods of killing a conversation which are more effective than this would be.

Of course, it is not necessary in practice to add comments to a million pre-existing clips or threads. The clips are posted over a period of years, rather than all at once. Every day, perhaps somewhere between several dozen and a couple hundred UFO clips might be posted. It would not require anywhere close to two hundred disinformation agents to cover this number of clips, plus most of the other internet forums which deal with UFO's on a regular basis.

A team of a dozen people might be able to handle the entire job. They could effectively discourage, divert or derail what would otherwise be pertinent UFO conversations across the entire country. In terms of efficiency and value, this provides tremendous bang for the buck from the point of view of those whose job is to maintain secrecy. They would surely be quick to take full advantage of this option and there is no reason to presume that they haven't.

We already know that many of the best film clips of UFO's really do contain legitimate alien spacecraft. People who do not believe alien contact to be a reality are unlikely to spend their time viewing and commenting on them. It is therefore logical to presume that the great majority of the disparaging, insulting comments which are attached to these clips do not represent genuine feedback from the public. They are, rather, acts of intentional sabotage by disinformation professionals posing as members of the public. Most who read them, however, will not realize that this is the case. The comments will then achieve their intended purpose and discourage people who may have been inclined to offer supportive statements from saying anything at all.

This is an example of using only a single technique. None of the relevant agencies are by any means limited to only this. Rather, they avail themselves of many different tools, all of which have been time-tested and proven to be highly effective against the public.

The military/intelligence services have now availed themselves of a new generation of weapons which are so high-tech that most people have trouble believing they even exist. They do indeed exist and they are used against targeted individuals within the borders of the United States.

Targeted individuals are people who have in some way made the powers that be nervous. They may be unwilling to accept the official lies and proceed to research matters on their own. If they get too close to the truth or make too loud a noise for the comfort of those in charge, they will be targeted. If someone happens to have a talent for thinking "out of the box" and can convince others to listen to him or her, this represents a clear danger to those who hold the power because it is precisely this out-of-the-box thinking which can lead to real solutions and can sometimes uncover secrets which would have otherwise remained well-concealed.

Conventional thinking is not a threat to those in charge of the disinformation and secrecy campaigns—conventional methods and conclusions have been thoroughly thought through long ago by those in power and have been well tended to. There is virtually no avenue one can take that leads from conventional-type thinking which has not been flooded with false turns, dead ends, confusion and infiltrators. It is designed specifically to waste the time and energy of any researcher. This will prevent them from being able to use it to learn something new and valuable.

Blocking those avenues is a matter of every-day routine for those who are professionals in the intelligence business. They are more skillful at carrying out their duties—and far more well-funded and numerous—than any individual or group of researchers has any realistic chance of even approaching. Trying to beat the NSA at its own game is hopeless, a pointless exercise in futility which is doomed to failure before it even begins. Attempting to do so will result only in wasting large amounts of precious time and energy. You will find yourself blockaded at every turn and filled with even more frustration than you felt before. The odds of success are analogous to the chance you have of beating a member of the Harlem Globetrotters in a trick shot contest: it's not impossible, but don't bet your house on it unless you want someone else to end up owning it.

People who think well out-of-the-box, however, are a different matter entirely from the perspective of those who hold the true power. Such people, by trying new methods and approaches, may well stumble onto something which has not been sufficiently guarded against and uncover information which was not well-defended against an unconventional or novel approach and may not have considered that such an approach could even be attempted.

Examples of people like this are Edward Snowden and Gary McKinnon, who utilized uncommon skill and determination to successfully breach layers of security which were not considered to be vulnerable to attack and came away with secret files belonging to the NSA and NASA. They attacked where they were not expected and by doing so encountered defenses which were far less robust than those arrayed against attacks which utilized conventional methods.

Anyone who is considered a possible threat due to their unconventional approach or who appears to be close to discovering hidden knowledge will become a target of covert surveillance. The agencies charged with guarding the most highly-protected and massively-secured information in human history are not concerned in any way about following civilian laws. They will not hesitate to violate the Constitutional or legal rights of their own citizens.

The National Security Agency was formed to oversee all information related to alien contact. It is officially allowed to break any law which does not specifically name the agency in the text of the law. This is virtually never done, leaving it immune to the threat of prosecution no matter what crimes may be committed. Phones can be tapped and people can be followed, threatened or even killed with impunity. These things are being done every minute of every day to American citizens who have committed no crime and who caused no harm to anyone.

The NSA is an organization which is out of control. It is subject to no laws, has unlimited funds available to it and employs people whose names can never be found on any personnel records to commit crimes against the people it supposedly is employed by. It is far from the only one: there are other groups within the military and intelligence worlds which can do the same thing and do so daily. In fact, though it may not be obvious to the casual observer, it is often the case that these groups take part in internecine turf wars. Rather than forming a single intelligence service which is united under a single leadership and has as its primary goal serving the needs and assuring the security of the American people and the nation, they instead can often be found engaged in conducting operations against each other. They compete constantly, struggling for power, funding and access—and each group has different goals and a different agenda.

These facts are relevant to the discussion of extra-terrestrial contact because those who study it are the primary targets of these lawless, invisible and highly lethal spy agencies. Researchers may go about their lives completely unaware that they have been noticed. They may have no reason to suspect that they have been targeted by megalithic power structures designed to silence them by any means necessary, including the use of deadly force.

Anyone who undertakes the study of alien contact in a serious way and anyone who is a witness, contactee or victim of what appears to be an alien abduction is, through no fault of their own, directly in the firing line. They are in harm's way.

There are governmental assets utilizing illegal--and completely unwarranted from any reasonable point of view—methods to silence or eliminate any members of society who happen to get too close to the truths which they jealously guard. Originally intended to guard the public against the dangers of totalitarianism and the establishment of a police state, they operate instead with the express purpose of ensuring that those very things will someday be put into place to subjugate the people they have been hired to protect.

One cannot hope to be able to successfully oppose such institutional monstrosities without recognizing the power and extent of the forces arrayed against them or the lengths to which they will go. If we fail to understand the enemy, we will have no chance of effectively protecting ourselves against him or recognizing his fingerprints when they are encountered.

It is extremely important that we make ourselves aware of the many tools which are at the disposal of the government and the various ways they are used against us if we are to have any hope of retaining our liberties. We deserve to be able to expect agents of our own federal government to act in our best interests, always. We have a right to expect them to protect and defend us from those who would subvert and violate the terms and provisions of the Constitution of the United States of America. We must demand that this is done without fail and that those who have failed to carry out this most basic responsibility of our government be immediately replaced no matter what position they might hold.

One of the critical things which a disinformation campaign MUST accomplish is the disruption of any rational, logical and fact-based discussion of the evidence. Such discussions often lead to the ability to correctly analyze the situation and draw accurate conclusions about it, conclusions which will, when drawn, reveal the truth about what happened and identify those who are behind it.

For this reason, from the point of view of those whose behind-the-scenes and often criminal actions were responsible for causing the situation, such discussions cannot be allowed to take place in an unimpeded manner. A disinformation campaign must be launched which will have the effect of obscuring or distorting the relevant facts and disrupt any factual discussion of the events in question. It will simulate evidence which will lead people away from the truth or serve to conceal it. Objections will be manufactured which discredit or ridicule the original source of the information.

There are many tools available to those who are engaged in the disinformation trade. All of them will be put into play as needed and combined with each other whenever possible. The fact that the public has not been educated about their methods and is unable to defend against them gives the intelligence agencies a huge advantage. These methods and tools are time-tested and proven to be very effective. They are employed time after time with great success, often at little cost and with a minimum of effort necessary on the part of those who are familiar with how to use them effectively.

One of the most powerful of these tools is the ability to control the mass media. No one should ever make the mistake of believing that what they are told by elements of the mass media represents the actual truth of the subject—and yet this mistake is made constantly by almost everyone. It is an indisputable fact that the media has for many decades been thoroughly infiltrated at high levels by disinformation professionals and is subject to their direct control in many ways.

The CIA itself has publicly stated that it "owns" the American mass media and controls the content it makes available to the public whenever it is deemed necessary to do so. Editors, publishers, analysts, news anchors, columnists and reporters are all subject to this influence and are in many cases paid or influenced indirectly by agents of the governmental services. Sometimes the reporters themselves are covert employees of those agencies posing as legitimate figures.

They make a big noise about the free press in this country, but a big noise is all it is. The American press has never been free during my lifetime and it becomes less free with each passing hour. Virtually the entire mass media is controlled by a half dozen corporations, all of which support the NWO and are in league with the government censors. Nothing will appear in the American mass media unless the government allows it to.

A good example of governmental control of information can be made about Area 51. Both Russia and China have taken a huge number of detailed photographs of Area 51 from their spy satellites. They have had the ability to do so for many years. They are well-aware of the layout of the facility can look at high-resolution photographs of it any time they want to.

The American public, on the other hand, has almost never seen a high-quality photograph of the base and if we attempt to approach it we are certain to be confronted by heavily armed security guards. Depending on the situation, we will be either turned back, arrested or shot.

So, the Russians and the Chinese can have a look at the layout of Area 51 any time they want to…but the American public is not even allowed to take a snapshot of the sand and tumbleweeds around its perimeter without putting themselves in legal jeopardy and possibly also placing themselves at physical risk. We paid for it. Russia and China can take high-resolution photographs of it. But we can't even go up to the fence and look in without committing a federal crime.

The information the press constantly floods the public with has nothing to do with truth or reality. It is all propaganda, a deliberate shaping and manipulation of public attitudes and beliefs into those the powerful few wish it to have. These attitudes and beliefs are specifically designed to promote, protect and glorify the agenda of a small club of multi-billionaires. Their interests have nothing in common with ours. They are members of the Illuminati. Most or all of them are alien-human hybrids, members of "bloodline families" or their cohorts, who are doing the bidding of their alien masters.

If the government does not want the public to be aware of certain information, it can and certainly will make sure that no mention of such information is ever allowed to appear within the American media. If it does, it is soundly ridiculed by official sources and then quickly disappears, never to resurface. If something is important enough, the President could call the presidents of our TV networks and tell them that if a certain subject is mentioned on television they will have their broadcast licenses revoked by the FCC and will be out of business tomorrow.

If you think that such a threat would never be made, you are quite mistaken and have seriously under-estimated the level of importance which is attached to the subject of alien contact by those who are in the know. They can, they have and they will continue to make full use of any and every tool and option available to them when it comes to stifling discussion and concealing accurate knowledge of the subject from the public. They have not hesitated to kill people to prevent them from speaking out about it…and they will not hesitate to kill us if we get too close to the truth.

I have included this discourse in a manuscript which is intended to deal with the subject of alien contact because I believe it is necessary for everyone involved in researching it to be fully informed about the massive array of weapons which are being used against us every hour of every day. Underestimate or ignore them at your own peril, for they certainly are being employed against you even as you read these words.

It is a dangerous and paranoid world we live in and there exist technologies and capabilities you might well believe to be unlikely or even impossible but which are in fact not only entirely possible but are also completely operational as we speak. They are controlled by invisible forces behind the scenes, people whose names you do not know and will never be able to find and whose agenda has nothing whatsoever to do with your safety or welfare. It has everything to do with making certain you are kept in a state of ignorance and confusion and thus rendered ineffective in terms of interfering with or stopping their plans.

There is nothing which is too expensive, too difficult, too immoral or too violent for them to employ. They have proven time after time that they are all too willing to kill anyone who gets in their way, even when those people are among the most powerful and influential to be found in government or society. They killed Kennedy, they pulled off the attacks of 9/11 and you will be nothing but a very small fish to them if they ever have reason to turn their eyes to you. That is the bottom line truth, the reality of the world we live in and the dangers grow stronger with each passing day.

Members of these groups are literally committing acts of war against the American public and the United States every single day. They are given permission to continue to do so by an apathetic and dumbed-down public who refuse to take the steps necessary to bring the problem to an end.

With each passing day, their power over us increases and our ability to put an end to the constant, intentional abuses of our freedoms and threats to our safety diminishes. It is foolish to underestimate the tremendous power wielded by these shadow organizations. It is nothing less than suicidal to be unaware of the massive influence which long-term psychological warfare operations exert on all members of society.

It makes no difference which of our two major political parties holds power at any given time. Neither of them can reign in or control the actions of these groups and any attempt to do so will result in the demise of whoever happens to attempt it. For all practical purposes, both the Democrats and the Republicans are owned and controlled by the same group of individuals.

The reason the government takes no action to protect or defend the American people is simple: they are not working for the American people. They are working to promote the agenda of the invisible shadow government—in other words, the Illuminati. If this were not the case, would the Federal Reserve Bank, which exists only to keep the nation in debt and drain away its wealth, even exist?

The only effective and realistic way to solve this problem is to force a complete restructuring and rebuilding of all these organizations from the ground up. The existing structures must be shattered into a thousand pieces and those who control them must be relieved of their duties and, in some cases, prosecuted for their crimes against both the American people and humanity. Anything less than this will be insufficient to the task—the most it would be capable of achieving are cosmetic changes while the main body of the monster remained unaffected and intact.

While the American people continue to allow the major political parties to influence their thinking and garner their support, no solution to this problem can be instituted in practice. It has taken almost a hundred years for these organizations to amass the power and influence they currently hold. It will not be negated easily or quickly and they will absolutely use every tool at their disposal to prevent such a thing from taking place.

This leaves the public in a very dangerous and precarious position. The necessary changes are so incredibly difficult to implement and oversee in practice that it is almost always felt to be more trouble--or to involve more danger--than it is worth by the members of the public. Unfortunately, failure to take whatever actions are necessary to dismantle and completely restructure these malignant and criminal organizations will result in the so-called "land of the free" descending into an unending tyranny, a police state under which tens and possibly hundreds of millions of people will either be put to death or allowed to die through one of the multiple causes which have been intentionally put into place to shorten their lifespans and hasten their demise. The few who remain will be forced into an involuntary servitude which they will not be able to avoid or end. This is the inevitable price of allowing government to grow to a point where it becomes a tool of oppression which is beyond the ability of the citizens to control.

I will now list some of the other standard methods of disinformation which are in play. They can be seen in action every single day by anyone who is aware of them and who cares to look for them. Their effectiveness has long been a matter of proven fact. Knowing that the public is oblivious to the use of these techniques must fill members of the disinformation community with joy. It continues to make their job less difficult and their actions more effective.

One classic and highly-effective disinformation technique is to intentionally change the subject without addressing the actual issues, attempting thereby to sabotage the discussion in a way which will not be noticed. This is done constantly on internet forums and discussion groups, at public gatherings and political speeches and many other places. If one can divert the conversation away from a topic they do not wish to have discussed, the disinformation operation has been successful. To the people in the audience, however, it will only be seen as a comment from an audience member, possibly an annoying one but certainly not a disinformation agent who has been planted in their midst for the specific purpose of derailing their conversation.

Another common technique is to utilize a "straw man" argument. This refers to misrepresenting the original argument or position by replacing it with one which is superficially similar but is not really the same. They then argue against this substitute idea and demonstrate why it is wrong. If people accept the false argument as the actual argument which was originally made, the straw man technique will then be successful.

An example of this would be someone who makes a statement in favor of strengthening the security of our national borders to guard against illegal immigration. This person might then be accused of being anti-immigration in general and it might be inferred that they are racially bigoted. Both these things are examples of "straw men": there is nothing about a desire to strengthen the security of our borders which implies that someone is opposed to legal immigration or is a racist. If people can be made to believe otherwise, however, that person will be forced to defend themselves against words they never said and positions they never supported.

Disinformation specialists will often accuse the witness of spreading disinformation themselves, without having any proof that this is the case. This is an attempt to discredit the messenger and therefore imply that the message itself is somehow not to be trusted. Proving that someone is spreading disinformation is a difficult thing to do…but accusing someone of it is as easy as pointing a finger and shouting.

Another common technique is to pose as members of the public and act outraged over and offended by statements someone makes. This is also known as the "how dare you?" technique. The idea behind it is that if your idea causes someone else to be outraged or offended, you are to blame for having said something which was way out of line or somehow otherwise insulted the people around you. Please note that it is not necessary for any of them to *be* outraged or insulted for this tactic to work effectively—it is only necessary for them to *pretend* to be.

It is very common to see disinformation agents attack the qualifications, honesty or credibility of the witness, without addressing the actual issues. They will attempt to cast a shadow of dishonesty, incompetence, gullibility, criminality or any other negative character trait upon someone who comes forward with information or states an opinion which they wish to suppress.

If they are successful in doing so, others will be naturally hesitant to take that person's side or publicly agree with anything they say for fear of having the same label applied to themselves. The point of the original statement can be swept under the rug. It will get lost in the shuffle and ultimately forgotten in the ensuing confusion. All that is required is to attack the credibility of the witness and throw in some anonymous slander. This is a tremendously effective technique of psychological warfare which is used constantly, as often as the opportunity arises.

Disinformation agents will sometimes claim that certain statements are "old news" which has already been discredited and is not worthy of further discussion by serious people. This has the effect of negating the point or making it seem irrelevant.

They will use any possible method to eliminate or disparage evidence or witnesses—if it isn't there, it isn't proof of anything.

Each of these techniques—and others as well--are intended to create a diversion which results in preventing the conversation from addressing the issues which are important. Avoiding those points and the discussion that may result is a key requirement of any disinformation campaign.

Our freedoms and liberties are being attacked constantly by agents of the very government which was established to safeguard those freedoms. The greatest threat to America comes not from some foreign nation but from within. Those who have amassed great wealth and power threaten all of us in their quest to acquire ever more of those things regardless of the cost to their fellow citizens and their country. Their loyalty is not to America but to themselves alone and their agenda and concerns have nothing at all to do with the agenda and concerns of ordinary people. They have insinuated themselves into every aspect of our government and economy and have colluded among themselves to the point that they control virtually all of life's necessities and can access and directly influence the leaders not just of this nation but of all nations. Even the freedom of thought has been rescinded and taken away from us and their minions abound in all levels of society to carry out their will.

Psychological warfare is by this point in time a well-established science and an integral part of the larger scheme of control and domination which is being carried out against us. Entire books could be—and have been—written about the art and science of disinformation. I only have time to speak of it briefly here, to give the barest outline. It is a topic which is well worth studying further, and I recommend that every person who reads this book make a point of doing so. It is an insidious, subtle, multi-faceted and incredible effective tool of power and manipulation. By utilizing all the possibilities inherent within the field of disinformation, a small handful of people can influence and control nations. They can literally control the sweep of history…and they are doing so, even as you read these words.

These few people, whose wealth and power is to us beyond imagination, threaten everything we believe in and everything we hold true. And who pulls *their* strings? That is a question every thinking person should certainly consider seriously, because if those who already effectively control our world are in turn controlled by external powers of hostile intent…a bad situation becomes suddenly infinitely worse.

CHAPTER 7: BACKGROUND CHECK

"If there is anything that is important to a reporter, it is integrity.
It is credibility."
-- Mike Wallace, investigative journalist

"Every time that I look in the mirror
All these lines on my face getting clearer
The past is gone
It went by like dusk to dawn
Isn't that the way?
Everybody's got their dues in life to pay."
--Aerosmith

I was about 18, in the late 1970's, when I first started to notice that I appeared to be burning out street lights. It would happen when I approached them, not every time but far more often than it should have. It happened when I was walking or jogging near them and even when I approached them while driving my car. Sometimes it seemed that I would cause three street lights to go dark on a single city block simply by walking down it.

I had no idea at the time that this is considered a classic indicator of someone who has been abducted by aliens. It seemed quite strange to me, but I had no memories of anything which seemed to be abduction-related and no reason to believe it was a category which applied to me. In the end, I didn't pursue the matter any further and didn't make the connection between phenomena like this and alien abductions.

I continued to notice this unaccountable effect on street lights until the early-to-mid 1990's, so the total time it was occurring that I am aware of was around twenty-five years. I do not notice it happening any more, though it is also true that I don't get out as much as I used to and so I don't approach as many streetlights as I once did. But to the best of my knowledge it is no longer happening; I am no longer causing street lights to go dark as I approach them and have not done so for several years.

It seems that our body's electrical field or aura is somehow tampered with during abduction events, at least in some cases. It appears that the result is to make the aura extend a significantly greater distance outward, away from our bodies and that this is what causes the interference with street lights as we draw near to them.

It is also well-known and established that a high number of abductees burn out electronic devices such as computers, digital watches, etc., far more quickly than would be considered normal. Some cannot wear digital watches at all for this reason. I have noticed this problem and it persists to this day. I was burning up a computer every eighteen months like clockwork, for years. Finally, I purchased a heavy-duty system which cost twice as much. It did have a significantly longer lifespan, but not what it should have--eventually it burned up too and had to be replaced with another heavy-duty system.

When I first noticed the problem in about 1984 I had no idea that such a thing might be related to alien abductions. It was another abduction indicator which I basically overlooked by accident, not knowing any better at the time.

At some point during the mid-1990's I became involved with one of the internet's first chatroom features. It was called Internet Relay Chat, "IRC" for short. I found the largest UFO-related channel around and began going into it to listen and try to learn all I could about the subject. I had already been studying it for many years, but had not specifically studied much about alien abductions at the time. I had read "Missing Time" by Budd Hopkins and "Abduction" by Dr. John Mack. I knew about Betty and Barney Hill and some other people. It was not something which applied to me as far as I was aware and the literature about it at the time was scarce and contained far more questions than answers.

I met some nice people in that IRC channel. One day, however, I saw something happen in that chat group, an incident which may have seemed minor at the time to others who observed it but which in the end brought about other events which changed my life in ways I could never have predicted or imagined would come to pass.

A person came into the channel one afternoon, someone who had never been there before and who had found it that day by searching for the term "UFO" on the channel listing. He appeared to be frantic, almost panicky. He stated that a large UFO had just passed over his house at a low altitude and asked who he should report it to or talk to about it.

The response by the members of this UFO channel, including several administrators who were present, was something which both greatly surprised me and struck me as extremely unhelpful and inappropriate, especially considering the frantic state of this person who had appeared asking for good advice.

It was nothing but a giant duck," someone remarked.

"Yeah. Or a weather balloon. Forget about it," another chimed in.

"They are all giant ducks, you know," offered a third person. "Or frogs. I think some of them are great big frogs."

The person who had come in asking for a little help and some good advice fled without another word.

I decided on the spot that a response like this from a supposedly reputable UFO discussion group was totally unacceptable and that, since it was tolerated by the channel admins, they were also totally unacceptable. The whole bunch of them needed to be replaced, if that was the best they could be bothered to do when an apparently legitimate witness asked them a very basic and indisputably relevant question about the subject.

Having no way to replace the admins, ban the offending channel members or do anything at all which would affect the actions and attitudes of this group, I decided to start a UFO discussion group of my own, a parallel group but one with an important difference. My group would be a safe place for such people as the frantic stranger to come, a place where they would be taken seriously and advised in a serious manner to the best of my ability. It would also be a sanctuary for alien abductees, I decided, a place where they could be among friends and feel safe talking with others about their experiences without fear of being ostracized or ridiculed.

Forming a discussion group was, fortunately, a very quick and easy thing to accomplish. A few minutes later I was the proud owner of a shiny new UFO discussion group which had exactly one member: me.

I didn't figure there was any way for me to compete with the bigger channels. In my mind, the idea of competing against another UFO-related channel was never a factor. My only intention was to provide people with an alternate forum, one where serious people would be taken seriously rather than treated with indifference.

There was no reason for me to think that anyone would even be able to locate a small, new channel such as this, much less decide to go to it and give it a try. But it had cost me nothing to form and couldn't hurt anything by being there, so I just sat in it for a while and waited to see what, if anything, would happen. I invited two or three people I had thought highly of who were members of the other group to stop by my new channel sometime, just so I could have someone in there with me to talk to.

They did stop in…and somehow a few more people found the channel that afternoon and they stopped in too. That evening a few more showed up. The next day, everyone who had been there the previous day once again showed up and a few more people discovered the channel and came by to give it a try. We had some good conversations about a variety of UFO-related subjects. Some of them claimed to be abductees and, just as I had intended, I treated them politely and took them quite seriously, offering to assist them in any way I could or to just be someone who would listen to them if they felt the need to talk about their experiences.

They seemed thrilled to have such an opportunity, which was no doubt difficult to find in those days. The subject of alien abductions was not taken seriously by many people at the time and there were almost no support groups or counselors available for them to make use of.

The next day, everyone who had been there before came back. There must have been almost two dozen people in my new chat room, much to my surprise. And more people were finding it and coming by.

The larger it grew, the more people wanted to come in and see what the group was like…and it grew very quickly indeed, far more quickly than I had ever imagined would be possible. The format was a hit with people and before long we had all types coming in, from housewives to airline pilots, artists to servicemen who had witnessed UFO's, young and old. We even ended up having an engineer whom I will refer to as "Bill" who was contracted by NASA and the USAF to reverse engineer technology found at UFO crash sites become a regular member within the first week or so of the channel's existence.

He and I eventually became the best of friends. I made him an admin and we worked together brilliantly with a natural chemistry, each of us having strengths which counterbalanced a weakness in the other one. Bill knew a lot about the technical aspects of UFO's, I was more well-informed about abductions and how to communicate with people in distress. He had knowledge of aspects about alien contact which mystified even the government. I had the ability to analyze it in new ways and sometimes apparently to figure out something they had missed.

Each time Bill added information to our database, another piece of the puzzle fell into place. Every time I analyzed it correctly or another abductee filed a report, more pieces fell into place. We each were blessed with a certain amount of personal charisma, and when we were operating together as a team this effect was multiplied.

The group quickly gathered momentum like a snowball rolling downhill. People came in at all hours of the day and night. Our attendance skyrocketed in almost no time. Before I knew it, completely without intending to, I found I was the owner of the largest and apparently by far the most popular UFO-related channel on IRC. I seemed to be in constant demand by the people who came in to join the discussion. Information of all kinds began to come my way. I absorbed all of it like a sponge and came back for more.

I quickly found that I had drastically underestimated the number of people who believed themselves to be victims of alien abductions.

I had presumed it would be only a relatively small number of people. I suppose I imagined that there might be at most a couple dozen in all of IRC.

I was very wrong about that. The number of people claiming to be abductees swelled rapidly. It became apparent before long that what I was dealing with here was a virtually unlimited number of people, a never-ending human wave of abductees. They began to flood the place at all hours, wanting someone to talk to about their experiences or just a place to relax among friends without worry or stress.

It quickly became apparent that there was no way I could handle the volume of people all by myself and no way I could be there 24 hours a day in any case. I added some people I trusted from among our regular visitors as administrators, to help keep things running smoothly. The channel continued to grow both in numbers and in reputation. In a very short time, without ever intending to, I became the IRC equivalent of a rock star.

I was completely unprepared for any of this, having thought originally that I would be lucky if even three or four people total found my new channel. I decided to contact the man who was at the time considered to be the top authority on alien abductions in the civilian world, Budd Hopkins, and ask for some additional information about the subject.

Budd was kind enough to reply to me and to offer to help in any way he could, including having me refer people to him as needed. His partner, John Velez, also became involved and I spoke to him on a regular basis, several times a week usually. Both were sincere in their wish to help people who were victims of alien abduction.

Budd, as it turned out, had a rather large and critical blind spot when it came to the subject, one which ultimately prevented him from gaining a full and proper understanding of what was really taking place. He refused to listen to anything which had to do with any type of conspiracy or the idea of governmental contact or interaction with alien races. He simply was not interested in such things in the least and would have no part of discussing them, ever. I don't think he believed that such contact could be taking place and therefore he arbitrarily eliminated it as a valid possibility. The result was that Budd wanted no part of any discussions about things which in his opinion did not actually occur in the first place.

He was unfortunately quite mistaken in that belief and his refusal to take seriously the possibility that alien-governmental interaction might indeed be taking place resulted in an incomplete and inaccurate understanding of the situation. Even so, Budd Hopkins did important research and his books did much to open the door to a greater acceptance by the public of the abduction phenomenon.

I stayed with this IRC channel for about a year and a half, during which time it continued to grow and thrive. During that time, I spoke personally with over 2000 people who reported being abductees. It served as training under fire and before long I got quite good at it. Of all those I spoke with, it was my opinion that only three of them were not legitimate abductees. One was clearly psychotic, one appeared to be trying to gain attention or favor by reporting something that wasn't true and one was a member of the military who later admitted that his job was to monitor and infiltrate as many UFO-related IRC groups as possible, keep logs of everything that was said there and pass the logs on to his superior at the end of his shift. His URL indicated that he was logged on at minot.com, a server located near Minot Air Force Base in North Dakota.

As some time went by and the number of people I interviewed rapidly climbed, it soon became clear to me that by and large I was hearing the same story over and over. People who were complete strangers to each other, from all over the country and from all walks of life, were all basically telling me the same thing, with only the minor details changed. I could have switched their reports with those of many others and there would have been little difference between them.

Some of them described their abductors: short grey beings with large, black, almond-shaped eyes who always spoke to them telepathically rather than aloud. Almost all of them remembered being abducted multiple times, beginning in early childhood and on throughout their adult lives until late middle age.

I kept hearing the same basic story, with only minor details changed, over and over. Those who described their experiences to me were completely unaware that I had already heard the same thing hundreds of times from other people. It was clear that they all believed what they were saying to be the truth.

It was also quite evident that I was not dealing with a group of delusional crazies. These people were sane, rational and sincere. They ran the gamut from housewives to artists, professional airline or military pilots to college professors. A couple of them were employed by NASA and were still trying to understand just what was happening to them and why.

I noticed some things which generally appeared to be factors which connected them to each other, things they had in common. One was that they almost always seemed to have a high degree of intelligence. Some were clearly geniuses, but of those who weren't I would still estimate that the great majority of them would have qualified as "gifted", meaning an IQ somewhere between 130 and 150.

Another thing that many of them had in common was that they were people who possessed a high degree of creativity in some form or another. Some were visual or graphics artists, some were composers, some painted or played music as a lifelong hobby, some were writers or poets or inventors. The bulk of them claimed that their first contact experience had occurred when they were around the age of six or seven. Many of the people who spoke of being abducted by aliens had at some point gone through a near-death experience.

It was obvious that the aliens were not abducting people at random. They were looking for individuals who had certain characteristics and selectively abducting those people. Furthermore, it became apparent that the aliens were keeping track of certain bloodlines within the human population. If someone had been abducted, there was a very high chance that at least one of their parents or grandparents had been abducted too. The same thing applied to their children and grandchildren.

Though it sometimes appeared to skip a generation, abductees were being chosen based on their genetics. When they found a genetic line that suited them, it seemed, the aliens would follow it through the generations, abducting what they felt were the most suitable offspring for their purposes.

This was clearly not a matter of medical examinations which were being performed on a random sample of the population. It was a long-term project that extended over many generations and very probably over many centuries. Certain high-priority humans were being targeted as part of a carefully-planned program which could, for all we knew, have been in place for literally thousands of years.

I will return to the topic of abductions and examine it in more detail in a later chapter. Even during this early stage of my research, however, it seemed there was little doubt that whatever the purpose behind alien abductions turned out to be, it had little or nothing to do with the best interests of those it victimized.

These people were being utilized as though they were lab rats by non-human intruders who appeared to be completely unconcerned about their pain, terror, comfort or any psychological issues which may have resulted from their experiences. These were not the actions of a friend; they were capital crimes. They were acts of war directed against innocent and undeserving civilians.

IRC in those days was an internet war zone. Many scripts were available for download which had the ability blow other IRC users completely offline. It wasn't long before the attacks against members of our channel—and myself in particular—began coming. At the time, I was using a notably under-powered computer which had only

4M of RAM and offered me no way to defend myself against such attacks. I was an easy target. I got blown offline—disconnected from my server—frequently, many times each day, and others had similar problems.

In addition, people began to spoof our IRC nicknames, pretending to be one of the administrators I had appointed to help me with the workload and then proceeding to kick people out of the channel, accompanied by privately-sent insulting messages which the victims believed were from one of our actual administrators.

The constant inflow of abductees and others to the channel combined with the struggle to stay online and try to prevent them from hijacking the nicknames of my administrators was something I had not anticipated and was totally unprepared for.

I felt quite protective of both my channel and the people who chose to regularly frequent it. Because of that I began putting in far too many hours and sleeping as little as possible so I could be online and somehow at least attempt to protect it as well as I was able to. It was a bad situation which got progressively worse as time passed.

Bill, the engineer who was by now a good friend of mine, lived a relatively short distance from me, just a few hour's drive. Several times I drove down to spend long weekends at his lovely home, which was surrounded by forest. He had been employed by NASA and the Air Force as a contractor for about sixteen years at the time I met him, was very good at his job and came equipped with some impressive security clearances.

Bill knew how interested I was in the topics of UFO's and alien contact and had seen first-hand how hard I worked at it. He knew how hard I pushed myself in an effort both to learn all I could and to keep our channel a safe and comfortable place for abductees to come and talk with others about their experiences. Eventually he felt comfortable enough with me and was sufficiently convinced of my determination and sincerity that he began to share things with me that would certainly be considered "insider information" and which clearly would have been subject to a high degree of security classification.

We remained close friends for years and he educated me about many things…and then one day, still at a relatively young age, he was suddenly gone, the victim of an apparent heart attack as he slept.

Maybe that's what really happened, but it is also well known that a heart attack (as well as many other fatal conditions) can be remotely triggered through classified technology. This technology is often used to dispose of people who have been determined to either pose a security risk or to have outlived their usefulness to the government and whose silence must be assured by killing them. I will never know which of those things happened.

Along the way, early on in our friendship, he did me one of the greatest and most unexpected favors anyone has ever done for me regarding the subject of alien contact. He quietly mentioned my name to some of his associates and superiors in the military whom he happened to know were dissatisfied with the way the government was handling the issue of alien contact and who wanted to make the public aware of the truth but were prevented from doing so due to their rank or positions.

These people contacted me privately, sometimes by e-mail or telephone and sometimes in person, and spoke to me of their concerns. They insisted that their names never be used and that our conversations be considered off-the-record. All of them wanted certain information they had to be presented to the public by a person of integrity and high credibility and they had, they told me, determined that I was that person.

I would make note here of the fact that I never sought out any of these people, nor did I ever ask anyone to violate any oaths or security restrictions they may have operated under. They came to me and spoke to me of whatever it was that was on their mind. I didn't ask whether any of the information given to me in such conversations was covered by security restrictions and none of them ever told me one way or another.

It doesn't take a genius to figure out that most of it was almost certainly highly classified. I have no way of knowing that for certain, however, and no official source has ever made it known to me that such information is classified. Until and unless that happens, I feel I have the right to pass along such parts of it as I see fit to others. Certain things I will never speak of to anyone because of my belief that they may represent legitimate national security concerns if they got into the wrong hands and I would never knowingly do anything which might harm or endanger my country. But certain other things are in my opinion both right and necessary to discuss in a public manner and I will do so later in this manuscript.

Having access to sources such as these, some of which were very high-ranking sources indeed, is a UFO investigator's dream come true. It is something which occurred partly due to hard work and dedication but which it seems to me was also a matter of luck, the luck of being in the right place at the right time to meet the right person and make the right impression on him. The chance that one would somehow find themselves in that situation is obviously quite remote. I do not know of any way a person could plan for such a thing or how one would go about trying to make such a situation come to pass.

It was far more than I had ever expected would come my way and the chance of such a thing happening to me seemed so unlikely that I had never even seriously considered it as a possibility. But life will have its own way and sometimes things happen which we would not reasonably expect to occur. Some people buy the winning lottery ticket, purely by accident. Some are struck by lightning while playing a round of golf. Some people get inside sources who talk to them about UFO's and aliens. Much to my surprise, I happened to be one of those people and it changed my life forever. That's just how it goes sometimes.

It was around this time that I decided to write a book about the subject, having come into so much information which was new to me and having by this time had the opportunity to speak with many people who claimed to be victims of alien abduction (I stopped counting at two thousand—the number is surely over three thousand at the time this book is being written). I made a basic—and, looking back on it, a very foolish—mistake: I let my plans be known in the IRC channel, already knowing it was being monitored by the government. I suppose I didn't think I was someone who was important enough for them to bother harassing. I was apparently quite wrong in that assumption.

A short time later, my phone was tapped. Whenever I picked it up I could hear a tell-tale click through the line every few seconds. My e-mail was hacked and spoofed as well: messages were sent to people which were horrible and insulting and which appeared to have come from my e-mail address, though I had no idea such e-mails had ever been written, much less sent. My online chat sessions, which I had thought were private, were broken into by third parties. I could not see the messages they sent, which appeared to come from me…but the other person in the chat could see them. It caused me no end of problems.

They even went so far as to send nasty, vicious e-mails from my address to my girlfriend, who naturally thought I had written them. At one point, they called her on the telephone and advised her to have nothing further to do with me, telling her that I was not what I appeared to be and was nothing but trouble. They eventually succeeded in frightening her enough that she broke up with me.

Sometimes it seemed to me that they would find new ways to make my life difficult not because they had any reason to do so, but just to show me that they could bring me pain and misery any time they wanted to. The government has a very large toolbox when it comes to inflicting pain on someone they have decided to target. I wasn't quite sure what I had done wrong…but whatever it was, they were coming after me for it anyway.

One morning a pair of well-dressed men in suits wearing dark sunglasses showed up at my front door, claiming to be couriers from a Certain Intelligence Agency. "You seem to be a guru," they told me. "You appear to have all the answers."

I suppose a person could see a statement like that as some form of compliment, but it did not seem that way to me. In the first place, I have never been any type of "guru" nor have I ever wanted to become one. Gurus depend upon a cult of personality, something I have no interest in being a part of. The important aspect of UFO research has always been the information itself, in my opinion. It should never be about personalities. Furthermore, I have never once claimed to have all the answers nor has that thought ever come into my head for even a split second. I know better. The most I can ever hope for is to be able to find *some* of the answers—many more questions will always remain unanswered than I will ever be able to find solutions for.

"We don't have a problem with what you're doing for the abductees," one of them said. "You're trying to help them and we think that's a real nice thing. It's something somebody should have done for them a long time ago. But you sent some chapters of the book you are writing to other people. They have been intercepted and read.

We were sent to deliver a message to you. Every day, people vanish and are never heard from again. Every day, people commit suicide. If you attempt to publish that information, you might very well end up being one of those people."

At this point I did something they surely didn't expect. I laughed at them. "You can kill me if you want to," I replied. "I know that. I know I can't stop you. You can kill me...but you can't scare me. I don't let anybody tell me what I am allowed to say or to write. I can not be scared into deciding not to publish my book. But I probably *can* be paid off. It will cost you seven figures, but that's nothing to a group like yours--it's just pocket change. Come up with that and I'll never publish a word."

The other man smiled grimly. "Tomorrow morning, there will be a paper bag sitting out near your trash can," he told me. "The money will be there. In unmarked bills."

"Sure it will."

He laughed. "We are just intermediaries, sent here to deliver a message. We have done that," he stated, his smile gone. "Don't forget what we said."

And then they left. I never saw either of them again. Were they really couriers for that infamous intelligence agency? I have no way of knowing. It really doesn't matter much, in my opinion. The literary agent who had agreed to help market my book to publishing companies never spoke to me again after those men came to my door, not even to tell me to get lost. It seems that someone got to him too.

In the end, they got their way: the unexpected pressures from all directions combined with the stress of writing the book and getting almost no sleep eventually drove me to a nervous breakdown. The book was never published.

Eventually things got to a point where I decided to give it all up for the sake of my health. Without announcing my intention in advance, I transferred ownership of the IRC channel to one of the administrators I had appointed, then I walked away from it and never went back. I isolated myself and stopped making any type of public statements about UFO's or alien contact.

With all those things accomplished and all that damage done, the harassment ended. My phone was no longer tapped and as best I was able to determine they went away and left me alone.

As I stated before, I certainly do not have all the answers about anything in life. I can, however, tell you one thing for sure: it is no fun at all to be hassled by the United States government and I highly recommend you avoid becoming a target of theirs if it is within your power to do so. If you have something to do which necessitates taking that risk, be aware that they are very serious people who can bring a lot of pain your way if they want to.

As private citizens, there is very little we can do to stop them. We have no way to protect ourselves from people whose names we will never know who have been given immunity from the law, the latest in high-tech gadgetry and an unlimited budget. If they want us dead, dead is what we will surely be. It may look like a suicide, a heart attack, a robbery attempt or an unfortunate car accident...but dead is what we will be.

Within these circles, silence is the price of survival. It is also the reason many good people are deprived of life. Kill one and you can scare a thousand more into being silent about what they know. But what is the price of this enforced silence? If no one is willing to step forward and speak the truth, nothing prevents the government from continuing to get away with this type of behavior forever. If the public is not informed about what is really happening behind closed doors and what is being done in its name, it will never attempt to stop them. Somebody somewhere must tell.

Deciding to be a whistle blower is a lousy life choice. The price paid is far too high and it is almost always far out of line with the value of the information one comes forward with. Whistle blowers are harassed, threatened, persecuted, slandered and they very often end up dying long before their time. For all this risk and trouble— trouble which often involves sacrificing their own lives for the sake of making information available to the public—almost nobody pays attention to what they say. Almost nobody seems to care.

Whistle blowers, witnesses and researchers put their lives on the line for a public which appears to be mired in apathy and completely self-absorbed. The information which was bought at the cost of the lives of honorable people who have committed no crime will in the end be almost totally ignored. It will be either ridiculed or vilified by the mass media, then swept under the rug and treated as though it didn't even exist in the first place.

These people come forward at great personal risk out of a feeling of responsibility and an honest desire to help their brothers and sisters. They wanted them to be aware of information which has been improperly withheld from them. They wanted people to know that crimes including violence, perjury, conspiracy, treason, kidnapping and murder are being committed against them by agents of their own government.

For their trouble, they are for the most part ignored by the very people they risked so much to try to help. If agents of the shadow government decide to have them killed, no one will be held to account. No charges will ever be filed and nobody will demand justice.

In the end, life will continue as it was before. The government will continue to get away with abusing the public trust, murdering innocent citizens and paying the killer's salaries with tax monies collected from the very people the whistle blower sacrificed their life to try to help escape from their chains.

Considering all this, one is well within their rights to question whether the society for which these people gave their lives is really one which is worth saving. I used to think it was...but in all honesty, I am no longer sure. I am no longer convinced that a society which would allow its most courageous members to be killed without so much as lifting a finger either to help them or to demand justice for their murders is one which is worth saving.

It is a thought which breaks my heart even as something deep inside me confirms the truth of that idea: we are giving up our lives for people who do not appreciate what we do at all and who do not even seem to care. It is difficult to escape the conclusion that we deserve far better than this kind of treatment.

We deserve far better. America itself deserves far better than to have her people sit silently by without even attempting to defend themselves as the lofty principles upon which this once-great nation was founded are undermined and the freedoms they once enjoyed are systematically stripped from them, never to be returned. I fear that one day very soon we will awaken to find that our freedom has vanished forever, replaced by a police state.

It goes without saying that all of us deserve far better than to be betrayed by people who are willing—anxious, even—to bring down what was once the world's greatest example of freedom, liberty and hope. That they would do so for personal gain, though they already control fortunes that would make Midas green with envy, surely constitutes one of the greatest crimes in the history of humanity.

If the American people had any sense of self-preservation at all, they would round up the whole bunch of them and put them to death, by lynching if necessary, since the court system will obviously never be willing to touch them at all. To allow them to survive is to wish ruin upon yourselves and your nation.

It is the sad truth of things that difficult actions must sometimes be taken during difficult times. Those actions, which may not be allowable under the law of the land, are sometimes necessary anyway. In the end, they can make the difference between enslavement and survival.

When the legal system has been subverted and is turned against the people themselves, there is no choice but direct action for those who wish to save themselves from oppression and tyranny.

A police state is unquestionably the direction that America, my beloved nation and my only home, is headed. No efforts on my part will in any way be sufficient to the task of changing that. No sacrifice on my part will in the end make any difference or result in slowing down the steady drumbeat of authoritarian rule. I know that. But if one does not consider freedom and liberty to be worth fighting and dying for, if one does not love their people and their country enough to be willing to make the ultimate sacrifice for them, what could there possibly be which *is* worth fighting and dying for?

I have no answer to that question. I know of nothing better to do than to try as best I can to awaken my fellow citizens while there may still be time for them to save themselves. I do not believe that there is any realistic chance that I will be successful in doing so. I think that the people of America will continue to act like a herd of obedient sheep or brainwashed zombies until they have lost everything they once took for granted and the nation that was once a bastion of liberty and an example to the entire world of what the human spirit could accomplish is nothing but a faded memory in the dustbin of history.

I think that you, who are reading this book, will take no appreciable action to help save yourself and will in the end be sucked down the drain with the rest of what used to be the greatest nation in the world. As I said, these are ideas which break my heart to even consider, much less believe.

In the very first chapter of this book, I stated clearly that the search for truth is my primary concern, regardless of what that truth may turn out to be. As is so often the case, the truth I have found has turned out to be bitter and tragic, something which I do not want to believe and which is a source of great sadness to me. It is something I would do anything in my power to change if I could.

Former President of the United States James Garfield once stated that "The truth will set you free...but first it will make you miserable." It has not been my experience that the first part of his statement was accurate: I have found no reason to believe that the truth has set me free. There is no question, however, that it has made me miserable. Garfield certainly appears to have been right about that.

CHAPTER 8: HOW TO MAKE A SKEPTIC CRY

*"When you have eliminated the impossible, whatever remains,
however improbable, must be the truth."*
-- *Sir Arthur Conan Doyle*

*"It's a habit I have,
I don't get pushed around."*
--Bernie Taupin

Of all those who claim they do not "believe in" the presence of aliens and alien spacecraft on and around our world, none are as deeply dug in to their position and apparently so personally invested in defending & maintaining it as mainstream scientists. Many of them are brilliant, talented and highly respected experts in their fields. One would think they should be among the first to take a keen interest in the subject. They should be motivated to do everything within their power to carefully investigate the evidence in a fair, logical and unbiased manner.

It seems rather obvious and inescapable to me that scientists would not rest until they could honestly say they knew for sure one way or the other. It seems they would want to investigate all aspects of the UFO situation in search of the truth. That is, after all, what scientists do for a living and we've got many of the best scientists in the world who are already being paid their salaries out of public monies. The possibility that we have already contacted extra-terrestrials and that they are already here should be more than enough to attract the attention of any inquisitive mind.

Contact with intelligent races capable of somehow traversing the unthinkably vast distances between the stars would unquestionably be the most important and profound event in human history. When there is reason to believe that such contact is taking place at this very moment, scientists of all types would be dispatched to investigate the evidence fully and with extreme care. Universities would line up for the chance to take part in it. They would offer classes about it for science credit. It is, after all, a new frontier of human knowledge and a transition to an entirely new paradigm. It will bring about a complete revision of our views about humanity and its place in a universe which not only contains other intelligent civilizations but the means to travel interstellar distances quickly.

If the presence of extra-terrestrials could be firmly established, it would be the dawning of a new age and there could be no going back. Our societies and belief structures would be forever transformed, changed almost beyond recognition in some cases. It is impossible to overstate the epochal nature of the change represented by contact with extra-terrestrials of superior intelligence and incredibly-advanced technologies. Scientists would not only be eager to fully investigate the possibility using all the tools at their disposal, it seems there would be nothing which could stop them from doing so.

Well, that isn't quite true. As it turns out, there is one thing which could stop them from doing so: a long-term psychological warfare operation dedicated to destroying the lives and careers of any who spoke out about UFO's combined with the threat of having their federal research grants cut off. Once those things come into play, the government has the capacity to stifle, smother and kill anything or anyone who poses a threat to their interests—including the biggest story in human history.

This is exactly what has been done. The result is that only a small handful of scientists appear to care about UFO's. They are strongly discouraged from speaking publicly about it. To do so means risking one's career and reputation, at the very least.

Instead of seeing hordes of mainstream scientists clamoring at the bit to study alien contact and UFO's, what we have is an almost universal denial and silence from all corners. Universities refuse to offer any classes about it and the scientists they employ refuse to discuss the subject other than to dismiss it and belittle any who take it seriously.

This is ironic, since the so-called "science" they claim proves their case has nothing to do with science and often requires tossing basic scientific principles and methods to the wind. It is doubly ironic because their position is full of more holes than Swiss cheese and those who, as scientific professionals, should be the first to notice this don't appear to notice it at all.

That being the case, it falls to me—a non-scientist—to chastise and lecture professional scientists about how to do their jobs. It should not be necessary for me to have to remind them of some of the most basic principles of science, which they seem to have completely forgotten about in their rush to secure federal funding. Apparently, however, it is. I do so now, with great reluctance and only because it seems that nobody else will step forward to do it.

Those within the mainstream scientific community often describe themselves as "skeptics". In fact, that is almost never true.

A skeptic is someone who refuses to believe something before being shown evidence which indicates it is true. When such evidence is put forth and cannot be disqualified for a legitimate reason, a true skeptic is required to accept the evidence as valid. An example of a true skeptic is the late Dr. J. Allen Hynek. He began as a disbeliever and was put in charge of Project Bluebook. Later, upon learning that there was sufficient evidence to prove the case, he changed his mind.

It is very rare these days that one will encounter a true skeptic. Most who style themselves as skeptics are really what I like to call "pseudo-skeptics". A pseudo-skeptic demands that he be provided with evidence. Then, when evidence is presented, he either ignores it or declares it to be fake without bothering to investigate it.

Those who call themselves "debunkers" also have an Achilles heel. Debunking is a necessary and valuable thing when it is performed in a legitimate way. There is no question that there are some individuals who will intentionally lie about seeing UFO's or who will falsify photographs or films. This problem has become increasingly more difficult to spot with the advent of high-quality professional tools such as Photoshop and easy access to powerful personal computers.

It is also true that many reported sightings turn out to be explainable as either natural or man-made objects. It must be remembered as well that human memory is fallible and that even the most well-intentioned people sometimes make mistakes. In such cases, a valid explanation for the sighting is called for. Frauds and misidentifications have no useful place within the database other than as a statistic. The sooner they are eliminated, the better for all concerned.

Faked photos and films are the bane of the UFO community. They cause legitimate sightings to be unfairly and incorrectly lumped together with them into a group in which all reported sightings are considered either frauds or to have a conventional explanation. There are innumerable people out there who are more than eager to prove photographs and films which purport to show alien spacecraft to be fakes or hoaxes of some type. They will jump at any chance to do so.

It is fair to say that there is nobody who detests hoaxes more than those who have had legitimate sightings of what are clearly alien spacecraft. It is already extremely difficult to have such sightings taken seriously by scientists or the public at large. Every time a sighting is faked it becomes even more difficult and those who report such things are given less credibility. As researchers, we have no interest in hoaxes or sightings which are explainable in conventional terms other than to identify them as such and eliminate them from consideration.

To members of the debunking community, these so-called sightings are a matter of mirth and glee—they give them another reason to laugh at and dismiss all other sightings in a wholesale manner. For those who have seen an alien spacecraft, it's far more personal. There will surely always be sightings which are explainable in conventional terms--this is to be expected and is unavoidable. Those who intentionally fake such sightings, however, make an already highly difficult job even more so and are despised by those within the UFO community.

The first major problem concerning debunkers comes up when false explanations are used to "debunk" legitimate sightings. This occurs with regularity. Sightings are declared to be weather balloons, headlights reflecting off clouds, military aircraft or the result of delusion when there is no evidence to show that such is the case. They are then, arbitrarily and with a semblance of great authority, dismissed and rejected. This rejection is almost never accompanied by a proper investigation of the sightings in question.

When this happens, debunking is not what has taken place. What has happened is called "cooking the data": changing or ignoring parts of the data to make it conform to your belief or inserting "solutions" which do not actually fit the data and then pronouncing that the sighting has been "debunked". This is dishonest, unscientific in the extreme and unfair to those who have had real sightings and honestly reported them. Scientists would like us to believe that they are above such things as cooking the data, but in fact they engage in it constantly. It is a historical fact that scientists have often been far more concerned with defending the status quo than they are with seeking the truth and upholding a high standard of scientific integrity.

Today we will turn the tables on those who cook the data and those who use their positions to falsify explanations and intimidate the public into accepting them. We will use the methods of those who hide behind the veneer of science, while carrying out procedures which are anathema to science, against them. When that is done, it will be seen that their so-called "position" turns out to be pretty much nothing but hot air and the loud noise they make will be replaced by an embarrassed silence.

The first thing that must be considered is that there are different forms of proof. There is scientific proof, in which case evidence can be gained and evaluated under laboratory conditions which will show something to be true. The second type of proof is what we will term "legal proof", in which case we are talking about establishing the truth of something beyond reasonable doubt. These two kinds of proof are very different in their approach, but when used properly they can both be made to demonstrate convincingly that something is in fact true.

The bottom line is that not every question can be answered accurately by utilizing a strictly scientific form of proof. There are things which cannot be tested under laboratory conditions, things which are true but which cannot be proven using standard scientific methodology. The scientific method was designed to be used to measure or evaluate things which are not subject to randomness or dependent upon personal choices. It works brilliantly when it is applied to determining when an eclipse will occur or measuring the speed of light. It does not work at all, on the other hand, if one attempts to use the scientific method to predict the winning numbers in tomorrow's lottery or tries to determine how many people briefly considered robbing a bank yesterday but then thought better of it.

If such limitations on the utility of the scientific method did not exist, there would be no need for a standard of proof beyond a reasonable doubt in a court of law. The scientific method would be used to prove the guilt or innocence of every defendant, and it would do so perfectly every time.

The scientific method is an extremely powerful tool when applied properly, but like any tool it is completely unsuitable for tasks it was not designed to for. Scientists themselves should be the first to realize these limitations. They should be the first to understand that the scientific method has no means of determining whether alien contact has been achieved unless an alien being shows up at MIT and volunteers to be tested and the tests are then repeated and verified by other top labs around the world.

Until and unless that occurs, there is nothing for the scientific method to measure and therefore nothing it can be used to prove or disprove. One may as well swing a baseball bat and attempt to hit a home run with the moon.

To insist that the scientific method is the one and only acceptable way to determine the truth about alien contact, then, is intellectually insulting and dishonest. When such insistence comes from scientists, it is a display of either an incredible degree of hypocrisy or complete incompetence on their part. They use the scientific method every day, like a firefighter uses a water hose. Knowing its limitations is part of their job, just as knowing that a squirt gun isn't the right tool to use on an office fire is part of a fireman's job.

One example of something which does not conform to lab standards is the matter of repeatability. Scientists insist that a certain result or event be repeatable in order that it can be confirmed as true and legitimate. This is fine...if you are in control of the parameters of the experiment. Otherwise it cannot be made to apply and it is pointless to expect that it would.

Let's imagine, for instance, that you fly an F-15 fighter over the head of a primitive tribesman in the Amazon who is out hunting for food. He returns to his village and excitedly describes what he saw to the people there. They refuse to believe his story unless the event is repeatable—in other words, until they see it too they aren't going to accept his word about it.

Is the event repeatable? Absolutely...provided you own the F-15. You can repeat it as many times as you like. You can repeat it daily, weekly, hourly, etc., on any schedule you care to set. The villagers, however, cannot make it *ever* repeat—nor is there any logical reason to expect it to. It is completely out of their control: they have no way of influencing what the pilot of the F-15 may decide to do and no way of inducing him to return and fly over the same area again.

In this case, the sighting was honestly reported and accurate but it was at the same time completely impossible to cause or to expect the

F-15 to return for an encore. The situation is the same when it comes to UFO sightings. Insisting that a UFO sighting be repeatable is ignorant and insulting: we do not control the UFO and have no way of convincing its pilot to return to the same place to provide confirmation of his existence to scientists.

Repeatability is something which can legitimately be required in a science lab when one controls all the parameters of the experiment. It can neither be asked for nor expected when a key element of the equation—in this case, the ability to control the UFO—is absent.

Skeptics will always also ask for physical proof—they see that as their ace-in-the-hole, knowing that it is virtually impossible for anyone to produce it. How, after all, would one come by such proof? Steal an interstellar engine from a UFO crash? Not likely. Anyone who tried to escape from the scene of a crashed alien spaceship with so much as a small scrap of metal would at the very least be arrested on the spot.

There is no other way for anyone to produce physical proof that they might think has even a reasonable chance of being accepted as legitimate by the skeptical community. Going back to our example of the primitive tribesman, it would be like insisting that he provide physical evidence that an F-15 flew over his head that day. He would have no way whatsoever of providing such evidence...and yet the F-15 did in fact fly over his head.

Even if someone could do such a thing as produce a piece of metal from a crashed spaceship--a sample of an unknown alloy, perhaps--it would do them no good as far as the skeptics are concerned. They would then insist that the person compellingly prove that the metal wasn't manufactured on Earth. How exactly is one expected to do such a thing? Even if it were an alloy never seen by humans, there is no way to prove that it was manufactured on another world and used in an alien spacecraft. Anyone involved in the field of science knows that it is impossible to prove a negative—in other words, to prove that the metal was not manufactured by humans—and they have now put the person who produced it in what they know to be an impossible position while pretending to be fair and unbiased.

The disinformation agents would immediately spring into action, some claiming that it was manufactured in orbit aboard the space station, others claiming it didn't really exist at all and the whole thing was nothing but a hoax. The reputation and credibility of the person who produced the metal would be attacked from all sides without regard to the truth, attempting to ruin both and thereby isolate the person.

People would be intimidated and ridiculed at all points if they spoke out about believing the metal was really what it was claimed to be. They would become leery of defending either the metal or the person who produced it for fear of being publicly called out and accused of being a gullible fool. Conversations in forums and at conventions which mentioned the subject would be quickly rerouted or diverted to a different subject. Anyone who attempted to defend the evidence as being legitimate would be hooted and jeered at until they were forced into an embarrassed silence. And one fine day the person who had originally produced the scrap of metal would probably find that it had gone missing, stolen.

The same basic problems are all still present if someone produces what they claim is a legitimate photograph or film of an alien being. Most people will not be inclined to take any such photo or film seriously and it is impossible to prove that any photograph or film clip contains an actual alien being. Once again, a person would find themselves in the impossible situation of trying to prove a negative: "prove it's NOT a fake!"

By invoking the "requirement" of proving a negative—a requirement they would never allow themselves to be forced into, knowing as they do that such a thing cannot be done by anyone, ever—they have effectively eliminated the possibility of having to admit that any type of evidence is legitimate as well as ensuring that all purported photos/films of extra-terrestrial beings can be ignored or dismissed with impunity. From their point of view, this is much like betting that a coin flip will come up heads while using a two-headed coin. If they can successfully use this method to prevent any type of physical or photographic evidence from being accepted, their position will remain bulletproof forever. For all practical purposes, they will have forced those who come forward with evidence to bet that a two-headed coin will come up tails. They will have made themselves invincible. What they will *not* have done is engage in legitimate scientific practices.

The classic elements of the scientific method are designed to measure and analyze natural processes and events. A "theory" is something which is possible but which remains unproven. For a theory to be proven a series of measurements must be taken, all of which must match the predictions made by the theory. These measurements must then be repeated by others and the same results must be obtained.

As this process is repeated and more and more measurements are taken which all match the predictions of the theory, the theory gains traction and credibility. Once sufficient measurements have been made, all of which agree with the predictions made by the theory, the theory may be promoted to the status of an indisputable fact, a scientific principle or even a universal law.

If at any point along the way measurements are taken which are at odds with the predictions made by the theory, they must be carefully checked and repeated. It must be shown with certainty whether they do in fact contradict the predictions of the theory or were simply the results of some type of error which made its way into the process of measurement. If the results are deemed to be accurate and do not support the predictions made by the theory, the theory itself is then considered to be in error. It must either be revised until a new version of the theory is obtained which can account for the measurements or it must be considered disproven and discarded altogether.

The scientific method is *not* designed or intended to be able to test for or prove the existence of advanced extra-terrestrials. This is especially true when neither the extra-terrestrials nor the government want their existence to be provable and do everything within their power to make such a proof impossible. The scientific method relies on and requires the ability to make accurate measurements and to have those measurements verified by other independent tests which show the same results for the same procedures.

In the case of testing for the presence of advanced extra-terrestrial beings on and around our world, it is not possible for the scientific method to be utilized until an alien--along with his interstellar spacecraft—chooses to show up and present himself for examination at a scientific institution of impeccable credibility.

Without solid, undeniable physical evidence that this alien and his spacecraft do in fact exist, science has nothing to bite its teeth into.

Until there is something which can be accurately measured and observed, the scientific method has no traction and there is no way to apply it to the situation in question. It is for all practical purposes unsuited to the job at hand and useless when it comes to analyzing the question in a way which could reasonably be expected to yield accurate conclusions.

Please note, however, that both the extra-terrestrials and their interstellar spacecraft have existed the whole time. They have not chosen to provide the scientific establishment with undeniable proof of their existence. Like the F-15 mentioned a moment ago, however, our inability to obtain one of their engines and subject it to scientific examination does not imply that it isn't there.

Having an alien spacecraft or an F-15 fly over your head has absolutely nothing to do with whether you will be able to haul one of its engines home with you. A prudent person would surely guess that you would have no opportunity to do such a thing. A scientist would insist that you produce the engine and then declare the sighting to be a hoax and you to be a fraud when you failed to do so. That is a major difference.

In the absence of something which can be subjected to repeated measurements, tests and observation there is nothing to which the scientific method can be applied. It is designed to be applied to objects, processes or forces which can be examined or tested by many different people in many different places and which will always yield the same results when they are.

The scientific method also requires that a theory must be able to make accurate predictions based upon its precepts. What kind of predictions might they expect us to make, based upon sightings of alien spacecraft? Since the activities of alien visitors and spacecraft are beyond our ability to predict accurately, there is nothing we can offer in the form of testable predictions and nothing we could reasonably be expected to come up with. One again, the scientific method was not designed for this type of situation and does not apply to it.

Utilizing a tool which is not suitable for the job cannot be expected to yield answers which are accurate. To insist that it is the only allowable tool is to engage in a process which is flawed from the start. It is all but guaranteed to generate conclusions which must be similarly flawed and to then accept those conclusions as valid. This cannot be considered a proper application of the scientific method. It is a backhanded method of cooking the data in advance to ensure that the result will match a predetermined conclusion.

The fact that the conclusion is completely inaccurate and is based on a methodology which is inapplicable to the situation makes no difference to the scientists themselves. Their only interest was in "proving" their own position—a position which is entirely based on inductive reasoning. It has nothing to do with a thorough, honest and unbiased investigation into the matter or with any type of scientifically-valid testing. Neither of those things have taken place at all.

The position of mainstream science regarding an alien presence has a fatal weakness, one which cannot be eradicated: the moment anything which purports to show evidence that an alien presence does in fact exist is accepted as valid or legitimate, their entire position vanishes forever. All it takes is one photograph or film, a single radar contact which shows--or just one of the 150-million-plus people who have reported UFO sightings to have really seen--an alien spacecraft and everyone who is invested in the idea that such things do not exist is proven wrong at the same time and the argument they have defended and promoted for so long—decades, in some cases, or even entire careers—falls instantly.

For that reason, no evidence of any kind, no matter what the source or how convincing the evidence may appear to be, can ever be accepted by the pseudo-skeptics as legitimate. For their position to be correct every single photograph and film which appears to show an alien spacecraft must be either a mistake or a hoax of some kind, every radar record which appears to show an intelligently-guided air vehicle of hyper-advanced capabilities must be the result of a faulty radar unit and every witness who claims to have seen what can only reasonably be thought to be an alien spacecraft must be delusional, lying or drastically mistaken.

The basic assumption on the part of the pseudo-skeptics, then, is that mistakes, faulty equipment, hoaxes, delusion or dishonesty are the explanation for every report. There is no scientific reason whatsoever to assume this and no reason at all to believe it to be true...yet no other solution is seriously considered or will be accepted by the pseudo-skeptics, who will at the same time insist that their approach is based on "science" while laughing at UFO "believers" and accusing them of practicing pseudo-science, being gullible simpletons or of being mentally unbalanced.

Yet before even looking at the evidence the pseudo-skeptics have themselves abandoned any pretense of legitimate scientific procedures and begun cooking the data until it gives them an apparently-valid reason to ignore what it shows. Every photograph and film is considered fake, every witness statement either a lie or a case of faulty memory and every radar contact an equipment malfunction. This deeply flawed belief allows them to arbitrarily reject all types of possible evidence even though there is nothing which indicates their assumptions are in fact correct and no logical or scientific reason to think they would be.

Professional scientists should logically be expected to be the first to notice this massive detour from proper methodology and valid investigative procedures. They should be the first to point out that any so-called investigation which makes such blanket assumptions without a legitimate reason for doing so and before even beginning to look at the proposed evidence can in no way be termed 'scientific". They should know clearly that a skewed and one-sided examination of any subject whatsoever cannot be expected to lead one to the truth. To proceed as if it can be expected to find the truth rather than to intentionally evade or obscure it is intellectually dishonest: it treats a false expectation as the truth.

It is impossible for me to believe that the many brilliant and accomplished men and women of science who continually engage in this practice do not notice the fact that they are violating some of the most basic rules and procedures of their profession. I do not accept that there are eminent scientists and university professors, people of genius, who fail to understand that they are making mistakes that would cause a seventh-grade student to be given a failing grade on his science project. And this is only the beginning of the major problems inherent in the position of mainstream science regarding the subject of UFO's and alien contact.

Scientists will tell you that they always prefer the most likely explanation, when given a choice between several possibilities. This makes sense and is a logical approach. Let's see how it works in this case: What are the chances that well over 150 million people claim to have seen something and not one of them was intelligent or competent enough to correctly identify what they were looking at?

The entire position of mainstream science here is based upon the assumption that this is precisely what has happened. But nothing which even vaguely approaches such a situation has occurred even a single time in human history. Rather than choosing the most likely explanation, mainstream science has concluded that something which has never happened before--and which there is no scientific reason to believe has happened now--has happened now anyway. The odds of that idea being correct are so vanishingly small that they approach impossibility. This is not science--it is an act of desperation.

The most likely explanation clearly is that at least one person who claims to have seen an alien spacecraft is correct. Science, however, is institutionally unable to admit that the alien spacecraft idea is even a valid possibility. Despite almost a hundred years of sightings and mountains of evidence that they refuse to admit exists, the pseudo-skeptics choose to do something akin to spending their last dollar on a Lotto ticket which has a one in sixty-five million chance to win.

Where does science and logic end and denialism and voodoo begin? Don't ask them, because they clearly have no idea.

The skeptics position becomes even more difficult, if such a thing is possible, when considering the photographic evidence. What are the odds that every photograph and film which purports to show an alien spacecraft is in fact a fake? The odds are zero, because many of those photos and films have been thoroughly tested and are known to be unaltered and genuine. Some have stood the test of time for over a half century. Others come from the official records and films of NASA space missions—if we cannot accept unaltered NASA mission films to be a legitimate source, there is no source which can ever be accepted. But if only one single frame of a film or one photo shows an actual alien spacecraft, we've got company...and the position of the so-called skeptics evaporates into thin air immediately.

If one wants to choose the most likely option, bet that at least one photograph or film which shows an object which clearly appears to be an alien spacecraft and which demonstrates performance characteristics vastly superior to anything yet achieved by humans is an alien spacecraft. Any self-respecting gambler, when given the chance to bet all he owns that exactly zero alien spacecraft have ever been photographed or filmed, would turn and walk away from the bet. But science took that bet and went all-in. That speaks for itself—and the words it is saying are not "legitimate scientific investigation", much less "most likely explanation".

Scientists like to use a logical device known as Occam's razor to find the most likely solution to difficult problems. Occam's razor states that the simplest explanation is the best explanation and that any part of an explanation which is unnecessary or superfluous should be trimmed away.

Occam's razor is commonly invoked by mainstream scientists when the discussion turns to UFO's. The simplest explanation, they point out, is that UFO sightings can all be properly identified by conventional explanations, whether it be an honest mistake, a malfunctioning radar console, a delusion, hallucination or mirage of some kind, a natural or man-made object or out-and-out fraud rather than the actual presence of aliens and alien spacecraft on and around Earth. This sounds like a logical and reasonable argument—and it is...provided you are working with accurate data and assumptions. Unfortunately for mainstream science, this is not the case.

As we saw when we discussed psychological warfare in the previous chapter, an important element in any psychological operation is to provide the target with false data which points to false conclusions and to convince the target that the data itself is both accurate and verified. If the target can be convinced that he is working with accurate data when the data in question has been carefully and intentionally falsified by highly competent professionals for a specific purpose, he will draw conclusions which he will be certain must represent bottom-line truths but which will be completely mistaken. Moreover, the conclusions he draws will be precisely the conclusions he was intended to draw by those behind the psy-op who made certain that the inaccurate data they provided would unerringly lead to a certain set of conclusions while making it impossible to ever find the actual truth within the distorted mess of disinformation which the target has been convinced to accept as legitimate data.

In this way, even the most brilliant and well-intentioned of people can be misled and forever deceived, convinced they have analyzed the problem in a sufficiently careful manner and arrived at the only possible logical conclusion. They will believe that the evidence supports their position solidly and will be quite happy to promptly go about defending it and digging themselves into a deep hole without ever realizing there is a problem.

They will often continue doing this all throughout their lives, provided more accurate data does not come along which compellingly proves their position wrong. Those tasked with running and maintaining the psychological warfare operation will, of course, make sure that such data is never allowed to surface and that the initial data set continues to be supported and accepted as the truth.

What sort of data might be falsified and used to that end in this case?

The first thing to deal with will be the belief that Einstein's Theory of Relativity prohibits any object from traveling at or beyond the speed of light. This is a widely-accepted idea which is thought by many to be an integral and well-documented principle of proper physics, one which it is not possible to violate or reasonably dispute in any intelligent conversation.

That assumption is, unfortunately, not correct—nor is it what the Theory of Relativity states. The Theory of Relativity states that information can not travel faster than the velocity of light. It does not refer to physical objects, although it is assumed by many that physical objects (such as living beings or spacecraft) would also be forever limited by the light-speed barrier. This would mean that travel through the unthinkably vast distance of interstellar space represents a tremendously time-consuming undertaking at best. For everything other than a few nearby stars, it would mean that interstellar travel in a reasonable time frame is simply not possible.

We now have a chain of logic which appears on the surface reasonable, scientifically sound and all but impossible to argue with. It goes like this: Even if a spacecraft can be accelerated to .999 of light speed, the vast distances between stars would require so much time to successfully traverse that interstellar travel, as a practical matter, would at best be far more trouble than it is worth. It would for all intents and purposes be an investment of time and resources which could never be expected to pay off. It would effectively be money poured down the drain chasing an impossible dream.

Add to that the fact that the fastest man-made object to date has achieved a top speed of around 18,000 miles per hour—less than one thirty-seven thousandth of the speed of light—and it becomes clear that the idea of interstellar travel is nothing more than a pipe dream. To presume that some hypothetical alien civilization had somehow found a way to get around the inherent light-speed limit which is part of the fabric of the universe itself, the argument goes, is illogical and fantastical since there is no evidence that this is the case.

Alien civilizations almost certainly do exist somewhere out there, as all competent scientists will agree...but they're not here because they can't get here, therefore all purported sightings of alien spacecraft must be false for one or another reason and there is no practical point in wasting time evaluating and disproving every single report. Scientists are busy people, after all, and funds are limited—there is no compelling reason to waste time and money looking for the presence of aliens on or around Earth when there is no way for them to get here in the first place.

It sounds quite reasonable and logical, when put in those terms. But along the way to this seemingly bulletproof argument something has happened which has not been noticed...and it changes everything.

So smoothly and subtly that it has escaped the notice of even the most intelligent targets—in this case, mainstream scientists—an age-old sales technique known as the "bait and switch" has been invoked. Scientists have been manipulated into asking a completely different question than the one they originally set out to find an answer to. They have been convinced to re-frame the question without even noticing that it happened. They are now asking "How could an intelligent alien civilization get here without violating Einstein's equations?" and they have been provided with what appears to be a satisfactory and scientifically-supported answer: "They can't." Anyone who dares to question or disagree with this answer will be immediately ridiculed, their credibility blasted to pieces, their reputation demeaned and possibly their career will come to an end just for having the temerity to voice such an idea publicly.

Having convinced themselves that there is no practical method for an alien civilization to navigate the interstellar distances, they will have no further reason to wonder about whether they are actually here.

They will see no reason to waste their valuable time considering such an apparently ridiculous proposition.

And yet the original question was not "How could an alien civilization get here?"—in fact, that is a question that nobody even asked. The question was "Are aliens already here?"—a very different question indeed and one with vastly different implications. If it should turn out that the answer to this question is "yes", the entire chain of logic which leads to the conclusion that they can't get here becomes instantly irrelevant. If they are already here, then someone has obviously found a way to get here.

How they accomplished that isn't the point--that is a question for another time and one which, like all reasonable and logical questions, has a reasonable and logical answer. It is not necessary to be able to describe the method of interstellar travel utilized by an advanced alien civilization to have members of that alien civilization orbiting our world and establishing bases on the moon. It is currently impossible for us to traverse the enormous distances of interstellar space in a reasonable time...but that does not necessarily imply it's impossible to do. If extra-terrestrials are in fact here right now, we may take it for granted that such a method exists and has been found—we may not have found it, we may not even know what it is...but somebody clearly found it and is using it.

The original question has been lost, buried in a flurry of scientific assumptions and logical fallacies which appear solid and logical enough to fool even professional scientists. It has been replaced by a completely different question, one which comes with a solution which conveniently prevents any further serious consideration of the original question. Instead, the question is transformed into something which nobody originally asked about and which—if an alien presence here is a fact—is not even relevant.

There are many other places where inaccurate data can be substituted for valid data in ways which can convince people that the lies they were just told were true. The United States Air Force, for example, has stated that at least 95% of all UFO sightings are explainable by conventional methods. I doubt that is the case. There is no question that many UFO sightings can be resolved using conventional explanations. A figure of 95%, however, is difficult for me to swallow. I don't think people are that dumb or that clueless.

I know that 95% of my own UFO sightings certainly were not explainable as natural objects. One was possibly a man-made object—it could in theory have been a helicopter. One was beyond question an alien spacecraft. The others were either alien spacecraft or human-designed vehicles which made use of alien technology. If they were vehicles which used alien technology it represents a hit--a piece of evidence for alien contact—no matter who was at the controls. So, in my case the percentage which could possibly—not certainly—be explained by conventional methods is one out of six: around 15%.

That is a far different thing than 95%. If one assumes an error rate of 95%, it becomes easy for the remaining 5% to be casually dismissed as probably just mistakes of some kind. If the error rate is really closer to 15%, with 150 million-plus sightings, you've got a situation which demands some serious attention from the military and some honest answers by the government.

The question becomes "Why would we believe the numbers which originated from the same military organization which has a vested interest in denying that alien spacecraft exist?" Wouldn't they above all people be the first to want to release false data about the percentage of sightings which were debunked or disproved? We have no way of knowing what the real percentage of error may be when it comes to UFO sightings. The only place which has a relatively complete collection of UFO sightings on a nationwide basis stretching clear back to the 1940's is the Air Force, the same place which wants to make sure you don't know such things even exist. Would you assume that the statistic of 95% is accurate? I would assume the opposite, that it is inaccurate and designed to further discourage conversation on the subject as well as discouraging witnesses from reporting their experiences in a public manner.

The Air Force also controls, ultimately, all the radar records for the entire country. That includes civilian radar records, because by stepping in and declaring any radar record or case to be a matter of national security they can attain both the original copy of any record and the copies which were made from it. They can declare any radar to have had a glitch, any case to have been solved or they can cause any evidence to disappear.

They can also quite often silence any witnesses by using one of various measures. In other words, there is no way for members of the public to check the validity of any numbers or statistics the Air Force or the government in general release and there is no reason at all to assume any of those numbers would be accurate. There is more than plenty of motivation, however, for the Air Force or other government agencies to distort, falsify, redact or completely invent all information which applies to the subject.

In this case, the smart money will presume that all their proffered facts and figures are bogus in some way because there is no reason to believe otherwise. Science took the opposite approach: they believe all of them because they are not able to scientifically prove that the government is lying without having access to the original documents, which they are never going to get.

The same is the case with numbers and data related to anything beyond Earth's orbit. NASA is the big name in that game...and one which is engaged in ensuring that the public is kept out of the loop as far as alien contact is concerned.

The most powerful telescopes and computers belong to the government in one form or another. The nation's university science departments depend upon governmental funding grants for their survival. This is a combination which allows for potentially all kinds of fudged numbers and data to be introduced to the public and quickly accepted by universities as the truth. They have no way of knowing, however, whether it is really the truth. They have no way of checking on it because they don't own the equipment—and, of course, nobody wants to argue with the hand that dispenses their federal funding.

In the end, there is no reason at all to presume that the numbers science is relying on to form its opinions are accurate or represent the truth of the situation. If one considers the very serious possibility that none of them are accurate because the government wishes to conceal the truth, there is every reason not to accept any of that data at face value and to question all of it. That, one would think, would be the logical presumption from a purely scientific standpoint.

But when one combines the eternal thirst for federal funding and the intentional refusal by the scientific community to seriously investigate the best evidence (or to even consider it might possibly be valid), one has a situation which is ripe for misconduct.

If science accepts at face value the data generated by the federal government, it makes it quite easy to build a case that the idea of alien contact is just a delusion. Repeat the supposed statistic that 95% of all reports are bogus, arbitrarily choose to ignore other data or possibilities, dismiss the "unsolved' cases with a roll of the eyes and a chuckle...and the scientific community has constructed a safe refuge from reality and a perfect means of protecting their all-important funding source permanently.

It's an easy, convenient solution which serves them well and, as far as they are concerned, does no harm. They just depend on the idea that members of the public will trust them blindly because of their expertise and positions while failing to notice that what they have just done is basically the exact opposite of applying proper scientific procedure and logic to the situation.

What they have done instead is manipulate the situation. They make sure that the answers they come up with will not jeopardize their federal funding because they correlate with the available data. Data which, of course, largely originated at places which are clearly inherently untrustworthy when it comes to generating accurate data about UFO's and making it available to the public.

When scientists explain their position, they claim it is scientifically the only valid and logical position one can reasonably hold. When I explain it, on the other hand, I can demonstrate that scientifically valid investigative techniques, the requirement that all possibilities be fairly considered in an unbiased manner and the necessity that all data be accounted for and explained properly have all been arbitrarily thrown out the window and abandoned in favor of an answer which has almost a zero percent possibility of being accurate but which guarantees federal funding will continue to be channeled their way.

Disinformation is a subtle and devastatingly effective art form. Those who are the best in the world at it work for the military/ intelligence services. They are dedicated to keeping even the best and brightest minds from asking the questions that matter most and, perhaps, finding answers to them.

Never underestimate the skill and competence of those who have been placed in charge of undertaking the most pervasive, complex, long-term act of psychological warfare in history. They are the best at what they do. In fact, they do it so well that even the most observant of their targets will almost never suspect that such people even exist or that such an operation is in fact taking place.

We have not even come to the most problematic aspect of the position promoted by mainstream science: a double standard of evidence.

One thing mainstream scientists will often invoke is the following truism, traditionally spoken in hushed tones and with great reverence: "Extraordinary claims require extraordinary evidence". That is not, despite what they might like you to believe, a principle of science. It is a quotation of something once said by Dr. Carl Sagan...and it is not in any way true.

Why should extraordinary claims require any more evidence than any other claim? Evidence is, after all, evidence. It is useful to remember at this point that we are speaking of people who devoutly believe in such things as dark matter, which can never be seen, touched or measured. I think it is hard to deny that this is quite an extraordinary thing for a scientist to believe in, since it can never be detected or verified by any known process.

Where is the extraordinary evidence which supports their belief in dark matter? The answer is simple: it doesn't exist. Their entire belief in this inherently unprovable hypothetical substance—which they claim makes up 85% of the mass of the entire universe—is based on some mathematical calculations which may very well be mistaken. Yet they do not hesitate to pull Sagan's statement out and use it against those who claim to have witnessed an alien spacecraft in our atmosphere. Apparently over 150 million witnesses and literally millions of photographs and films which cannot be debunked do not indicate to scientists that anything of importance might be taking place.

Even if the supposed requirement for extraordinary evidence exists—which it does not—it has been met and easily exceeded by any reasonable standard. For mainstream science, however, this statistic is completely ignored, it is treated as though it doesn't even exist so that they can continue to rail on about how UFO proponents have no evidence and need to provide an extraordinary amount of it if they wish to be taken seriously. At the same time, they believe in dark matter while never having seen or measured such a thing and having no solid basis for anyone to believe it exists other than an equation which is almost certainly not even accurate.

This is the game that mainstream science is continually running against anyone who dares to speak up about alien contact—and they run it quite successfully indeed, using the weight of their offices and the presumed authority of their credentials and positions to intimidate and browbeat anyone foolish and careless enough to disagree with their devoutly held, unbelievably hypocritical and simple-minded belief that NASA astronauts and the greatest rocket scientist of all time can testify to the reality of alien spacecraft on and around our world but that nothing is actually there.

Does such a position make sense? No. But to them it makes perfect sense...which just goes to show that geniuses can be incredibly thick-witted at times and fail to see even the most obvious and gaping holes in their own position. The main flaws in the position of mainstream science, it seems, is that its position has nothing at all to do with science and everything to do with denial. It combines a refusal to investigate the evidence with institutional blindness, intellectual dishonesty and the fact that far too many of them have abandoned science in favor of the far more lucrative profession of being funding whores.

Now we come to the matter of witness testimony. While it is true that the statement of even a witness of impeccable credibility has no value as scientific proof, it is enough to send a defendant in a murder trial to Death Row. When the best-trained, most carefully screened and highly qualified people in the world publicly state that alien spacecraft are real and are present on and around Earth, one would think it is at the very least an issue which ought to be examined extremely closely and considered with the utmost care.

There have been innumerable witnesses of such high credibility come forth, but for the sake of argument let's disregard all of them except statements by astronauts, cosmonauts, high-level NASA officials, military officials of the highest rank and those who hold governmental positions equating to Minister of Defense or higher. There does not exist anyone in the world who is in a better position to know the truth of the matter or who is better qualified to accurately identify all types of military aircraft as well as accurately identify objects which can only be explainable as intelligently-guided spacecraft of unknown origin which exhibit capabilities far greater than the best humanity can produce.

When such people state unequivocally and for the record that alien spacecraft are here or that alien contact is a fact, a serious investigator is required to treat these statements with the utmost seriousness and investigate them in the greatest possible detail. To do otherwise is to arbitrarily ignore the best judgments of the most qualified people in the world. It is done without cause and without producing any evidence which might indicate those people were mistaken.

Science has now dug itself into a hole which is ominously deep and has no apparent means of extricating itself. When we are finished, mainstream science will have created for itself a black hole of logic, a position from which is impossible to escape.

In an apparent attempt to abandon all pretense of logic and common sense and to toss away any possible resemblance to valid scientific procedure, mainstream scientists refuse to investigate the cases which represent the best evidence for alien contact. They will only investigate cases which are clearly and obviously hoaxes or which have simple conventional solutions. They refuse to touch—or even acknowledge the existence of—those which cannot be explained or debunked. These are, in the end, the only cases which matter. They are the cases which scientists should be most interested in investigating and getting to the bottom of. Instead, they are completely ignored.

The technical term for this practice is "cherry picking" and it is something which is normally carried out by those who are unable or unwilling to deal with the most important and convincing data. By choosing easily-falsifiable events, they then give themselves an excuse to ignore all the best evidence. They congratulate themselves for having solved the cases which are easily debunked—and, therefore, do not matter—while managing to completely avoid the evidence they cannot explain.

Once again it is clear to see that what we are dealing with here is not in any way related to proper scientific procedure. What we have is an arbitrary refusal to acknowledge data which conflicts with their preferred, predetermined solution. What we have is a systematic denial of the facts which is supported at all levels of the scientific establishment. In cruder terms, what we are dealing with is a massive, widespread and fully intentional fraud on the part of scientists who are almost always ultimately found to be on the public payroll. We are being lied to by the people we trust to inform us of the truth and who are quite literally our employees.

To hold the so-called "skeptical position" regarding the matter of alien contact, one must be willing to do various things, any one of which would disqualify them as an unbiased scientific investigator capable of producing an accurate analysis of the situation.

They must first believe that they can determine the correct answer to the question without taking the time to collect data or analyze it. If data is produced which conflicts with their predetermined solution they must be willing either to ignore it completely, distort it until it conforms to their preferred solution or arbitrarily reject it without valid cause for doing so. They must insist upon standards of evidence which are impossible to satisfy and which they would never agree to operate under themselves.

They must refuse to take part in unbiased investigative procedures which are designed to honestly examine the best evidence to find the truth. Instead, they must be willing to examine only evidence which can be proven fraudulent or otherwise dismissed for cause. They must then use these fraudulent cases as a valid reason not to investigate cases which are well-documented and impossible to disprove. This is analogous to making the claim that the little boy who cried "wolf!" provides scientific proof that wolves do not exist.

Each of these things is incompatible with the proper application of scientific methodology. Each ensures that any conclusions they reach will be inaccurate, unfairly biased, hypocritical, intellectually dishonest and terminally flawed.

There is no other way to hold the "skeptical"—more correctly called the "pseudo-skeptical"—position. These things are being done every day by even the most reputable and highly-esteemed members of the mainstream scientific community...and they get away with it because nobody has the backbone necessary to challenge them on their own turf.

When forced to conform to their own standards of evidence, mainstream science will find it is completely unable to prove that the Hindenburg exploded, that the Titanic sank or that World War II took place. All documents relating to any of those events will be arbitrarily rejected as forgeries on the basis that there is no way for them to prove they are *not* forgeries. Any witness statements will be summarily disqualified—the statement of a witness is not scientific proof of anything. Besides, we must assume that their witnesses are either lying, mistaken, psychotic, drugged or undergoing a mass hallucination. The fact that "mass hallucinations" do not actually exist makes no difference to us.

Any photographs or films they may produce which purport to show evidence of any of these events will be considered fraudulent and rejected immediately. They will be forced to prove that this material is *not* fraudulent, something they will find it is impossible to ever do. If they produce experts who say the photographs are unaltered, we will simply assume that there is something the experts have missed.

Photoshop is, after all, an extremely powerful tool which is fully capable of fooling even the experts when used by skilled professionals.

The testimony of historians will simply constitute an example of "appeal to authority", something which is strictly forbidden when constructing a scientific proof. Any physical evidence which might be produced will also be rejected: a rusted diving bell does not prove that a ship sank, a burned piece of wood does not prove that a zeppelin exploded and a derelict gas chamber does not prove that a world war took place.

If they say they have located the wreckage of the Titanic on the sea floor, they will be required to prove that they didn't put it there themselves for the purposes of defrauding our honest scientific investigation. How can they prove they didn't sneak in at night and plant that wreckage and all those bones just because they wanted to fool us? They can't. There is no way to prove such a thing.

The standards of evidence, which are identical to those which are forced upon the UFO community, are impossible to satisfy. Nothing can ever be proven while they remain in place. This, we shall inform them, is *science*—and nothing less will be acceptable to a serious person.

What will they do then? How can they ever hope to prove that World War II took place, when every type of evidence they produce is deemed unacceptable and rejected out of hand? They will find that their job has been made impossible by applying methodology and standards which prevent any type of evidence from ever being accepted as legitimate.

It is important to note that the problem here has nothing to do with the idea that none of these events took place. The fact that they did is well-known and is part of the historical record. The problem is that, just as with alien contact, the scientific method was not designed to be utilized to prove or disprove such things and is incapable of doing so.

These events have nothing to do with natural processes or universal laws, the things the scientific method was intended to be applied to. They cannot be subjected to testing in a laboratory. They cannot be proven by mathematics or repeated observations. They cannot be forced to provide us with physical evidence which would serve to prove their reality beyond any possibility of question or doubt.

We are not dealing here with questions of science, we are dealing with matters of history and of events which are dependent upon the actions of self-directed individuals rather than immutable universal laws or inherent physical properties. In such cases the scientific method is incapable of navigating the terrain, it has no way to analyze the data and arrive at the correct solution to the problem. It is inapplicable, unsuited for the job and is therefore completely irrelevant.

By attempting to force the use of the scientific method on things it was neither designed for nor capable of addressing in a meaningful fashion, the proponents of mainstream science have accomplished something which is as rare as it is embarrassing. After declaring themselves to be Grandmasters, they have managed to checkmate themselves with their own pieces.

CHAPTER 9: TYPE I GREYS

"To my knowledge, no NASA astronaut has ever reported seeing a UFO in space, let alone having a confrontation with aliens."
-- David Morrison, who I certainly hope is not a heart surgeon or a firearm safety instructor, in an article from The Skeptical Inquirer

"At no time when the astronauts were in space were they alone: there was a constant surveillance by UFO's."
–Scott Carpenter, Mercury astronaut and the second American to orbit the Earth

According to the best information I can find, the Roswell Event was technically not a "crash"—it was a planned takedown of an alien craft by the military. They had discovered early on that their powerful military radars interfered with the guidance system of these alien craft, sometimes causing the pilots to lose control of the vehicle and crash. It is believed by many that this is what occurred that day—the military picked the craft up and intentionally caused it to crash by activating their most powerful surface-to-air radar units in the area.

It has also been reported by Lockheed's Senior Research Engineer, the late Boyd Bushman, that many years after the event a military pilot had claimed he shot the craft down during a high-speed pursuit. According to that story, it was a Naval aviator who happened to be closest to the object when it was picked up on radar and he was diverted from his course and ordered to intercept the craft. He achieved both radar lock and visual contact with the craft, the story goes, and then the craft began to accelerate away from him. The pilot requested permission to fire on it over his radio. When the base commander asked why he felt the need to open fire on the alien craft, he replied "There are two possibilities: either it's friendly or it isn't. And if it was friendly, it wouldn't be trying to run away from me." The senior officer agreed. The pilot was given permission to open fire. He launched a missile at the craft which struck it and caused it to crash to the ground.

I have no way of knowing personally which—if either—of those stories is true. If the craft was brought down intentionally, it is difficult to understand why they Air Force does not seem to have been aware of it until local rancher Mac Brazel reported finding the spacecraft and a debris field later. On the other hand, it is said to be common knowledge within the black ops community that the Roswell disk was brought down intentionally. Having no way to know what occurred, I chose to include those accounts for your consideration (and because I found them both to be interesting).

The bodies—as well as the extra-terrestrial survivor—from the Roswell crash were about four and a half to five feet tall. They had large, hairless heads, round eyes and arms which were long by human standards, extending downward to about the level of their knees.

There is a video clip which can be found at YouTube and various other sites which purports to have been leaked from the KGB. It shows what appears to be one of these extra-terrestrials, who is said to have been captured by the Russians from a crash site in the USSR and held prisoner. The being was given the nickname "Skinny Bob" by someone and it stuck.

Unlike most clips which claim to show an extra-terrestrial being, this one has never been debunked to the best of my knowledge and it appears to be legitimate. If not, it is by far the best fake I have ever seen. It certainly appears that what we are looking at is an alien being and not a puppet created by some special effects department.

There were clearly legitimate concerns which directly involved national security that led to the initial denial and cover-up by the military and the government. The extremely advanced level of technology found at the crash site as well as the fact that this and other presumably alien spacecraft had easily and seemingly effortlessly outperformed our best airborne fighters in all the ways that mattered. They were faster, more maneuverable, could attain higher altitude and appeared to literally pop into being out of nowhere and vanish the same way.

When combined with the fact that they were operating with impunity in American national airspace, this would surely have been sufficient reason to justify the initial cover-up. So would the fact that it was not known with certainty whether the intentions of the beings who piloted these vehicles was friendly or hostile. If they turned out to be hostile, there it was unlikely we could defend ourselves adequately against them. After taking all this into account, utilizing the highest possible level of security classification was a no-brainer for General Ramey, commander of the Roswell base.

It was learned that the alien captive—who was called E.B.E. (short for extra-terrestrial biological entity) belonged to a race which came from a planet in the Zeta Reticuli star system. This race is often confused with the "classic" E.T.'s, the ones with large, dark, almond-shaped eyes that we call the Greys. That is incorrect—that particular race was not involved with the Roswell event and had nothing to do with it. To avoid confusion, I will refer to this extra-terrestrial race as the "Type I Greys" and to the classic E.T.'s as "Type II Greys".

If I simply call them "Greys", I will always be speaking about the Type II Greys. We will get around to taking a close look at the Type II Greys—and there are more types as well—later in the book as well as in the follow up book. It should also be noted that many people believe it is the Type II Greys, with the large, wraparound eyes, which originate from the Zeta Reticuli star system. I think that is incorrect, for reasons which will make themselves clear later in the text. In fact, since it is known that the Type II Greys are only able to reproduce by cloning rather than natural methods, and since it is also known that they are cloned by the thousands in underground bases here on Earth, it would probably be technically accurate if they were to think of this planet as their place of origin. Many and perhaps most of them would have lived their entire lives here, just as we have.

Returning to the Type I Greys, it soon became evident that EBE was an inveterate liar. He answered questions in the way he thought his captors would want them answered, without regard to the truth. It was a long time before the Army learned much of value from him, though it is reported that in later years EBE became more cooperative and began to provide some accurate information when questioned.

When the Greada Treaty—also sometimes known as the Greada Accord—was signed in 1954, it was still hoped that the beings which piloted these spacecraft might turn out to have peaceful intentions. The possibility that they might well have hostile intent, considering the already-evident technology gap, would have left us exposed to attack by beings with a technology we had no effective means of defending ourselves against.

The idea that these extra-terrestrials had come to our world with friendly intentions was a rather misplaced hope, considering something which had been found among the crash debris at the Roswell crash site. What the military crash investigators had found there, among other things, was a very large vat filled with human blood in which dismembered human body parts were floating. Hands, feet, legs, various organs and other parts were suspended within the liquid contained in the vat.

I have no way of knowing just what was going through the minds of our military leadership at the time, but if someone had asked me I'm quite certain I would have observed that beings with peaceful intentions do not fly around with dismembered human body parts floating in vats of human blood. Those which do are presumed to be hostile, lethal and highly dangerous. But that's just me. I'm funny about things like that, I suppose.

This race of alien beings are members of a group known as the Collective, which is an alliance of several E.T. races which work together with the intention of ultimately taking over our world for themselves. Indeed, they have already gone far toward making that goal a reality. There is little question that the members of the Collective are dominant among the alien races which are known to visit or inhabit Earth. They are far more influential, numerous and powerful here than any of the races or groups which are considered friendly toward humanity. Their acts and intentions, especially when combined with those of other members of the Cooperative such as the Draco (a race which will be discussed in detail in the second book), can not in my opinion be considered anything other than hostile, invasive and decidedly unwelcome.

Unknown to authorities at the time, we may have ultimately been better off if these aliens had simply decided to start blasting our cities apart from orbit. It may well have been quicker and far kinder than what eventually took place.

CHAPTER 10: FRIENDS AND ENEMIES

"If aliens visited us, the outcome would be much as when Columbus landed in America, which didn't turn out well for the Native Americans."
-- Stephen Hawking

"Where are all the friends who used to talk to me?
All they ever told me was good news
People that I've never seen are kind to me
Is it any wonder I'm confused?"
-- The Alan Parsons Project

It is not known to me exactly how many different alien races are known to the United States government. It is surely a number which will be different depending upon how inclusive one wants to be. If we decide to count such things as robots, androids, hybrids, synths and other forms of artificial intelligence the number will of course increase. If, in addition, we choose to make a separate entry for each of the distinct groups or divisions which exist, both within individual races and among groups of allied or cooperating races, it will become even larger still.

I do not know which method of counting will prove to be the most useful to us in the end, so it seems best in my opinion to attempt to come up with two distinct numbers. For one number I will utilize a method which counts one for each race but does not add to the total for different divisions or groupings which may exist, either within any particular race or between cooperating races. I will also not add anything for such things as androids, hybrids, etc. For the second number I will include everything, with the possible exception of human-E.T. hybrids.

In this way, we can hope to have at least some general idea about how many different cultures and civilizations we are dealing with when it comes to the total number of races which are known to have contacted and interacted in some way with humanity, either now or in the past. We will be able to utilize the second number to get some idea of how many competing groups we may be facing, and also a rough idea of how many possibly-conflicting alien agendas are in play.

There is no way for me to be able to ascertain the precise number, of course. Any number I am eventually able to come up with is bound to be inaccurate to a greater or lesser degree. I would presume that my numbers will miss the actual correct number on the low side—in other words, that there are almost certainly alien races which exist and which are known to our government that will be unknown to me. I will have no way to include them, nor will I have any way of knowing how much I missed the mark by.

While it is of course possible that there are races which have been reported that do not actually exist in the real world, it seems likely to me that the number of such races will probably be quite low. If we accept the existence of only races which have been either reported by multiple credible sources or which have been reported by just a single source of very high credibility, it is not likely that we are going to end up with a lot of extra-terrestrial races on our list which do not actually exist.

I have heard, at various times, numbers as low as 32 and as high as 160+ when it comes to the total number of distinct extra-terrestrial types that the United States government is currently aware of. It is clearly going to be a number which has steadily increased with the passage of time. New entries would be added as time passed and additional races were discovered.

When the so-called "modern UFO era" was starting up in the period of the late 1930's and early 1940's, the number of alien races the government was aware of surely amounted to no more than a mere handful. This probably continued to be the case until at least the time that we began detonating nuclear weapons on and below the surface of our world.

That was a decision which seems to quite clearly have generated a great deal of additional interest in us among the inhabitants of the galaxy and it was not long at all before a wide variety of alien races which had never been reported previously began to be reported in association with sighting and contact events which spanned the globe. As soon as we started blowing up atomic weapons on the surface of our only home planet, extra-terrestrials we had no idea even existed basically came running to check us out and try to ascertain just what we were up to and what we were thinking of.

The non-human intelligent entities with which we are dealing can be classified in much the same way we humans classify foreign nations or groups. Some appear to be friendly, many appear to be either neutral or basically uninterested in us one way or another, and some appear to be overtly hostile and highly dangerous. Workers at Area 51 like to describe them as being either "wranglers" or "rustlers". The wranglers are E.T.'s who are generally considered to be either friendly or at least non-threatening. The rustlers are E.T.'s who are known to be hostile, unfriendly, invasive, harmful or otherwise dangerous to humanity as a whole.

The accurate classification of alien races and groups is made more difficult by the fact that, just as humans are, each alien race is composed of many individual members. They do not all always agree with each other about issues such as how to feel about Homo Sapiens or the planet Earth. Divisions exist within their societies and their individual members and some members of a given race may well react with hostility or aggression upon encountering humans while others may choose to refrain from contact or even extend the hand (or claw, tentacle, proboscis or what-have-you) of friendship.

It is not the intention of this chapter to produce a detailed list of all the alien races which the American government (and others) are aware of. I hope to be able to do that at some point in a future volume. What I want to do here is to make the reader aware of some basic groupings which are known in terms of both different general attitudes regarding the human species and different general origins which are known to apply to our non-human visitors.

Attempting to produce a detailed list of each non-human race which is believed to be interacting with humanity would be premature at this point. It is more useful, in my opinion, to continue to build a framework which will allow the reader the best chance of making good use of the complete list when it is produced.

It is an inescapable fact that the topic of alien contact ultimately affects and includes a large and diverse variety of different disciplines and fields of knowledge. It also requires us to consider a wide range of important issues and unavoidable realities associated with such contact.

Making it even more difficult is the fact that so much of it lies far beyond anything in our ordinary experience. It is difficult to wrap the mind around things like this. Many of their capabilities involve things which we consider to be impossible, and yet without drastically redefining the things we accept as possible there is no way to come to an understanding of these ancient beings and their technological prowess.

That is, to put it mildly, a major challenge for even the best of people and the brightest of minds to take on. As we attempt to do so, we will certainly need all the help we can get.

I have attempted to render some assistance in this regard by taking great care as far as the general layout of the books and the order in which the information I wish to share and discuss is presented. It was a matter of considerable difficulty and required quite a few revisions and even a couple wholesale overhauls.

There is quite a bit of groundwork which is necessary before we can take on the more complex, intricate--and sometimes downright radical--concepts and situations which are of immense importance in terms of assessing the situation. All the data we can accumulate must be considered to enable us to at last arrive at an accurate and comprehensive understanding of the Big Picture regarding alien contact and all it implies.

There is no question that alien contact represents the most important and profound story in human history. There is nothing else which can even remotely compare with it in terms of the massive, unavoidable, radical and revolutionary effect it will have on human society.

Much of what mankind has believed and assumed to be true since ancient times will be instantly turned on its head. Many scientific and social disciplines will be invalidated or become irrelevant overnight. Others must be completely re-examined and rebuilt from the ground up.

It is an unfortunate fact that, if full disclosure were to take place, we would find to our immense surprise that most of the things we were taught in school and have accepted as truth throughout our lives have been nothing but an intentional deception. They are an intricate and pervasive snow job whose only purpose was to mislead, cheat and victimize society on a global basis.

Within the black ops community, non-human entities are often said to fall into one of several general groups. The first group consists of those extra-terrestrials which are considered either neutral in their attitude toward humanity or who appear to be completely uninterested in us for some reason. Members of this group are not believed to pose an imminent threat to us, nor are they considered likely to render us any assistance. It is reasonable to expect that there would be some aliens who would not find humans to be particularly interesting or relevant as far as they were concerned, and this does indeed seem to be the case.

There are some members of the galactic community whose interest in Earth is purely scientific. They come here to study (and to take samples of) the many diverse species of plant and animal life which inhabit our world. Although their craft are sometimes observed, they do not normally choose to interact with humans if such interactions can be avoided. These visitors often select landing sites which are sparsely inhabited by humans. If this is not possible, they normally prefer to land during the hours of darkness, carry out their business and then leave.

There are also some visitors who are generally considered to be of a friendly or positive nature as far as their interactions with humanity are concerned. It is not believed that they represent a serious threat to us or that they operate from an agenda which is either malignant or harmful to the humans they encounter. Contact reports involving humans and members of the group categorized as "wranglers" are generally of a positive nature and are sometimes said to be beneficial to the humans who are involved. Some contactees report being taught new skills, given some type of advice or otherwise assisted by the aliens they encounter.

As is discussed in another chapter, I do not personally feel confident that all the extra-terrestrials who claim to have our best interests at heart are telling the truth. We are dealing, even in the best case, with beings whom we ought to presume can out-think, out-fight and out-strategize us. It does not seem prudent to me that we accept much of anything at face value when it comes to dealing with them.

There are many different possible methods of manipulating humans, both individually and as a group, and we would be best served by remembering that it is almost certainly the case that the extra-terrestrials understand us to a far greater degree than we understand any of them. What appears on its surface to be a friendly attitude could be just part of a massive set-up, a way of convincing us to drop our guard or to become dependent upon their assistance. If we become dependent on their assistance, we become subject to their control.

As is mentioned in another chapter, the evidence that so-called "friendly aliens" have truly helped us to any significant degree is at best sorely lacking. Although we have certainly gained both knowledge and advanced technologies from our alien visitors, they appear to have come either from the recovery and subsequent analysis of crashed alien spacecraft, or to have been given to us by entities who are of a hostile nature and whose motives have nothing to do with our long-term benefit. That fact alone ought to be enough to give us serious pause when it comes to the matter of the intentions of any group of alien beings.

We are alone and terribly vulnerable here on Earth. The location of our only home planet is known to dozens of alien races at a bare minimum, all of which presumably can crush our civilization into the dust if they choose to. We would be extremely foolish to forget that the potential to do great and permanent harm to human civilization lies within the capabilities of even the friendliest and most non-violent appearing alien beings.

Whether we like it or not, the fact is that we are participating in a game in which there may be no meaningful second chances and it is only sensible to conclude that we are operating from a position of permanent weakness when compared to any group of aliens who has the power to travel here in the first place. Any interactions we have with these alien beings, including even the friendliest among them, must necessarily be considered with great care and attention to detail if we are to hope to have any chance of a successful outcome.

Within the galactic community, there exists nobody who is required to hold our hand, be our cosmic babysitters or assist us in any way. While it is possible that some may in fact assist us, we must remember that absolutely none of them are *required* to do so and that any such assistance is therefore strictly voluntary and could end at any time. Any significant mistake on our part could in theory be enough to bring our world crashing down around our shoulders and the brief, troubled era of humanity could come to a brutal and permanent end.

It appears that we have already made some major mistakes in our dealings with extra-terrestrials Those mistakes appear to have put all of us in a very difficult situation, one which there is no easy way to extricate ourselves from.

It seems to me that the only sensible way of approaching any potential interactions with extra-terrestrials, whether as individuals or a people, is to do so with an abundance of caution. We need to utilize a great deal of foresight and extreme care. All the wisdom we can bring to bear should be focused intently on the matter.

We cannot afford to allow the discussion to be dominated by those whose primary interest is personal, political, financial or military. We have been clearly shown that those types of people cannot be trusted to guard our best interests. They cannot be trusted to concern themselves with our long-term welfare or that of our world. They have proven beyond any doubt that, when given the ability to do so, they were more than happy to sacrifice our best interests and even our lives for their own profit.

Those people must never again be allowed to control the situation. By the same token, I see little reason to believe that scientists have earned the right to assume any type of leadership position themselves. For almost a hundred years, with the evidence literally floating in the skies above their heads, they have proven to be disinterested, unaware, hypocritical, incompetent and dishonest. It could also be fairly said that they appear to be quite a bit less intelligent as a group than they are given credit for being.

These are people who have proven that they can examine photographs and films—including NASA mission films—which clearly show alien spacecraft and see nothing unusual about them at all. They can be shown photographs of a fleet of alien spacecraft performing maneuvers over the Eisenhower White House and conclude that those craft did not exist.

Putting people like this in charge of the situation would give them credit for intelligence they do not seem to have and common sense they do not appear to possess. It would elevate them to a position of leadership which their words and actions over the last sixty-plus years have clearly demonstrated they did not earn and do not deserve.

The other classification which is often used for various extra-terrestrials which are known to visit of inhabit Earth is that of "rustlers". Members of this group are considered unfriendly or hostile when it comes to their attitudes and interactions with humanity. Some are known to be extremely dangerous to encounter, with such encounters often resulting in the death or permanent disappearance of the humans involved.

Activities such as the abduction of humans for purposes of hybridization or medical experimentation are commonly reported by those who have—almost always involuntarily—encountered members of this group. It has also been reliably reported that some of the "rustlers" are known to abduct humans and either sell them as slaves on the galactic black market or utilize them as slaves themselves. Several extra-terrestrial races are known to utilize us as a food item and are quite capable of killing and eating the humans they contact if they wish to. At least one group, a reptilian race commonly known as the Draco, are known to brutally torture human captives and then quite literally eat them alive.

Some among the rustlers are known to be invasive, aggressive and to interfere with human societies and individuals. They have historically been responsible for the death of uncounted thousands of humans and continue to be responsible for the death of many in the present day. Some of them inhabit bases within our solar system or deep beneath the surface of our land or oceans and appear to have no intention of leaving in the foreseeable future.

There may be some type of agreement between the non-human civilizations—or, at least, among those which are known to visit Earth—which does not allow direct conquest of planets with military force. It could also be the case that they simply do not wish to do this because they have found a better means of conquest, one which does not involve the wholesale destruction of cities.

There is no question that any of these alien civilizations can potentially level our cities at any time of their choosing. None of our technology is likely to be able to prevent them from doing so. Judging by the present situation, it appears that certain parts of our military forces would join the aliens in attacking us rather than attempting to defend us.

It seems that direct attacks on human cities have occurred more than once in the distant past. The historical record contains accounts of cities and even entire civilizations which were destroyed.

Archeological evidence reveals civilizations which achieved high levels of advancement and then suddenly, for no apparent cause, completely vanished. Nothing today remains of once-mighty civilizations such as the Mayans other than the devastated ruins of vast cities which have over the centuries been overgrown and retaken by the jungle.

How exactly does one manage to forget about a civilization such as the Mayans? It would seem to be especially unlikely that they would be completely forgotten if, once they were gone, the locals had to take up residence once again in the primitive jungle. How does one forget entire civilizations which seem to have existed and thrived in areas which are now covered by the sea? It would be somewhat like abandoning New York City and then expecting the rest of America to completely forget that it ever existed.

Ideas like this make no logical sense. There is only one way which is known to me that could cause these great ancient civilizations to be completely forgotten: genocide. Exterminating the locals and letting others who happened to wander into the area later take their place. That would do it. Nobody would remember the Mayans if the jungle had overgrown their ancient cities and none of the locals had ever lived there during their reign.

If that is really the case, who could have been responsible for such a widespread and efficient elimination of the residents of the area? The answer suggests itself.

Ancient historical texts in India known as the Vedas contain what can only be described as a record of a nuclear explosion destroying an ancient city. The details are so accurate that they could be used to describe the destruction of the Japanese city of Hiroshima and the after-effects of the radiation on those who survived the initial blast.

The idea that aliens apparently destroyed at least one human city with an atomic bomb thousands of years in the past should give us pause. Perhaps the most valuable thing a pawn can do for itself is to clearly understand that it is a pawn and that it is surrounded by pieces of far greater power than its own. There should be no question about who the pawns are in this game and we should be under no illusions that they are somebody other than ourselves.

We have become accustomed to thinking of humanity as the one and only most dominant force ever to occupy our world, and to thinking of aliens as theoretical beings who may or may not really exist. To start with that perspective and change to one where humans occupy a position at or near the bottom in terms of technological capabilities, intelligence, experience and scientific concepts is a paradigm shift of massive proportions. It is, so far at least, one which has proven to be too great for most people to successfully make.

Their inability to adjust to this idea makes no difference in terms of the ultimate reality of the situation. The bottom line truths regarding humanity's interaction with alien life forms is not in the least affected by the failure of some to come to grips with it. The only thing which is affected are the people in question, who will be inevitably—and possibly permanently—behind the curve when it comes to these matters and will have no way of even knowing it.

It is unavoidable that vast numbers of people will be members of this group. They will be the last to understand the situation we find ourselves in and the least helpful in terms of adapting to a new reality. They can be expected to be highly vocal, to stubbornly resist change and to consistently be responsible for putting obstacles and objections in the path of progress. Their arguments will sound entirely logical and reasonable at first glance, but will be based on ignorance and will ultimately be of little value to the rest of us. They will have the effect of slowing us all down at a time when we can least afford it.

Sadly, it is the case that this is already happening at present and that many of the members of this group which is unable to adapt to a new reality are among our most intelligent and capable people. They have, unknown to themselves, been victimized by the interminable psychological warfare operations. Their worldview has been determined by others and is by this time stubbornly resistant to change or modification.

They will of course stridently deny that such is the case or that they have been affected in any significant way by psychological warfare. This is the problem which is encountered when we have too high an opinion about our own intelligence and too little understanding of and respect for the effectiveness of psychological warfare as practiced by professionals. It is a sad truth that it is precisely the people who believe themselves to be immune to the effects of psychological warfare who comprise the perfect targets and are the first to fall.

That is the position these people currently occupy…and it is a position they will never realize they are in. This will have the effect of causing them to stubbornly fight to the end of the battle and to do so for the wrong side. Their talents will be wasted and inadvertently spent on holding the rest of us back at a time when they could be doing us a lot of good.

It is an unfortunate truth that sometimes the brightest of people can act like the slowest people in the room. They are not immune to being influenced by propaganda, nor are they terribly difficult to manipulate or deceive, especially if they can be given false data and convinced to trust it.

In fact, it is often the case that many of the most intelligent people around will be significantly easier to manipulate than will the average citizen, since they have an even greater propensity for assuring themselves that they are protected from such influence by the relative superiority of their native intelligence. Serenely confident in their own invulnerability, they become the targets of a virtual army of highly-trained professional information warriors.

As was illustrated earlier in the chapter which dealt with the so-called skeptics and debunkers, they can be made to fall as though they were a line of dominoes. They will be the last to realize that they have been targeted and led astray. That is the price of believing yourself to be too clever to fall for the manipulations that others fall for.

By the time the error of their ways becomes obvious even to them, it will be far too late to do anything about it. The things they will attempt to do then are the things they should be attempting to do now, while the opportunity still exists for them to bring about meaningful change.

When they at last get around to trying to do so, the situation will be such that all their efforts will be doomed to failure. As the saying goes, they will be a day late and a dollar short. Those who depended upon them for leadership and expertise will pay the price for allowing the scientific community to become too comfortable with the status quo and too unwilling to rock the boat.

When the question "Why didn't you see this coming, decades ago?" is asked, the scientific and academic communities will be capable only of saying "We're sorry. It wasn't our fault. It was *someone else's* fault" and then hoping that this is taken as a sufficient explanation.

Considering the responsibilities entrusted to these people by the entire citizenry of the country, that is an answer which is as inadequate as it is unforgivable. They were given all the training necessary, they had access to the finest equipment money could buy and the most qualified experts the world could produce. They were being paid by the public to investigate matters such as this in a careful and thorough manner.

They were happy to accept those fat paychecks the whole time. But they steadfastly refused to even consider doing the things they were being paid to do and which we had every right to expect them to be doing. They never felt the need to bother doing any of those things. To them, it was all nothing but a big game…and all they had to do to collect from it is sit on the sidelines doing basically nothing, or being busily engaged in doing things which were of far less importance. This is what happens when people are certain they have the correct answers, when in fact they have not yet even started asking the right questions.

If extra-terrestrials judge humanity to be little more than dull-witted monkeys who are oblivious to what is taking place all around them, it will be difficult to argue with them. Still unaware that other dimensions capable of sustaining life even exist, we are surrounded by beings which have been navigating those realms for tens of millions of years. It is difficult to envision a winning scenario for us as members or competitors in this galactic society.

CHAPTER 11: ALIEN ORIGINS

"The universe is a symphony of strings, and the mind of God that Einstein eloquently wrote about for thirty years would be cosmic music resonating through eleven-dimensional hyper space."
-- Michio Kaku

"Far behind the music you can almost hear the sounds Of laughter, like the waves upon the shore Of infinity..."
-- Al Stewart

Most of the non-human visitors to our world are of an interstellar nature: they traveled here from another planet which orbits a distant star. This turns out not to be the only possibility, however. In fact, there are several others which are known. Some are counter-intuitive and will almost certainly come as a surprise to the average person, but each is important to understand and I would like to discuss them within this chapter.

As far as the extra-terrestrials which originate in other solar systems are concerned, it is apparent that they have developed a method of traveling through space which is far faster than the speed of light. Though they would have the option of using either generation ships or ships crewed by clones or synthetic life forms, it seems apparent that they are not limited to doing so. After the detonation of the first nuclear weapons here on Earth, the number of sighting reports increased drastically all over the world in a very short time. Wherever those craft may have originated, it did not take them long to get here. Clearly, they did not arrive via generation ships.

As UFO skeptics are quick to point out, the distances between the stars is so incredibly vast that—assuming one is limited forever to sub-light speeds—traveling to other stars would inevitably be a tortuously slow endeavor with only very limited utility. It seems highly unlikely that, if such were the case, there would be any ideas about interstellar trade routes or wars in space. It is highly unlikely that dozens of extra-terrestrial races would choose to send generation ships to a backward planet like our own in any case.

As will be discussed later, when we deal with the "secret space program", it is not necessary to speculate about whether hyper-light travel has been achieved. We know that it has. Ben Rich, former head of Lockheed Skunk Works, stated on his death bed that "we have everything you've seen in Star Trek and more. We now have the ability to take E.T. home again."

It is likely that most or all the extra-terrestrials we are dealing with have developed a method of interstellar travel independently from the others. In other words, there may be more than one possible way to span the distance between the stars and even the galaxies. Video evidence indicates that at least some alien craft can cause an Einstein-Rosen Bridge to form as needed. In other words, they appear to have generated a wormhole or a portal of some kind in the area in front of the craft. The craft then proceeded to enter the portal and vanish.

This could be an example of artificially-created wormholes being used for nearly instantaneous long-distance travel. I have no way of proving that, of course, or even of knowing with certainty that what was occurring represented the formation of a wormhole within our atmosphere.

I do not consider it to be written in stone that these craft can generate wormholes at will. However, when all the films I have seen and all the other information I have gathered are taken into consideration—including the alleged capability of human-built spacecraft to travel between the stars as well—I consider it to be highly likely that some type of wormhole technology is in use. Although mainstream science considers such things to be only theoretical possibilities, it is my best judgment that they exist, they do in fact work quite well in practice and are being used regularly within both our atmosphere and our solar system.

There is an interesting statement regarding this idea which was made by the late Boyd Bushman a number of years ago. Bushman was the chief research engineer for Lockheed at the time, though he had previously worked for other prominent, cutting edge corporations prior to his employment at Lockheed. He was known as "the father of the Stinger missile" because he invented the guidance system for it. He held eighteen patents for technology-related inventions he had devised.

He held a security clearance which allowed him to have intimate knowledge of projects—and to work directly with exotic technologies—which were designated as being "code-word compartmentalized information". This is another way of saying that they were classified at a level which was well beyond Top Secret.

To be cleared for things like this requires a person to not only have a "Top Secret" clearance and an unblemished record as far as maintaining security protocols is concerned, but also to have an unambiguous need to know information about certain things in order to be able to perform his job. Even after his retirement, Bushman kept his security clearances.

Boyd Bushman was one of the most senior men in the industry. He was a brilliant, innovative thinker who was respected by all who knew him. He agreed to take part in a fascinating interview hosted by another man of brilliance, multi-talented author and intellectual David Sereda.

At one point during the interview, after demonstrating an anti-gravity device as the cameras filmed him, Bushman made a statement which I found to be fascinating. As they were discussing the possibility of faster-than-light travel, Bushman said, in a seemingly casual and offhand manner, "There was a mistake in Einstein's equations, which we have identified and corrected." The implication was that the equations which appeared to prove that nothing could travel faster than the speed of light contained an error which, once it had been corrected, did in fact allow for faster-than-light travel to be possible in practical terms. It also implied that not only can at least some extra-terrestrials travel at speeds far faster than that of light, we also have technology which allows spacecraft which are part of our so-called "secret space program" to travel at speeds which are faster than light too.

Some of the visitors are time travelers who have traveled here from some point in the future. That is a difficult proposition for the average person to accept—I fully realize that. It is, however, the objective truth of the matter and to those involved in black ops it is a known and long-established fact.

No, you haven't been told about it and you almost certainly never will be, if the government has its way. It is true anyway.

Time travel is available to both the American military and many alien races and is used when necessary by all of them. I am in no position to explain just how it is accomplished and I will not attempt to. But I know that time travel technology is very real. How can I know such a thing? Because it was used on me on multiple occasions during abduction events, which I will describe later in the book.

You are under no obligation to believe that, of course. If I were the only person to claim such a thing about time travel, the wisest course of action per the methodology I laid out in the first chapter would be to file my report away as an interesting possibility…but not to invest your belief in it.

I am aware of the inherent paradoxes which appear to make the topic of time travel impractical or even beyond the limits of possibility, depending upon whom you ask. I am not qualified to even venture a guess when it comes to the technical nature of a time travel device and will not attempt to do so. Others surely have that knowledge, but I do not. I am also unable to give a first-hand description of what such technology looks like: although it is possible that I have seen it, if so I have no memory of it whatsoever and therefore have no way to describe it.

What I do have are memories of being sent through time on several different occasions, all of them against my will, during abduction scenarios. I also have corroborating testimony from additional witnesses of good reputation and high integrity, some of whom are known to me personally and some of whom I consider to be my close friends. Some have gone on record with statements much like mine, which describe being sent through time during an abduction. Others describe time travel from the other side, having utilized it during their time serving in the black ops segment of the military.

It is my opinion that the topic should be taken very seriously by researchers and that, at the very least, they leave themselves open to the possibility that it is taking place. If one chooses to accept the statements of myself and other whistle blowers as being factual reports, it will be possible to answer some questions which they were unable to find answers to previously.

As far as the military's technology is concerned, I do not know where it came from. It is possible that it was technology which was either gifted to them by an alien race or reverse engineered from tech found at a crash site. I have heard, though, that the military's time travel technology is based upon some of the records and papers which belonged to Nikola Tesla and which were immediately confiscated by the government when he died. It is believed that Tesla had either solved the technical problems and found a method by which a working time machine could be constructed, or that he had managed to build one himself.

I do not know which, if either, of those things is true. But my instincts tell me that the military's time travel technology is not alien in origin and did indeed come from information gained when Tesla's papers were seized upon his death.

As I understand it, there are at least two different methods which are used to travel through time. One of them allows a person's consciousness to be present, somewhat like being in holographic form, but the person will be completely invisible to others and unable to interact with the people or effect the events that they are witness to. In other words, they could watch Abraham Lincoln get shot, but it would be impossible for them to warn him about it, prevent it from occurring or interact with the world of that time in any other way.

The other method, I am told, does allow changes to be made when one travels into the past. Apparently, the idea that we exist in a universe which contains many different timelines, each dependent upon events unique to itself, is correct.

It is believed that certain alien races have traveled into our own past and taken actions there which were intended to alter the world as we experience it today. The intention was to change the past in ways which would lead to a world which was easier for the aliens to influence, control and dominate than other timelines might have been. It is said that this is exactly what they have accomplished and that it led to the world we live in today. It is also said that they have promised to refrain from taking such actions again.

If these things are true, and though I have no way of knowing for certain whether that is the case I believe it is very likely that they are, I know of no reason we should trust them not to continue to take such actions until the modern world is in a condition which meets their needs.

I do not have any reason to trust in the good intentions of alien beings or to take them at their word when matters of our own security and safety are on the line. I presume that any alien race will always take whatever actions it deems necessary to serve its own agenda, regardless of whether such actions are acceptable to us or not. To assume otherwise is, it seems to me, a foolish risk which is not worth taking. To imagine that any race of intelligent, non-human beings would put our interests ahead of their own is, in my view, an idea which makes no logical sense and which should never be presumed to be true.

I do not possess the technical chops to accurately discuss either the theoretical or practical intricacies relating to the topic of time travel, and I am not comfortable speculating about them in the absence of such knowledge. I will leave that to others who are more qualified. I will simply state that this technology has been used on me several times during military abductions and that I have two good friends who utilized the technology when they worked in the black ops segment of the military.

It is not necessary for the average researcher to be able to explain the technical details of building a time travel device, nor is it reasonable to expect them to do so. It is only necessary that they be aware that such technology does in fact already exist and that it is possessed by both alien races and our own black ops military forces. That being the case, there clearly *are* people qualified to both understand and explain the technical side of the issue, as well as people who can construct such a device and have it perform effectively. As a practical matter, it is only necessary to be aware that time travel is an option which is available to these groups and is used regularly by them.

The idea of time travel will be difficult for many to accept as being true. I understand this completely. It was a difficult thing for me to accept as well. But, as was stated earlier, out-of-the-box is what this stuff is all about. Things we do not believe to be possible are being done every day by those who have access to highly-advanced technology. The fact that they have not seen fit to tell us it exists is par for the course. It should not be taken as an indication that these technologies have not been developed covertly.

Just because we do not understand something does not in any way imply that it does not exist. We are, after all, perfectly capable of doing innumerable things today, easily and inexpensively, which were believed to be impossible by the best scientific minds of the past. It will be no different in the future, where things we see as impossible will by then be commonplace. It is simply a matter of allowing our knowledge of the physical universe and the laws by which it operates to advance sufficiently. When they do, today's impossible will become tomorrow's commonplace.

There is another method of travel which is utilized by certain alien races and groups. It is by far the most difficult for us to accurately visualize because it involves concepts which are not normally a part of our daily lives or our worldview. It involves yet another instance where we are required to go outside the box to come to a proper understanding of the situation. And so, once again, out of the box is where we will go.

There are other dimensions—more properly, it should be said that there are other vibrational frequencies—which are capable of sustaining life. Ours is not the only one. As these dimensions go, ours exists at a lower frequency than some others. Objects which are solid in our dimension would not be solid to beings who exist in a higher frequency state. When these beings are not fully materialized into our dimension of reality, they can pass through solid objects without any sense of contact. This is one reason they can do such things as walk through doors and walls. I understand there is also a device which attaches to the belt and makes this possible for humans to do as well, though it operates by altering the density of objects rather than moving between dimensions.

It has been reliably reported that all known planets, moon, stars and galaxies also exist in these so-called "higher dimensions", but that within those dimensions their form and attributes are completely changed. The planet Jupiter, for example, when seen in a higher dimension is a completely different color and, rather than being a gas giant, is a solid planet. The same source stated that the way this is known is because NASA has developed a method by which a craft can "jump" into this higher dimension for a very brief amount of time.

Most of the objects reported as UFO's which are commonly presumed to have traveled across vast distance of space are in fact "jumpers", meaning craft which are hyper-dimensional. The beings which build and pilot these craft originate in a dimension which has a higher vibrational state than does ours and have developed the ability to "jump" between the dimension which they are native to and our own.

This is the explanation for why UFO's are so often reported to "appear as if out of nowhere" or "instantly vanish". What is happening is that these craft are traveling between dimensions. They could be physically present in a certain location in a higher dimension, one which is not visible to our senses, and remain completely hidden from sight.

When they jump through into our dimension, the effect is that an alien spacecraft appears suddenly in plain view where there had been absolutely nothing visible a split second before. Similarly, they can jump from our dimension into a higher dimension and instantly vanish from sight.

This does not imply that they have left the vicinity, however, as they are technically still in the same place. Because they are now vibrating at a frequency which is too high for our eyes to detect, they are invisible to us and we have no way of knowing they are there at all.

There is reportedly at least one dimension NASA is aware of which exists at a vibrational state which is lower than our own. It is possible that there is more than one, though it appears that as dimensions go our vibrational state is low enough that there are not likely many more which are lower than ours.

Extra-terrestrial visitors can be (and usually are) a combination of more than one of these things. They can be (and often are) beings who originate in places very far from Earth—other worlds, other constellations—in higher dimensions. They combine, in that case, interstellar and interdimensional characteristics. The same thing can be said for beings which travel here through time: they can also be from other dimensions or from distant solar systems.

This is an important piece of information, because the inter-dimensional nature of these entities allows them great latitude in behavior--once they arrive at our location we will have no idea they are even here. This is also true if they jump through into our dimension individually, rather than aboard a craft of some kind. At least some alien races are reported to be able to do exactly that, though the method by which it is done is not yet understood. It is possible, for example, for a member of the Reptilian race known as the Draco—a race which will be covered in detail in the volume which follows this one—to be literally standing in the same room with us and be completely invisible to our sight.

The topic of inter-dimensionality is one which is difficult to understand fully. I am the first to admit that my understanding of it is by no means either comprehensive or complete. As was the case with time travel, I will not attempt to speak about it here other than to make the reader aware that it is very real. It is something which conventional science currently lacks an understanding of, but a large percentage of the non-human visitations which are taking place on and around Earth involve inter-dimensional jumps as well as interstellar travel or time travel.

Despite the confidence demonstrated by mainstream science regarding their view of the universe, the truth of the matter is that our conventional knowledge of physics is extremely limited in its scope. Though far more advanced in modern times than it was in the past, physics is a science which is still in its infancy. We are very far from being able to claim a complete understanding of either the nature of reality or the laws and forces which are present within what we call our universe. Those who describe it as a "multiverse" are technically correct: it is comprised of many different dimensions of reality, all of which exist together and yet are at the same time separate from one another.

Making it even more complicated, each of those dimensions appears to have what amounts to an infinite number of unique individual timelines being carried out simultaneously. There are surely timelines where the Germans won the Second World War, where Lincoln didn't go to the theater on that fateful night, etc., and all of them led to a future world which is fully populated and going about its business at this very moment…on the same planet we live on, in the same spaces we inhabit, completely invisible and inaccessible to us.

The fact that we are being visited by beings who can travel here from other dimensions demonstrates the difference which exists between their levels of technology and our own. It should also serve as an indication of the difference in natural intelligence between them and us.

Other than the Type II Greys, it seems likely that every alien race known to us has far greater intellectual capabilities than our own. They utilize technologies which are, it would appear, at least hundreds of thousands of years more advanced than ours. I think we would not be wrong to presume that they are in some cases literally millions of years ahead of us. The difference between a stone age tribe living in the jungle and the world's most modern military force would certainly be far less than the difference between our technological level and that of the aliens.

Their capabilities are beyond anything we can even imagine. Their motivations and agenda originate from minds which are distinctly *not* human and which we therefore have no accurate way to predict or guess about. The blunt fact of the matter is that even the least advanced and the most friendly-appearing of them could have motives and agendas which are very different from what they appear to be. If that were the case, we would probably never understand them until it was too late to matter.

As stated above, even the least advanced, friendliest-appearing non-human civilization must be presumed able to eliminate the human race--and to do so quickly and easily, should they make the decision to. If that decision is made, it is quite unlikely that there is anything we could do to save ourselves. Much like the citizens of an ant farm, we continue to live only at their sufferance.

We have become accustomed to thinking that our fate is in our own hands and that we can choose how the future will look. This is a human conceit, something which is not true at all. Where our future lies and the shape it will take, rather than being something we have the power to control, appears to depend almost entirely on the choices that are made regarding us by ancient, highly advanced, non-human entities of unknown intent. We live or we die, both as individuals and as a race, at their pleasure. We do not own the ant farm, we are the ants. That is an idea we had better all get used to. We are going to have to live with it for a very long time.

It does not require more than a quick look around at the world we live in to clearly understand that, despite the many ways we find to flatter ourselves, we are not a very impressive bunch. If that isn't a thought worthy of careful consideration and long reflection, I don't know what is.

CHAPTER 12: THE PLEIADIANS

*"Welcome to the official site of the Nibiruan Council, a
multidimensional off-world council whose members are connected
to the people of the planet Nibiru and the Nibiruans' ancient
ancestors, the 9D Nibiruans. "*
-- The Nibiruan Council, Serving the Worlds of the Galactic
Federation (a website)

*"I thought that they were angels,
But much to my surprise
They climbed aboard their starship
And headed for the skies!"*
-- Styx

There is an extra-terrestrial race known as the Pleiadians
(sometimes spelled "Pleiadeans") whose existence has been well-
established by this point in time. They are quite like humans in their
appearance, although not identical. The Pleiadians are generally taller
than humans and have very pale skin, blonde hair and blue eyes. They
are considered by those who have met them to be a very good-looking
race by our standards and are always reported as being trim and
athletic in appearance, with well-toned muscles. This is the same race
which was referred to by Billy Meier as "Plejarens".

The Pleiadians are believed to originate on a planet called Erra,
which orbits the star we call 10-Tauri. Sometimes called Taygeta, 10-
Tauri is part of the constellation Taurus and is slightly larger and
slightly more luminous than Earth's sun. It appears to be considerably
older than our sun as well, leading to speculation by astronomers that
it may be nearing the end of its main sequence.

If true, this implies that in a relatively short time the star in the
Pleiadians home system will evolve into a red giant, expanding
outward when the interior pressure is no longer counterbalanced by
the pressure at the star's surface. The expansion of the star means that
the heat it radiates is spread over a much larger surface area, resulting
in a cooler temperature overall. When our sun reaches the point where
it passes out of its main sequence it, too, will evolve into a red giant.

This race has occasionally been reported to contact humans on an individual basis, though such contact events are not a common occurrence. They occur with far less frequency, for example, than does contact with the classic Grey aliens, whose interaction with humans is often reported in association with abduction events.

It is generally believed within the UFO community that the Pleiadian race is friendly, sympathetic and genuinely helpful in terms of its interaction with humanity in general and individual humans as well. Contactees often report that their encounters with Pleiadians was positive, as well as sometimes claiming to have gained new skills from of such contact. Because of their physical beauty combined with the many interactions with humans which are reported to be of a positive nature, Pleiadians are commonly considered to be among the most peaceful of all known races, as far as their relationship with humans are is concerned.

The Pleiadian race is often confused with another race, one which is very similar in appearance but, rather than being blonde and blue-eyed, tend to have brown hair instead. The best information I have been able to find leads me to believe that these two groups represent distinct races, rather than being a single race with multiple hair colors. I do not consider that this is written in stone, but at this point I do consider it to be the most likely situation.

The Pleiadians are virtually always given the role of protagonist among the many groups discussed in a previous chapter. I will refer to some of those ideas here as well, for the sake of clarity, but most of what I had to say about that topic has already been covered.

I interact with members of the New Age movement on an almost daily basis. Some of them are engaged in attempts to contact the Pleiadians. They gather in open fields and beam their adoring welcomes outward into space, hoping that these friendly visitors will receive them and respond by making an appearance.

I want to be as fair as possible to the Pleiadians, of course, and I certainly do not want to be guilty of mistaking their intentions or misunderstanding their message. I took it upon myself, therefore, to follow the example of the believers. I attempted to project my thoughts outward into space in what I hoped was the general direction of these enlightened souls. I invited them to appear in my home and fill me in on their plans, so that I could be sure not to get it wrong in this book of mine. I offered to provide them with a delicious salad for dinner (presuming they are likely to be vegetarians). I even offered to provide them with a beverage which it seemed to me might be suitable to their tastes (home brewed beer, which I dubbed "blonde, blue-eyed, looks-like-a-Nordic Pleiadian Ultra-Pale Ale"). Apparently, my soul lacks the requisite degree of spiritual light, however, because my invitation never received a reply of any kind.

I tried. I gave them the opportunity to make sure that everything I said here about them reflects the absolute truth. I even named the pride of my cottage distillery after them. But as it turns out, I had to go it alone and hope for the best. That's the way life goes sometimes.

Far from being a race of superheroes who are going to come flying in on their glorious wonderships to save the day and rescue humanity from certain doom, the Pleiadians appear to adhere strictly to a policy of non-intervention. This is most likely due to agreements which they have made with other spacefaring civilizations, including presumably the Draco, the Sirians, the Mantids and the Type I Greys.

I am not privy to the details of such agreements, nor do I pretend to be. I have been told by inside sources, however, that such agreements do exist and are the primary reason the Pleiadians remain outside the arena for the most part as far as humanity is concerned. The fact that the Eisenhower administration declined an offer of assistance from them and chose instead to sign a treaty with aliens who turned out to be hostile, even after being warned about them in advance by the Pleiadians, is also believed to be a factor which is in play.

It appears that the United States has repeatedly attacked Pleiadian vessels within Earth's atmosphere with a variety of weapons systems. This is quite possibly another reason they are not inclined to offer us much assistance.

Why did we engage in such attacks? Possibly because the Pleiadians are believed to be at war against the Draco, and we did so attempting to please the race we foolishly signed a treaty with, a treaty which in effect granted the hostile alien powers official recognition and permission to occupy the United States and, by extension, the rest of the world as well. There is little question that approving the Greada Treaty was a poorly-advised, extremely unfortunate decision. We are still paying the price for it today.

Just as it is with humans, one cannot judge the motivations or agenda of an entire race by utilizing generalized statements which are intended to apply to all individuals within a certain group. Though it is certainly true that many people have reported encounters of a positive nature with Pleiadians, those are not the only types of reports which exist. Some have reported seeing and interacting with Pleiadians who do not appear to be friendly.

One can not presume to know the true intentions or attitude of a Pleiadian—or of any alien, for that matter—simply by being able to identify its race. This adds reinforcement to the warning given earlier in the book: "Do not attempt to interrupt or interfere with an alien being". Just as Pleiadians can be positive and pleasant to encounter, so too can they be negative and hostile. It is furthermore believed that the negatively-oriented Pleiadians engage in the practice of abducting and hybridizing humans just as the (far more commonly encountered) Type II Greys do.

Abductees have occasionally reported seeing Pleiadians present in the spacecraft when they have been abducted by Type II Greys. It is believed that they are either androids, synthetic beings, prisoners or clones of prisoners who were captured during the war which is said to be ongoing between the Pleiadians and the Draco Consortium.

As members of a race which appears to permanently occupy the position of supreme underdog regardless of which group of extra-terrestrials we are dealing with, it is surely unwise to presume that any of them have genuinely friendly intentions without first having a great deal more to go on than statements they may make to that effect. Manipulation can come in many forms, including offers of assistance which are designed to bring about either changes which are desired by the ET's themselves or dependence upon the technologies and commodities they might make available to us.

Isolated, backward, outclassed, outgunned and very much alone, it seems to me that an abundance of caution on our part is not only advisable, it is required if we possess even a modicum of instinct for self-preservation. These alien races know humans very well indeed— better than we know ourselves, in fact—and have observed us for untold thousands of years. We, on the other hand, know very little about them and it has already been demonstrated by the Greada Treaty that they can and do deceive and manipulate both our military and political leaders.

As much as some people may wish that the Pleiadians are going to step in and save us, there is no reason to believe that this is the case. If these problems are to be solved, it is clear to me that we must take the responsibility for solving them upon ourselves. We do not have the right to pass the burden to others who owe us nothing or blame them if we fail to find solutions on our own.

We have long been accustomed to thinking of ourselves as special and as more deserving of good things than any other creatures around. This has certainly been just one more example of self-delusion. By galactic standards, the only thing about us which is special is our DNA, which is valuable to the visitors for certain reasons. Other than that, we are very far from being special compared to virtually any of the ET races which surround us. Far from being the most favored creation of the gods, we appear to be little more than self-important cosmic mutts. Not only are we unlikely to be given any special favors, we are unlikely to get so much as an even break in our dealings with extra-terrestrials.

As will be seen later, it appears that many of the problems we face today as a global society are in fact problems which have been intentionally created by extra-terrestrial beings and their representatives. We are forced to contend against beings of higher intelligence and far more advanced capabilities than we possess. This puts us in a position from which it is very difficult to find a winning scenario. Like it or not, this is the position we occupy.

This will be illustrated in detail in the following volume, "Alien Contact: Paradigm Shift", and I highly recommend that each of you who is reading this volume make a point of reading that one too. Despite all my efforts to make certain this book contained as much useful information as I could find a way to pack into it, the best I could do was use it to set the stage for the book which is to follow it.

By reading this volume, you will have a sufficient understanding of the general outlines of the situation to allow you to fit the pieces of the puzzle neatly into place when they are presented to you later. The truth regarding alien contact is of tremendous importance. It is very much worth the investment of time and the cost of purchasing a couple of books to understand it.

Whether you think it directly affects your life or not, a day will come all too soon when it will be made clear that alien contact has an immense impact on your life and on our global society. When that day arrives, there will be two types of people in this world. The first will be the uninformed public, which includes most people. They will be trying as hard as they can to promote the wrong attitudes, information and actions. If they are successful, it is no exaggeration to say that humanity as we know it will come to an ignominious end. The world will indeed end not with a bang, but with a whimper.

The second type of people will be those who made the effort to become well-informed about both the alien agenda and the agenda of the hidden powers of this world before the situation came to a head. These people—and you will be one of them—will be in the minority. Rather than being deceived, they will be forewarned and able to identify the lies and propaganda which will be flooding the world during that time.

It is no exaggeration to say that the members of this group, which will find themselves persecuted and marginalized to no end, may very well represent the last and greatest hope humanity has for its survival. The stakes could not possibly be any higher. I therefore encourage everyone who is reading this to make certain they take in both volumes, not for my sake but for their own. The reasons for this will become clear later.

For all their positive attributes, the Pleiadians are not likely to be of much help in terms of solving our global problems, nor do we have the right to expect them to be. If we are worth saving, we can prove it by solving those problems on our own. We can take charge of our own destiny and do the things that must be done to bring about a better world. Our childhood is over, and the future that awaits us is both demanding and unforgiving. We must demonstrate that we are worthy to face it.

CHAPTER 13: THE COLONEL'S MESSAGE

"The truth will set you free, but first it will make you miserable."
-- James A. Garfield

"Welcome to the light
Now everything is okay
You run through the light of night
You come to the light of day"
-- Yes

The following is a partial transcript of conversations I had with one of my highest-ranking, most well-placed inside sources. In my judgment, he was also the individual who was the most motivated in terms of wanting to make certain information available to the public and firmly believed it was his duty to do so if possible.

Virtually nobody has access to complete and unfiltered information concerning extra-terrestrials. Some, however, do have access to a considerable amount because it is necessary for them to be able to carry out their responsibilities. That description is certainly applicable to this source and to the best of my knowledge he never said anything which was intended to mislead or deceive me in any way. I believe that when he spoke to me about these matters he was telling the truth to the best of his ability.

That does not necessarily mean that he himself was always given accurate information. It is standard practice that even very senior officers will sometimes be given only partial information. This is done to ensure that nobody other than the dozen or so people at the very top of the security clearance food chain would be able to piece the whole story together accurately.

I will state for the record that this source was among the most informative, helpful and well-informed of any I have ever spoken with. I always found it fascinating to listen to him speak about alien-related matters from his position as such a high-level insider. I hope that you, too, will find the things he had to say interesting and helpful. He held a rank which was equivalent to or higher than a full Colonel in the U.S. Air Force. I will refer to him simply as The Colonel. He spoke on the condition of anonymity. I will not name him, nor should it be presumed that his rank was technically that of a Colonel or that the USAF is necessarily the branch of service he was associated with.

The following conversations are verbatim, word for word transcriptions of our conversations, with the exception that they are incomplete. I have chosen to omit certain things which may touch upon matters of national security that I do not feel are appropriate to publish. Other than that, not a single word has been changed.

The Colonel: There is a group of people within the military who disagree with the actions and policies of our government. We do not approve of the way they treat our civilians or of their activities which involve the visitors. They do not represent our best interests and put us all in a great deal of danger. We are unable to speak publicly due to the positions we hold, but would like people to be aware of certain things which are being done without their knowledge or permission. There are things we feel the public should be informed about.

Since we cannot say these things ourselves, we need someone on the outside to relay the message for us. Someone who has no connection to either the military or the government. Someone like yourself. I want you to speak for us. I want you to say the things we are unable to say on our own, but which the public must be told.

The first thing I would like to make you aware of is that the business we are engaged in is highly lethal. We utilize people who have certain skills which we require and continue to do so for as long as they are of use to us. When their usefulness comes to an end, their lives often come to an end soon afterward.

Your friend Bill, for instance. We pay him quite well for his services because he has a set of skills we need. But eventually there will come a time when it is determined that his usefulness has come to an end. At that point we will either set him up in business at our expense or he will be shot. He is aware of this. He was informed about both possibilities before he began to work with restricted technology. Some people accept those conditions and some do not. Those who decline are allowed to walk away, but will never be given another opportunity to work with anything related to the visitors or their technology.

I am told, by the way, that you have taken an interest in the public statements of Bob Lazar. It has still not been decided for certain what will be done about him, meaning whether he will be terminated. If it is decided that termination is our best option, the method has already been planned. The entrances to his home will be sealed shut and he will be killed in an unfortunate fire which will erupt as he is sleeping.

It is my opinion that such action will not be undertaken. He has told everything he knows, all at once. There is no longer any way for him to hurt us. Killing him now would only serve to add credibility to his story, so it is my feeling that he will not be harmed.

But that is not a decision I will make, and as of now no final decision has been made regarding that issue.

[Author's Note: This conversation occurred a number of years ago and it seems that The Colonel was correct in his opinion that Bob Lazar would not be the victim of a military hit.]

I understand that you have some questions about crossbreeding. Crossbreeding is taking place and the government is involved in abductions. One hybrid is at Groom Lake and one is in Russia.

DT: Are you speaking of Grey/human hybrids, or of Reptilian/humans?

The Colonel: One is Grey, one is Sirian.

DT: Could you please describe the Sirians for me?

The Colonel: The Sirians look like a cross between a dinosaur and a human. Bipedal, like a small upright dinosaur, but human colored skin.

DT: Are they involved in abducting humans?

The Colonel: Derek, I don't like telling you this, but they don't abduct anyone. It is our own people doing it, using their technology.

DT: And now that you have told me this, I presume I must be killed. Would you mind if I ordered some pizza first?

The Colonel (completely deadpan): What would you like on your Tombstone?

DT: There are certainly a lot of people who have reported seeing aliens in their homes and I am one of them. And I must tell you, if our government is abducting private citizens that is a very serious problem.

The Colonel: Let's get a few things straight first. First, we have been using "undetermined technology" for quite some time. This is borrowed technology and we do not understand all of it. Furthermore, we have a strict guide of conduct between ourselves and our guests which is tightly adhered to by both parties, under penalty of death. Both sides have agreed to this.

DT: Drawn up by them or by us?

The Colonel: Derek, they drew it up and it was signed by President Eisenhower. We have modified it over the years to make it fairer to us and they have agreed to it. They are not bad people, just different, with a completely different sociological structure and set of values. It is a two-way situation. We have certain rules that they must follow and they have rules that we must follow. We are in constant communication with them.

DT: And they are allowed to do what, Colonel?

The Colonel: They are permitted to experiment with DNA in labs that we provide, under our supervision. They are permitted to cull out any animals, including humans, which both they and we deem unfit. In this case, unfit means subject to genetic problems.

The document gave them "permission" to overfly our country at will, to go where they pleased and do what they wished to do for the most part. They were also given permission to abduct a certain number of our citizens under the original terms of the agreement.

We agreed to construct, either on our own or with their assistance, underground and undersea bases for the use of our guests. Some of those bases are jointly occupied. Some connect with bases they already possessed here, most of which originated in large natural caverns or cave systems and were later enlarged by them.

Both sides agreed not to go public about their presence. It was felt it would make both our jobs more difficult were that to happen. They agreed not to interfere in our politics and to periodically provide us with advanced technologies.

Naturally we were primarily interested in technologies which could be developed or applied to some type of military application. They have given us such technologies, as well as others in the fields of medicine, advanced concepts of physics, fiber optics and microchips. Thanks to them, we are now able to cure virtually any disease known to us, including cancer. We have been given technology which allows us to clone humans and have been making use of it for many years.

Most of these technologies have not been released to the public. Those which have been are released only after we are certain we have a sufficient lead on anything which the public is made aware of that nobody can catch up to us. Anything they are made aware of will already be outdated technology as far as the military is concerned, several generations behind what we are capable of.

The usual method of releasing technologies to the public is to funnel them through a large company which does a lot of business with the government. We will release the technology to one of those companies and allow them to patent it and profit from it. In return they must agree never to reveal where it came from. They will claim to have come up with it through research and then take it to market.

The miniaturization of computer chips is one example of technology which has been made available to the public. Some other technologies we borrow from them. We do not entirely understand some of them and it is believed possible that we may not have the ability as a species to ever truly understand them. They are far more intelligent than we are and it is felt that their intellect can take them to places ours cannot go. Other races of visitors are not happy about the fact that we took the decision to make an agreement of this type with the Sirians and their allies.

There was an initial meeting between our President and the ambassador from a race which claimed to be interested in assisting us in solving our global problems, things such as overpopulation, energy and pollution. They also offered advanced medical technologies.

There was a condition attached to this offer of assistance: before they would begin to help us, we had to agree to eliminate all nuclear weapons first. We had no way to be sure that the intentions of these visitors really were peaceful. It was believed that, should they prove hostile, nuclear weapons might well be the only weapons available to us which would be effective against them. Because of that, this proposal was rejected by the President on the advice of the military.

At some point during the meeting a silent alarm was accidentally triggered, causing guards to rush into the room. Thinking the President was in danger, they opened fire on the ambassador, shooting him dead center in the chest and killing him instantly. They have never trusted us since that day. Considering the circumstances, I do not blame them. It is hoped that, with good behavior, we may be able to regain their trust in another 125 years or so.

DT: Can you describe what is being done at Dulce Base?

The Colonel: I'm sorry, Dulce Base is not something I have information about. If I did have information regarding Dulce Base, I feel certain that I would not be able to discuss it. That subject is off limits.

DT: Understood. What sort of DNA-related experiments are they doing?

The Colonel: So far, the best I know is that they are working on re-combining human DNA sequences to be more compatible with their own.

DT: That implies a threat, does it not?

The Colonel: Human DNA is much more common among life than we previously thought and can be found in many creatures. Their races are all dying. We are the youngest intelligent life in the known and explored universe. We are the new kids on the block. Our DNA sequences have not yet begun to degrade. That makes us exceptionally valuable to them. It is in their best interest to protect us. So, while there have been atrocities in the past, they have promised there will be none in the future. Our future health is their primary concern. We are the DNA farm. We are not unique. Our DNA structures can be found almost everywhere, but ours are in the best state of health. They are attempting to prolong their races longevity. It seems that within our DNA lies the code that will determine when our race will begin to die out as well. Their philosophy on this is that all races are allotted a particular amount of time…and they don't want to die off.

DT: What is the relationship between the Greys and the Sirians?

The Colonel: The Greys are an artificial life form, created by the Sirians some 5,000 years ago or so for DNA experimentation.

DT: What is the purpose, exactly, of the impregnation of abductees?

The Colonel: Impregnation is generally done by one of our own operatives, using borrowed technology to give them the appearance and capabilities of our guests. This is done to ensure that none of our own are ever caught. Furthermore, it is felt that by making it appear that our guests are doing this, people who report it will look foolish. Derek…you are very skeptical of their intentions for good reason, however I can assure you that they pose no threat to our species.

DT: The problem is that they DO pose a threat to the individuals who are "chosen" by them.

The Colonel: I must agree with you, Derek. We cannot get them to understand that. They believe that we should feel honored. They see us as emerging intellects, not yet fully formed.

DT: My thought is this: if they just asked for volunteers, wouldn't it make everything much easier for all concerned?

The Colonel: I'm afraid that is our government's doing. The general consensus is that people would panic if the truth were released. I disagree.

DT: Isn't all of this totally illegal, Colonel?

The Colonel: Yes, it certainly is. But who are you going to sue? You can't prove anything and you have no names to name even if you could. You have no means of forcing the military to disclose anything. If you ask for certain documents and the military says they do not exist, how will you prove that they do? I'm afraid our time is up, for now. I have things to attend to. Thanks for letting me talk with you. This meeting did not take place. I never said a word and will deny it if anyone puts it to my name.

*****

The Colonel: It was refreshing to once again speak to someone who would not write my name down in some little black book. Thank you for that opportunity. Mine is a job where paranoia is almost a requirement. Over the years, I've raised in rank, but at the cost of being able to speak freely. Officially, I must deny everything that is discussed here.

I understand and appreciate your desire to learn more about the extra-terrestrials and why they are here. Please believe me when I say that, for the most part, we can trust them. So far, they have not violated any of the established guidelines (although we have), have advanced our technological capabilities by at least 100 years and on occasion have proven their friendship with advances in medicine. We are the ones who have lied and cheated them. They have no reason to trust us.

It is my opinion that they are not hostile, however not entirely friendly. They are ambivalent towards us. We are viewed by them as a very young, emerging civilization that will one day take to the stars. For this reason, they were first attracted to us. It was no surprise to them that our DNA closely resembles their own, in the same manner that a chimp's DNA is 98% of ours. According to our guests, over 80% of the known civilizations share DNA to within 1% of each other. In most ways, we are all brothers.

The exception to this is the Sirians, who believe they are the first and only race to achieve true intelligence. To them, we are all trained monkeys. The "greys" were their attempt millennia ago to create artificial life upon which to conduct their experiments. Their objective was and still is to find a way for their race to interbreed with "mammalian" races in order for their race to continue.

We are the youngest, newest race in the established known cosmos. There are dozens of known and recorded races. Of these, almost all outdate us by well over 100,000 years. They believe we are the young, warlike race that will save them with an influx of new, young DNA.

Their medical sciences, which far outstrip our abilities, show clearly that all races have a DNA "time bomb" built in that causes the race to die out after a certain length of time. This is to preserve racial diversity by forcing new races to merge with old and is considered by ALL of them to be completely natural and as it should be.

Because our race was born later than anticipated, this event may or may not occur naturally and so their races will die out, leaving us alone in another 20,000 years. If this happens, Homo Sapiens will have no one else to merge with in 100,000 years and so we will be the last. When we are gone, there will most likely be no others. The reason for this is that we are the least common factor.

Let me explain what I mean. Here is what you REALLY want to hear. The reason our government is so completely and abjectly opposed to revealing their existence is because it means admitting that we are the LEAST advanced of all species and probably the last as well. Imagine the impact being the LAST would have on our people. It would eliminate all hope for the future. There would be no reason to continue, knowing that our future is limited and that none would come after us.

You see, of all the species our DNA is at its most simplified structure. We are the basic equation of intelligent life. All that came before us had infinitely more diverse and complex DNA sequences. We are the least common factor: the least advanced, the least intelligent. How does that make you feel?

Our guests intend to show themselves at some point, however our government plans to exterminate them on Earth before that can happen to protect our interests. They do not understand that this will cause a war we cannot even hope to win. It is a terrible thing that we do.

You must believe me, our only enemy where they are concerned is our own government.

DT: Last time we spoke, you told me that the aliens are not creating hybrids, that it is the military which creates them. I must admit it was a statement which took me very much by surprise— something I didn't expect to hear and which I had never considered before. Did I understand you correctly about that, Colonel?

The Colonel: Hybrids are OUR experiments, not theirs. Our guests are repulsed by these experiments and see us as barbaric and uncivilized for it. We do not represent ourselves well. We borrow their technology to make ourselves look like them, move as them and use their craft. We use their tech to pass through solid objects and fly. We use their technology to actually bend light around an object, rendering it invisible to sight. That's one reason our stealth bombers cost a billion dollars each: when the cloaking system is operational, you can look right at them as they pass overhead and you will see nothing but the sky. The plane itself will be completely invisible, hidden from sight and because of its design also hidden from radar. That is also why none have ever been shot down.

I'm sorry, Derek, they are much more civilized and considerate than we are. It does not feel good to realize that you belong to a race of low-class chimps surrounded by advanced intellects. But that is who we are and that is one reason why the government will not permit disclosure.

DT: Can you describe the Sirians for me please?

The Colonel: The Sirians average 6'6" and according to what I have seen range from about 6'2" to seven feet tall. Their average weight is in the 350-pound range. Most of their weight over 200 pounds is in their thighs and very short (about 12 inches) thick tail. They also have very thick necks and decidedly heavy skulls. They remind me of intelligent dinosaurs. If you are familiar with Star Trek, think of the Cardassians. They don't look that way by accident, except the Sirians don't have human-like faces.

They are not our enemies but I would not turn my back on them, either. They are congenial but not overly friendly. We work with them on a "friendly but not friends" basis. If they were to be considered hostile in any way, it's that they think we don't deserve their technology and they don't like giving it out, but that is part of the deal. It's like trying to work with people you don't like. You'll do it, but nobody is particularly happy about it.

Their view on us is that we are a relatively new species that will eventually take to the stars, as they did and others after them. They don't like that idea, but they recognize our right to do it, just as the others did. They're cold shouldered and treat us like we're not as good as they are, yet they constantly find us intriguing. They are snobs by every definition of the word. We are not their equals technologically and they seem to enjoy pointing that out. They have compared us to other races, but that tells us nothing as we know little to nothing about the races we were compared to. They are intellectual snobs, in my opinion. They have stated themselves that they do not associate with other species because everyone wants their technology and they are sick of it.

They are interested in us because the "greys" were a complete failure in genetic experimentation. They are incapable of reproducing themselves, so the Sirians gave up on that idea, subjugating them to slave status. The greys, according to the Sirians, are called Mobites. They are relatively unintelligent and possess limited social structure. For this reason, the Sirians have expressed interest in collecting DNA from our species because ours is the most compatible with the most life forms—including theirs.

We are the lowest common denominator, if that helps you to understand my meaning. I may have expressed myself inaccurately. That does not mean we are low or common. It means that we are the basic species. There is nothing wrong with that at all—in fact, it's good because it gives them a reason to keep us around. They have no intention THAT I KNOW OF to ranch us, however we do have plans to cover that scenario should it develop. We can modify our atmosphere by adding a combination of various salts and other elements to it. The result would be that we would barely notice the difference but it would render our atmosphere completely unbreathable to them. The hope is that at that point they would just give up and go away.

There are some minor differences in sequencing that they can fix. The two Sirians that I have met made me feel like a chimp surrounded by scientists. The Sirians have an average IQ of 200. They barely acknowledged me except that they understood I hold a position here and worked with me grudgingly, if I had to give it human terms. They speak fluently every language we know. Their own language is guttural, with lots of tongue clicking and body movements. Our analysis shows that it is akin to dolphin clicks and whale sounds, but it is not the same. They do not speak to our whales and dolphins. I just wanted to make that clear.

The Sirians represent approximately 25% of all guest activity. They prefer to stay on their craft and pursue science. They are mostly scientific in nature and are very inquisitive. Their culture is based on exploration and scientific achievement. Status in the Sirian culture, as best we can determine, is based on "What have you done for me TODAY?" They are highly regimented and we know nothing about their mating habits.

My conclusions are this—and this is all my *personal opinion*: I do not like them. I would not sit to eat with one. I don't want them in my home, on my planet or anywhere around me. Those are my personal feelings toward them. They are rude and obtuse, but they are not hostile…at least, not yet. I believe the day will come when we will have to fight with them. Not like a war, but rather we will need to let them know that we want them gone. Other races do not care for them. Their "superior snobbery" makes them just go away when confronted.

Unfortunately, our own people are more interested in their technology than in our own welfare. The Sirians do not pose an invading global threat, but they do give me reasons to think that they might try to impose their will on us someday *with* the cooperation of our government. Ours is the most willing government on Earth to cooperate with them.

The Mobites range from 3'4" to 4'6" and weigh from 70 to 120 pounds. They are warm-blooded but are not mammalian. Their life expectancy is 35 human years. I have met five in one meeting. They look exactly like we all know they do. They have four equal-length fingers and toes. They are proven to be technically inept and have IQ's by human terms of around 85. They are poor pilots and are responsible for most of the crashes we have found.

Bloolongs are from 4'6" to 5'6" and weigh around 130 pounds on average. They have silvery skin and look more like humans than any other species we are aware of. They are warm-blooded and very friendly. They genuinely like us and do not like the Sirians. No big surprise there—most of the other species don't. They are interested in us because they believe we are all related.

The Bloolongs have personally seeded several thousand planets. They claim success on all but 20% of them. Ours is not one of them. This is the only species that we know of which has made it to another galaxy. They will be our best allies against the Sirians if the situation degrades to the point of actual military warfare. Their technology is not far behind the Sirians. Their only shortcoming is their lifespan, which is ten human years. *(Author's note: This would appear to be the race which originates in the Andromeda galaxy and which is commonly referred to as "Andromedans" within ufology circles.)*

Girhads (there is a whistle sound at the end of their name). They average seven feet tall and weigh in at around 400 pounds. They are one of the older races and are strictly explorers and nothing else. They depend on several other races to trade information for food, textiles, etc. We don't know very much about them other than that they live close to 200 human years and are amazingly strong even for their size. I have never met one.

Egboldarians are a non-mammalian species that we have not been able to classify. They are strictly aquatic and vegetarian. I like to think of them as intelligent squid. Their technology is 100% organic. We think, but are not sure, that this is the tech that our engineers have been working on, which was recovered at the crash at Varginha (though the species involved in that crash were of another race). They cannot survive in our atmosphere and our oceans are too salty for them. They have lived for a limited time in fresh water we have provided, but had to add some organic compounds of their own. They have no interest in us whatsoever because we are too incompatible with them biologically.

Xtichxius (pronounced ex-tick-see-us). I don't know anything about them except that they absolutely detest the Sirians for creating the Mobites. They are in a trading relationship with the Girhads.

Braan are skinny, spidery-like humanoids in that their arms and legs are disproportionately long compared to their bodies. They eat living creatures such as mice, small birds, etc. They are very intelligent and are fond of us the way we are fond of our pets, yet they do not treat us like pets. Rather, they are always happy to be around us, they marvel at what we have achieved for such a young race and they also dislike the Sirians. They are roughly five feet tall and weigh in the 60-pound range.

Their culture is built on the concept that intellect will always rule over might. In many ways, their philosophies are much like ours. They are the only race we've met that have religion the way we do. They have their "savior", like we do, and call him Cherist (key-rist).

There are many more races, but I will not go into that now. Briefly, we are not in danger although we very well could be someday.

The Sirians are the only species we are concerned about. We are drawing a lot of fire from other races about our involvement with them. Our activities are not endearing us with anyone either, but they all seem to recognize that we are young and make mistakes. I would be more afraid of our government than of anyone else at this point.

SETI *[the Search for Extra-Terrestrial Intelligence, which scans the skies with a large array of radio telescopes]* is, of course, now controlled by the military. Do you really think we would let them possess a powerful technology like that without getting involved, without stepping in? SETI is now used, for the most part, as a very fortuitous place to hide large amounts of funding that are used for other projects.

It is also a fact that SETI has received signals from life in outer space. SETI has never been a privately-funded group, not really. It has been "absorbed", if you will, and any communications it receives are reported directly to us and immediately classified. The public will never hear a word about it.

If you look carefully at the tapes of the Martian landscape from the Pathfinder probe, you will see that the so-called "360-degree panorama" was not that at all. It was only a 270-degree view. The reason for that is because, a short distance behind the Pathfinder, on the surface of Mars, there was a large boulder estimated to weigh about four tons. It showed very clear signs of having been moved quite recently, of having been turned up on its side. Both the marks on the ground and on the face of the boulder confirmed this. We don't know why or how it was moved...but it was. So, you were never shown the backside of the Pathfinder, only the areas which did not include a view of the boulder.

There is a war in space between two alliances of aliens...and the Earth is at the center of the battlefield. It is a long-standing conflict.

Some battles took place not only in space, but on Earth itself. To the people of the time, they were thought of as the forces of Good and Evil, or of Darkness and Light. Some of the battles were seen by the people who were around then and were reported by them.

The Cydonia region of Mars contains the remnants of what is believed to be an alien base that was destroyed in that war. For that reason, we try to divert attention from Cydonia as much as possible. There are alien bases in our solar system, including bases on the so-called "dark side of the moon" and on Mars. This is another argument against sending a manned mission to Mars: because of the public interest in the "Mars face", any expedition to Mars would be under tremendous public pressure to investigate that site. If that were to happen, it would be nearly impossible to conceal what is there. It's not worth the risk.

The alien civilizations are very old. They have had advanced technology for much longer than we have had civilization. Some are more advanced than others. They do not get along very well with each other. Each have their individual reasons and methods for exploring and colonizing this region of space. They are separated, roughly, into two factions, with some races apparently remaining neutral or outside of the conflict.

Why have they come here? Some of them claim to have used Earth as a base long ago, in prehistory. They consider this planet to be their property and would like to take it back. But they all face, or soon will face, a big problem. Some of these races reproduce by cloning exclusively, they have done so for thousands and thousands of years. Their DNA is now deteriorating. They can no longer reproduce naturally. Their main purpose in coming here is to use human DNA, which is young and strong and extremely diverse, to save themselves. If they are unable to do that, some of these races will die out very soon, within the next several thousand years. Most of the others will die out as well, though maybe not quite so soon.

Their interest is scientific...but it's also a matter of intense personal interest. They need us to save themselves. They know that we will be the next race to achieve interstellar travel. So far, they have been unable to successfully modify human DNA in a way that will ensure their own survival. They recognize the possibility that they may never be able to achieve that and that they will eventually become extinct.

There is no real reason for them to want to destroy us; we can never be a threat to them. And, for now at least, they need us. But each of them wants to be remembered, should their race die out. Each of them wants their legacy to remain and they want us to carry it into the future for them. The issue then becomes "Whose legacy will we carry?" They each want it to be their own...and that is basically what they are fighting about.

At this point, there is another matter I want to mention. There is something I've wanted, for years, to do before I retire. I would like to take a qualified civilian researcher into one of our underground or underwater bases and give them a tour, let them have a look around at it for themselves. I have not yet done so because it is quite difficult to find the right person for the job, so to speak.

It would have to be a person with a high degree of intelligence and reliability. They would need to be able to understand just what it is they were being given access to. Most of the technology used in these bases is advanced far beyond anything seen in the civilian world and there would not be time for me to explain it in detail. The individual would have to be someone I trust implicitly to keep the whole thing secret. They would be unable to identify either myself or any of the other personnel at the base they might interact with and they would be required to act and speak as though the entire thing never took place.

They would be given the opportunity to see and learn things which are normally unavailable to members of the public, but in return they would be unable to describe those things to others or to speak of the incident at all. It would be a non-event, something which never happened. It is difficult to find such a person because of the risks involved and because of the personal attributes they would need to possess. I will ask you this question only one time, so I urge you to think carefully before you answer it. Would you be interested in being given such an opportunity?

DT: Of course I would! But there is something I don't understand. I don't have the security clearances that I'm sure would be necessary to get onto a base of that type. How would you be able to get me in the door?

The Colonel: The moment I set foot on the property I become the highest-ranking officer on the base. I also become the person with the highest level of security clearance. They do not tell ME who can enter the facility, I tell THEM. But if such a thing were to happen, it would be as I said. As far as anyone else is concerned, it never happened. You must agree to that condition or it will never be done.

DT: I understand. I do agree to those terms and will never speak of it to anyone. And thank you for considering me! I am honored.

The Colonel: I will hold you to your agreement. When the time comes, you will be contacted with the details.

****

It is believed by many that those people who are Rh-negative—in other words, who have a negative blood type—are thereby indicated as being the product of human/extra-terrestrial hybridization. It is believed that a negative blood type does not occur naturally in humans and is a direct result of the genetic cross between an alien and a human.

There is no question that people who possess a negative blood type are at a far higher risk of being abducted than those who do not. Though it seems clear that *all* humans are products of human/extra-terrestrial hybridization and genetic engineering in the distant past, the hybridization which is taking place in modern times is a far different thing and is being done for a very different purpose, one which is directly harmful and threatening to humanity as a whole and could theoretically lead to the end of humanity as we know it.

It seems to me that there are several extra-terrestrial races which are involved in creating or attempting to create modern hybrids between themselves and humans. It is my opinion that many such hybrids exist and that this activity has been ongoing for thousands of years, if the historical records are accurate. This implies a great number of hybrids being produced over time.

What is being done with those hybrids? Where are they?

It seems to me that many of them have been released into the general population to live and work beside us. Probably very few of them are even aware that they are hybrids and simply consider themselves to be ordinary humans. They are, however, not ordinary humans. They could be thought of as an invisible colonizing force, the members of which are unaware of both their origin and their ultimate purpose. Certainly, these people have committed no crimes and have not intentionally done any harm. But if they do indeed live and work among full-blooded humans, this necessarily implies that they also intermarry and produce children with ordinary humans, further spreading the DNA of the colonizing alien race out among the general human population.

All that is necessary in such a situation is time, patience and sufficient hybrids to release into the general population. As the extra-terrestrial DNA spreads out among the population of Earth, it will normally contain a smaller proportion of ET DNA each time a full-blooded human is involved in the reproduction cycle. It is nevertheless a fact that over time the genetic character of humanity will be modified, forever changed by sinister non-Terrestrial powers and races without our knowledge or consent. The more hybrids which are inserted into the population, the more effective this program becomes and the more extra-terrestrial DNA the average citizen of Earth will on average be carrying.

In theory, this is a way to conquer the population of a world without firing a single shot while at the same time resetting the genetic timer by creating a hybrid race which is partly extra-terrestrial. This is, it seems to me, a method a *truly* advanced race would employ if it wished to conquer a planet and had the luxury of taking it slow and working in a methodical manner.

CHAPTER 14: THE SUB-GLOBAL SYSTEM

"We have, indeed, been contacted - perhaps even visited - by extraterrestrial beings, and the U.S. government, in collusion with the other national powers of the earth, is determined to keep this information from the general public".
-- Victor Marchetti, former CIA official, 1979

"And you know, it makes me wonder
What's going on under the ground
Do you know? Don't you wonder
What's going on down under you?
We have all been here before,
We have all been here before."
-- David Crosby

The reader will most likely be wondering at this point whether the trip to a secret underground or underwater base ever actually took place. I have no recollection of being shown any of these installations. If such a visit did in fact occur, I would not be at liberty to speak about it.

If the reader wishes to observe that, had a trip like this not taken place, mentioning the possibility in this manuscript would be an unnecessary and utterly pointless waste of space, I will not argue with them. I have nothing else to say about it but that.

Because I feel that it is necessary for members of the public to be aware of the existence of these bases, why they were constructed and what they contain, I will describe them as best I can under these conditions. In doing so, I will make use of information drawn from a variety of sources, some of which are part of the public record and some drawn from interviews. Whether these descriptions are based on second-hand accounts or come from personal experience makes little difference, in my opinion, so long as the information itself is accurate. To the best of my ability to make it so, the following information is true and correct.

I will begin by saying that pretty much everything you may have heard about these underground installations from the reports of whistle blowers represents the truth. There is indeed a system of underground bases and fully-equipped underground cities. They are connected by a grid of roads and highways which are usually at least wide enough to allow two tractor trailers moving in opposite directions to safely pass by each other. In places where they are not sufficiently wide for this, there are parking lots or areas where traffic can pull to the side of the highway to let other traffic past before proceeding. The bases are often referred to as D.U.M.B.'s—Deep Underground Military Bases—and the entire network is called the Sub-Global System.

This underground world, which was built at a cost which is estimated to be over $12 *trillion* and is still being expanded, is intended to be a sanctuary, a refuge for the financial, political, corporate and military elite to take shelter in during times of extreme emergency. There is absolutely no intention to allow members of the public to have access to them during times of trouble. Some have been allowed access for the purposes of constructing the facilities which are located there and stocking them with a virtually inexhaustible amount of supplies of every conceivable type.

It was mentioned in the chapter entitled "National Treasury" that if the money allocated to the black budget were returned to the general fund, the United States could easily pay off its national debt tomorrow. Just the cost of the Sub-Global System alone, as you can see, is enough to pay off most of that debt all on its own.

Other secret projects which are ongoing have incurred expenses amounting to trillions of dollars each. Much of this is hidden within the budgets of other governmental agencies and secretly withdrawn from them. This makes it exceedingly difficult to trace or to put an exact number on.

Though we will not discuss the Secret Space Program until we get into the second volume, you can imagine the expenses associated with constructing, staffing and maintaining bases on the moon, Mars and other bodies over a period which extends already to almost a half century.

If you have ever wondered why this country is bankrupt, you may be assured that the reason has absolutely nothing to do with free school lunches for poor kids or the Social Security system. These are nothing more than scapegoats which are used to push the emotional buttons of voters while at the same time providing a convenient method of covering up the enormous expenditures which monopolize the treasury of the entire United States but are intended to benefit only a fraction of one percent of the population.

It has been estimated by some that the total expenditures of the covert projects which deal in some way with alien contact, alien technology or the secret space program consume over half of the federal budget each year, and have done so for decades. Though I have no way of confirming this, I do not have any reason to think this statement is not accurate.

These programs and activities are without question by far the most tremendously expensive project ever undertaken by humans. It is no exaggeration to state that the costs associated with them will eventually result in the bankrupting of the entire United States government's financial assets, including all lines of credit available to it. In fact, this is already happening. It is plain to see that our government is being financially run into the ground and our economy is being devastated. The true reason for this is hidden, but its effects are already crystal clear...and the situation will become worse in the future than it is now.

Consider carefully the fact that the advanced technologies controlled by this small group of unelected power brokers are kept secret, even though they have the power to vastly improve the quality of our lives if they were released. The benefits of these covert programs are also withheld from the public, made available only to a carefully-chosen handful of individuals. You and I will never be among them.

It is for this that the entire economy, wealth and financial stability of the United States has been knowingly sacrificed. It is for this that what was one the wealthiest nation the world has ever known will be driven into permanent bankruptcy and its population reduced to a state of poverty. Just because this even has not yet occurred at the time of this writing does not mean it will not happen. That it will happen is inevitable. It is a mathematical certainty.

The precise day is unknown, but sometime soon the economy of America will be toppled and come crashing to the ground. Unlike previous economic crashes, there will this time be no way for the American people to repair the damage or rebuild the economy. Once the dollar becomes devalued, the wealth of the nation will be decimated forever. This has all been carefully planned by the people who intend to emerge from the situation with full control of the nation in their hands. Freedom will be a thing of the past. The only thing people will be concerned with then is the ability to simply survive...and many of them will not be able to find a way to do so.

Multiple entrances to the Sub-Global System exist in every state. None of them are obvious and all are concealed in some manner. Most people are completely unaware of the presence of the Sub-Global System (SGS). They have no idea that such entrances even exist, much less the ability to locate them during times of need. They would not even know where to begin looking for them.

Some of the entrances are located on military bases. Some appear to be to be large doors to warehouses or storage facilities which might be located anywhere. When they are opened, however, rather than revealing the interior of a standard warehouse they provide access to secret highways which lead deep into the underground.

There are entrances which connect to secret and highly-restricted underground levels of facilities such as Los Alamos National Laboratories in New Mexico and the infamous and newly-constructed Denver Airport, which was built at a cost of many billions of dollars to serve a city which already had a perfectly good airport and no need for a new one. The walls of the new Denver Airport are covered with murals which depict scenes of devastation, gas-masked-equipped police and military troops controlling groups of terrified civilians. They depict urban warfare, mass death and slaughter. They include various New World Order symbols, as well as writing in a language which is unknown and appears to be alien.

If the implications of this are already enough to make the reader begin to feel queasy, the full description of the SGS will be enough to bring them almost to the point of downright panic. Though it is my intention to share knowledge rather than to spread fear, the truth is that some of the realities we face are downright terrifying when the facts are known. When the extent and configuration of the Sub-Global System become known to you, if it does not cause you to be afraid, you have not been paying sufficiently close attention.

Entrances to the subterranean world also exist in the form of what appear to be part of the natural landscape such as hillsides or sheer rock faces on mountains. As was stated in the introduction to this book, we live in a world of illusion and almost nothing is what it appears to be. Just as no expense has been spared in the construction and equipping of the bases which lie deep underground, so it is with many of the entrances to those bases. What appear to be sheer rock walls on the side of a mountain can literally be retracted into the mountain itself, much like a garage door is retracted into a garage.

Roads which appear to be blocked off or disused, or which in some cases are covered with soil and concealed but which can easily be utilized simply by running a piece of heavy equipment over the ground, moving the soil aside and exposing the roadway run into these entrances and then head downward at a steep angle, eventually connecting to the rest of the underground grid. In some cases, advanced holographic projectors are employed which can generate hillsides which appear to be completely natural, including trees and plants which sway in the breeze, to conceal entrances to the SGS. The state of the art in holographic capabilities which are available to the military is far beyond anything so far seen by the public. There is literally no way to tell whether what you are looking at is a natural landform or a hologram, when these capabilities are employed to their full effect.

It should not be imagined that accessing the Sub-Global System is as simple as being able to somehow locate an entrance, open what appears to be a standard shipping bay door at a warehouse and then step or drive inside. Far from it.

Sometimes the entrances take the form of massive, virtually indestructible blast doors of the same type which are used to secure the entrance to the NORAD facility located deep beneath Cheyenne Mountain in Wyoming. They are airtight, watertight, locked into position by several enormous pistons and capable of withstanding anything but a direct hit by a nuclear weapon.

These doors are composed of low-carbon steel, which provides protection against attempted intrusions by force, plague, chemical weapons, conventional explosives, radiation and blast waves. Weighing 25 tons each, these blast doors are so finely tuned and set into place that it only requires two people to swing them open or closed. Although a single blast door provides all the security one could imagine, that is still not felt to be sufficient by the powers that be. In most cases, the outermost blast door is backed up by a second and perhaps even a third identical door which is located a short distance down the passageway.

There are sets of high-strength gates, shaped in a way which allows them to lie flat against the curved walls of the tunnels when open, placed at periodic intervals. Though they are typically kept open, they can quickly be closed if the need arises, effectively preventing the passage of either vehicles or individuals. In this way, the entire underground network has been divided into a series of distinct compartments or areas of operation, each of which can be secured against any possible unwelcome intrusions by hostile forces.

Additionally, there are more of the massive, 25-ton blast doors installed at key locations which further serve to protect each individual section of the grid against possible threats. The people who built this system of underground bases and cities were clearly serious about being very certain that these areas are as secure as it is possible to make them.

The transportation grid comprises thousands of miles of paved roadways. It spans the entire length and breadth of the United States, deep underground and is used to move equipment and materials of every imaginable kind between the various facilities which have been constructed there. It is believed by many that the underground transportation grid does not stop at U.S. national borders but continues, underground, into other nations as well and that there is a checkpoint located at each national border. While I cannot know with certainty whether this is the case, I believe it to be extremely likely that it is.

If a map of the entire underground network were to be revealed, I believe it would be seen that there is a subterranean tunnel which runs underneath the sea bed of the Atlantic Ocean and connects the United States to Britain, which has its own system of underground bases. To presume that such a level of construction exceeds the technical capabilities of the United States government is a mistake—in fact, it is well within their power to accomplish such a thing and to do so without making any use of alien-based technologies at all. And remember, the name of all these interlocking tunnels, bases and cities is the Sub-*Global* Network, implying that is has worldwide reach, at least to a certain extent.

Parallel to the highway system, which is for the most part used to transport physical goods from place to place, there is an extremely high-tech subway system. It is what is called a mag-lev train, meaning it uses the force of magnetism to levitate the subway car above the rail. When the cars are in motion, there is no frictional resistance because the cars do not touch the track itself.

These subways are said to be capable of speeds between Mach 1 and Mach 2, which is twice the speed of sound. I have it on good authority that they can travel quite a bit faster than that. If one were to imagine that they could break Mach 3, it would probably be an accurate guess. These subways are used for the rapid transportation of people across long distances.

The only city in the world which utilizes this form of cutting edge technology in their subway system is a section of Tokyo. No American cities offer mag-lev subways, because the expense is too great. On the other hand, if the money it cost to install the mag-lev subways within the SGS were refunded in the form of grants to individual cities, the entire country would be riding on mag-levs right now. We would be able to board a train in Los Angeles and arrive in the nation's capital about three hours later.

The improvements to the nation's infrastructure which could have been provided for far less than the cost of the SGS boggles the mind. Instead, the nation's above-ground infrastructure has been left to decay without being repaired, upgraded or replaced while the Sub-Global System has been given cutting-edge technology at every possible opportunity, including technologies which the civilian world has not even been told exist.

Enormous tunnel boring machines, many of which can melt solid rock, have been used to drill these tunnels. They have also been used to excavate larger areas which comprise military bases, fully operational and fully equipped underground cities and enormous storage facilities for all types of munitions, food and medical supplies and all other necessities of life. When solid rock is melted, it is moved in liquid form around the entire outside perimeter of the circular tunnel boring machines (TBM's) and forms a smooth, shiny tunnel of solid rock through which people and vehicles can pass.

Though the depth of these facilities varies, they are located deep beneath the surface. The average depth is reported to be between five and seven miles underground. That is a depth which is worth giving some long thought to, in my opinion.

As will be described in the chapter which deals with abductions, I have personal knowledge that both alien races and our military possess the ability to travel through time, both forward and backward. As difficult as that may be to believe, it is nonetheless true. It is certainly worth considering the possibility that members of our military have traveled into the future and seen events which will—or are likely to—occur then, and then traveled back to report about them.

The construction of the Sub-Global System was almost certainly motivated by being in possession of knowledge of the possible future. That future clearly appears to involve some type of catastrophic devastation on a global scale which will cause the surface world to be uninhabitable for a long period. This underground refuge has been prepared in advance of such a devastating event as a shelter and place of refuge when it occurs.

Don't worry about not being able to find the entrances when the time comes. As was mentioned earlier, you won't even be told such entrances—or such a subterranean world—exist. Nobody intends to invite you to the party. You will be sacrificed, left alone aboveground in a world which has suddenly become uninhabitable. When that occurs, to be on the surface of the world will equate to being given a death sentence. This is the future which has been carefully and with forethought planned and prepared for the citizens of not just the United States of America, but of the entire world.

To state it another way, your taxes are being used to build facilities which will keep people who are perfectly willing to sacrifice the lives of you and your entire family safe from harm even as you are left to die on the surface. If the disaster was not considered to be something which would take place in the fairly near future, the extreme amount of money, manpower and materials necessary to construct the SGS would not have been budgeted for and allocated to a project like this.

It is not unreasonable at all to think that this event may very well occur at some point during your lifetime…and that, after that, the future will indeed look very different from the past. In fact, I can guarantee you that the world your grandchildren will inhabit will be completely unlike any world we have ever known before and one which is well beyond the ability of most people to imagine.

The roads and tunnels do not just connect a series of deep-underground military bases. Highly secure bases have also been constructed for the nation's most infamous intelligence agencies, including the CIA and the NSA and others. In addition, full-sized cities have been built miles underneath the surface, complete with malls, housing facilities, hospitals, parks and all manner of civic infrastructure and buildings.

These cities are in some cases as much as thirty miles across. By comparison, the city of Chicago metro area is less than ten miles across. They have everything needed to give residents the ability to stay underground for literally centuries if necessary.

There are power generation facilities with multiple backups, dedicated air and water purification systems, enormous wells and water storage facilities, warehouses pre-stocked with food and medicines of all types. Giant farming areas and hydroponic facilities, complete with artificial sunlight and automatic irrigation, are in place and ready to be activated with the flip of a few switches.

The hospitals have exotic technology available to them which is completely unknown to the civilian world, including devices capable of healing virtually any injury in a matter of seconds, cloning facilities and much more. These are based on technologies which were acquired from alien races through a combination of the terms of the Greada Treaty, signed in the late 1950's, and tech which was recovered from crashed alien spacecraft of various types.

I have heard it said that each base, while having all the necessary facilities for independent, long-term existence, is also intended to specialize in a certain area. Some, for instance, will be primarily military bases, others will concentrate on agricultural production, manufacturing, medical facilities, high technology or something else. I do not know for certain whether this is actually the case, but it makes sense that it would be.

In case the entrances to the SGS should happen to be breached somehow even after all the precautions which have been put into place, the potential for fast, lethal response has been put in place. Storage facilities containing military vehicles of all types, including armored personnel carriers and the latest generation of Abrams battle tanks, are fully stocked. The vehicles are fueled and armed. Hundreds of millions of rounds of hollow point ammo and other munitions are stored in bunkers, waiting to be utilized. Of those who will be allowed into the underground when disaster strikes, many of them will be highly-trained military units and their families. These units will be tasked with protecting the security by any means necessary including the use of deadly force against civilians.

Who will be running the show down there? Who will be responsible for issuing orders to the military commanders and troops? Will it be the political leaders we have elected and whom we assume are in charge?

Hardly. Those who give the orders when the underground grid is sealed off from the surface will be the same people who rule from the shadows even today. They will be the ranking members of the Illuminati and the orders they give will be followed on pain of death.

There are some people who, for one reason or another, are aware of the location of at least some of the entrances to this sub-global grid. During a time of extreme peril, they might well form a mob of armed citizens who were intent on gaining entry to these fully-stocked underground bunkers.

If this happened—and they presume that it probably would—the elite had to be sure there was absolutely no way for ordinary people to bypass their security measures and enter their publicly-funded survival bunkers. It is safe to presume that any military-grade blast door which was designed to withstand a near-miss by an atomic bomb would not be something the public could pry open with a crowbar or smash through with a vehicle.

They would certainly find that there was nothing available to them which would serve to breach one of these entrances. If they somehow breached it anyway, there is another one just like it only a short way in. Both would, we can safely guess, be protected by the most advanced sensors and monitors in the world. They would also be defended by military units equipped with state of the art body armor who possess a tremendous advantage in firepower (as well as a virtually unlimited supply of ammunition). They could never be overcome by civilian mobs—or, as we call them, groups of United States citizens who had been left to die while their leaders ran underground to save their own skins.

The underground cities are completely self-sufficient. They have large stocks of food and water stored within them. Residents will be able to produce their own food supplies by utilizing large caverns equipped with hydroponic systems, illuminated by industrial-sized metal halide and high-pressure sodium bulbs. Air would be circulated by means of large high-speed fans, both at ground level and built into the ceiling vents.

Massive generators are in place, since it is presumed that the national electrical grid may well be rendered non-functional and the bases and cities will be required to provide their own power. There would be plenty of extra generators on hand to replace any which fail with the passage of time.

There would be hospitals and medical supplies, bunkhouses and private residences, office buildings and stores. Water would be supplied by underground streams and, along with the air supply, be constantly cleaned and recirculated. There are number of extremely high-tech cloning centers, deep underground, which are part of the Sub-Global System. These cloning centers are used exclusively for the cloning of humans and they are staffed and fully operational even as you read these words. Just because mainstream science has not yet officially cloned humans does not mean that the military has not done so. In fact, the military has had the ability to clone humans for many decades and has made full use of it. Those who are judged to be among the elite are given access to these centers and full use of their capabilities. Some others, who are not counted among the ranks of the elite but who have been judged valuable for some reason, are also given access to the cloning centers. For them, however, the access comes with a price: they must agree to do as they are ordered and work to advance the secret agenda of the NOW/Illuminati during their normal civilian lives.

The cities and bases are equipped with a network of high-performance, state of the art computers which monitored the mechanical systems and the electrical grid, as well as facilitating communications between distant locations. Secure storage facilities contain large caches of both gold and silver, as well as other metals such as platinum and copper. There are also significant amounts of naturally-magnetic lodestone stored there.

In addition, there are a large quantity of military vehicles stored in large underground garages, the types used for troop movements as well as heavy armor like tanks. One reason for this is to prevent the public from being able to use those things against the inhabitants of the bunker system—if they can't get to them, they can't use them.

The other reason, of course, is to actively defend the tunnels against any possible intrusions which might occur. There are plenty of accommodations down below for military troops, virtually all of whom will be either willing to fire on American citizens if ordered to, thoroughly mind controlled or both. If given orders to kill, they will not hesitate to carry those orders out.

There is absolutely no question that those who will be in control of these underground locations are every bit as determined to keep members of the public out as they are to make certain their own subterranean sanctuary is the most well-stocked and highly secure series of bunkers ever constructed by humanity.

If the surface world becomes completely uninhabitable and the perimeter security of the SGS were maintained, those who entered before it was too late would have everything they need. They could survive there, without the need for any type of resupply, for centuries. The air and water can be purified and recycled. The necessary food can be grown hydroponically, the needed commodities can be produced in factories which are in place and ready to go. Everything to be found in the cities and bases is military-grade and state-of-the-art, which in most cases means that the technology and equipment available there is many generations of anything so far seen in the civilian world.

If you were allowed entry to this underground world, you would find once you arrived there that you had absolutely no power and absolutely no freedom to make decisions about anything that matters. You would be put to work and paid with enough food and water to get through the day and nothing more. You would find yourself in the position of being an expendable human resource, valuable only for your ability to carry out your assigned workload and given no consideration or thought beyond that by those who were in command of this underground world.

When their bodies finally became old, weak or damaged, they would be cloned and their consciousness removed from their old body and injected into a new, young, healthy one. When your body became old, weak or damaged, you would be classified as a useless eater who had outlived your usefulness and be disposed of as though you were a used Kleenex.

So just what is it that has the Masters of the Universe so worried? One can look around at the world as it is today and, without any special sources of information, reasonably deduce various calamitous situations which could occur. One can see that many of them could occur with little warning and little chance for those who are unprepared to save themselves. Preparing for the worst while hoping for the best is, it seems to me, unquestionably the correct course of action to take right now. There may well come a day when those who have prepared in advance can save themselves, or at least to prolong their lives, while others will be lost. It is a matter of common sense that we should be able to look at what is happening in the world and understand that a very bleak future could easily be in store for us all. Those who are both perceptive and wise will do all they can to prepare for such a future now, while the ability to do so still exists

CHAPTER 15: NATIONAL TREASURE

"It's clearly a budget. It's got a lot of numbers in it. "
-- President George W. Bush

"Out of the blue and into the black
They give you this, but you paid for that
And once you're gone, you can't come back
When you're out of the blue and into the black"
-- Neil Young

The government of the United States has a long, storied and well-documented history of subterfuge when it comes to providing the public with information about the things it does. The military and intelligence services have engaged in a wide variety of programs which have been kept secret from the public. Many of these activities have been directly harmful to U.S. citizens and are patently illegal. Though many of these operations have eventually been exposed, there are virtually no instances where those who were responsible them have been held responsible. Rather than being prosecuted as criminals, they have continued to serve and have often been promoted for their actions.

The American public, successfully rendered impotent by sustained propaganda and endless psychological warfare operations, have allowed this situation to go continue. The media, rather than acting a safeguard to public interests, has failed in its duty and contributed to the problem. It has buried stories associated with these crimes intentionally distracted the attention of the public by focusing on unrelated, usually trivial matters.

In addition to the criminal activities themselves, the costs associated with off-the-books programs and the enormous amounts of money consumed by what are known as "black ops" has been hidden. The average citizen, if asked, would have absolutely no clue as to the actual amount of money which has been secretly diverted from the budget and used to finance these programs.

If the figure in total dollars were known to them, they would without question be completely shocked. To allow these activities to continue unchecked is nothing less than a form of national suicide. It will very soon result in the permanent economic destruction of America.

In a previous chapter I discussed the true mission and purpose of "Never A Straight Answer" NASA. It seems appropriate to begin our discussion of these financial matters, then, by starting with the financing of NASA itself. As we look it over, it is helpful to remember that every single dollar spent by NASA was spent to intentionally deceive you and 8rob you of your hard-earned dollars. Everything that NASA has ever done has been intentionally and specifically designed to cause you to believe that certain things are true when they are in fact all nothing more than a carefully-manufactured edifice of lies.

Keep that in mind. After all, you paid for it.

Over the course of its existence, NASA has officially spent over a half trillion dollars of money from the national budget. This compared roughly to one year's budget for all our military forces combined. At its peak, NASA's budget accounted for around 4.5% of the total national budget. Its actual expenses were considerably lower than a half trillion dollars, though it is not possible to know by exactly how much. A considerable portion of NASA's official funding consists of dollars which are quietly funneled to the black ops programs rather than being used by NASA directly.

The expenses incurred by projects which come under the umbrella of being somehow related to alien contact or alien interactions with humanity can never be known with certainty because it is a number which is considered highly secret and is not included as part of the official national budget. Instead, various departments and agencies are allotted more funding than they require and the additional money is passed over to the black ops groups and added to their budget.

One can imagine the tremendous expense of secretly constructing a network of tunnels, bases and entire cities which can be as large as thirty miles across several miles underneath the ground. One can further imagine the tremendous cost of making certain that the entire network is fully stocked with food, medicine, ammunition, military vehicles, cutting edge communication systems, water and air purification systems and anything else they decided to stock up on.

The total cost of this program is believed to exceed $12 trillion, and the program is ongoing.

To take just a single example, the facilities associated with the Denver airport alone were responsible for costing taxpayers nearly $5 billion to construct a facility which was not needed and which appears to be intimately associated with the New World Order. It has underground levels which are inaccessible to the public. The airport walls are covered with inappropriate, disturbing murals which depict civil violence, government troops in gas masks, people being executed and other gruesome scenes. They depict a world where civil rights are a thing of the past and a police state is a reality.

As will be discussed in the follow-up to this book, America has long had an extensive (and hugely expensive!) space exploration and colonization effort which is entirely separate from NASA and is known as the "secret space program". It utilizes many different types of alien technology, including technology which allows American-built spacecraft to engage in interstellar travel. Unknown to the public, human colonies have been established in other solar systems by "breakaway civilizations" and the colonization programs are ongoing.

The military has also invested a tremendous amount of money into the chemtrails program, as well as programs which have worked with and developed exotic weapons and capabilities. These programs collectively represent what is far and away the most tremendously expensive project in human history.

Although it is impossible to find the exact amount, it can safely be estimated that the costs have run into the tens of Trillions of dollars. It has been estimated that these projects account for 60% of the entire federal budget, year after year. It is my opinion that this figure is quite likely to be an accurate representation of the tremendous expenses incurred by projects which are in some way related to alien contact and the technologies associated with it.

Think about that number carefully. Roll it around in your mind. Think about all the various things you have been told by politicians are to blame for America's national debt.

Offering free or reduced-price school lunches for our poorest children has been blamed, for example. This is nothing but an example of scapegoating our own impoverished children, for the sake of being able to continue to construct underground cities whose doors will be firmly closed to you when disaster strikes. Other reasons are sometimes given as well. None of them are true. Remember that the next time you hear a politician whining about this or that being the cause of our national debt. Think about the fact that these people are willing to deprive impoverished children of lunch and close the programs which you have paid into and which you expect to provide you with income during your retirement.

If the money spent on these programs were to be returned to the U.S. budget, we could easily repay the entire national debt tomorrow. The United States of America would instantly be transformed from a nation which has incurred what is by far the most massive debt in history to a nation which was comfortably in the black. There would be plenty of capital to fund programs like Social Security and Pell Grants. Furthermore, America would be nicely positioned to continue as the most dominant economic power on Earth during the 21st century.

To say that this is a change of epic proportions is a tremendous understatement. It becomes even more serious when one considers the tens of trillions of dollars in debt generated by the Federal Reserve Bank and deposited directly on the shoulders of the American middle class. Every penny of this debt is unconstitutional, as is the very existence of the Federal Reserve Bank itself.

Many people do not realize that the Fed is not a part of the United States government. It is a collective of large international banks which have illegally been given the power to create and print American dollars. This is a power which is clearly assigned by the Constitution to the Congress itself, not to a collection of private banks.

The banks which make up the Federal Reserve Bank have the power to literally create money out of thin air, simply by typing it into a computer database. These dollars are fiat currency. They are not backed by gold and have no intrinsic value.

This money, created by simply adding a line to their balance sheets, is then loaned to the United States government at interest and the loan is then transferred onto the backs of the American taxpayers. The interest on the loan of this nonexistent money is pure profit for the banks. It represents a debt so large that it is mathematically impossible for this country to ever repay.

At the time of this writing, the U.S. national debt is approaching $20 trillion and is increasing by the second. That is twenty thousand billion dollars that we owe to other nations which have loaned us money. The entire world is running out of money to loan by this point, but our spending continues to spiral out of control. There has been no serious effort by Congress to put a stop to deficit spending and put the budget back into the black. Nor will there be any such effort, regardless of which party controls the government.

The sheer amount of money which has been either wasted, stolen or spent in ways which provide benefits for only an elite few and offer none to the average person is truly staggering. The long-term economic agenda of TPTB is staggering as well. It is the complete destruction of the American dollar, the bankrupting of the citizens of the United States and the total wealth of the nation—along with all its resources, including food and water—in the hands of only a few hundred individuals. The fact is that this long-terms agenda is proceeding at a rapid pace and gathering speed all the time.

This kind of unrestrained, voracious greed combined with absolute brutality is unacceptable and intolerable. George H.W. Bush once said to an associate that if the people found out what they were really doing, they would chase them down in the street and lynch them. The people would be absolutely correct to do so and well within their rights. It is something which ought to be done, there is no question about it.

George W. Bush said "We'll all be long dead before some smart person figures out what really went on here in this office." He was quite wrong about that, as he was wrong about pretty much everything else he had an opinion on. Some of us have already figured it out. The trouble is, we are unable to bring him to justice with our legal system. We have no way to force him to testify and no means of accessing the evidence that has been buried under a mountain of secrecy or eliminated by eliminating the witnesses.

We do not have the financial resources necessary to prosecute these people in any case. Only the U.S. Department of Justice can do these things. It will never do them, because it will be forbidden by everyone who occupies the White House until it is far too late to matter or to do any good. Long before the Justice Department carries out its duty, the dollar will have been devalued until it is worth no more than tissue paper. Our economy will have been permanently crippled by these people and their henchmen. The future is going to be very different from the world we have known up until now, my friends, and it is not going to be pretty in any way.

It is a testament to the power of propaganda and brainwashing on a massive scale that three hundred million Americans watch these things being done to them without taking to the streets and demanding change. The tools to do so are in their hands. If they chose to, they could form a new political party which was beholden to nobody and controlled by no one and elect all their leaders from it. But they have not done so, nor will they. In one of history's greatest ironies, the American public's money is being used to impoverish and enslave it. That is the reality of the world we live in.

CHAPTER 16: MASTERS OF THE UNIVERSE

"More than 10,000 sightings have been reported, the majority of which cannot be accounted for by any 'scientific' explanation... I am convinced that these objects do exist and that they are not manufactured by any nation on earth. I can therefore see no alternative to accepting the theory that they come from some extraterrestrial source."
-- Air Chief Marshal Lord Dowding, Commander-in-Chief, RAF Fighter Command, 1954

"Your world was made for you by someone above
But you chose evil ways instead of love
You made me master of this world where you exist
The soul I took from you was not even missed"
-- Black Sabbath

Within the United States government there are three official levels which can be invoked to protect sensitive information: Restricted, Secret and Top Secret. There are, however, additional measures in place which provide additional layers of protection and further restrict access to certain information.

Being issued a "Top Secret" security clearance it an extensive process which takes time to accomplish and includes a detailed investigation of a person's background. In addition, it involves interviews with their friends, neighbors, previous employers and anyone else who it is felt may be able to provide information which is necessary to the process of determining whether a certain individual will eventually be given a "Top Secret" clearance.

Being issued a "Top Secret" security clearance, however, does not mean someone will be given access to all material which has been designated Top Secret. Information is provided only on a "need to know" basis. An individual will be made aware of as much classified information as they require to have the ability to carry out their duties...but no more than that.

If, for example, a person is required to analyze a set of aerial photographs of a Russian base which requires that he have Top Secret clearance to look at, he will be shown the photos and can then carry out his assignment. It is not necessary for him to be told whether the photos were taken by a satellite or a spy plane, when they were taken or even the location of the base itself—and he will not be given that information.

This system is designed to prevent even those who have been granted extremely high-level security clearances and who have been entrusted with extremely sensitive information—data which often either powerfully affects or directly influences issues critical to national security—from having access to a sufficient quantity of information to make it possible for them to reveal more than a very few secrets of importance should they take the decision to go public.

Even so, there are secrets and then there are Secrets. There are some types of information which are so sensitive and so closely-held that even someone who has met the qualifications for and been issued a "Top Secret" clearance is not considered qualified to have access to it. Additional safeguards are put in place to protect the confidentiality of such information. The result is that there are elevated levels of secrecy which are commonly referred to as "Above Top Secret" or "ATS".

The Manhattan Project was the code name for the program which involved America's best scientific minds working to design and develop the world's first nuclear weapons. The secrecy which surrounded it was unprecedented. Information relating to the program was protected by security protocols and procedures which were far beyond anything previously used in human history.

Secrets at this level are protected by what is known as "compartmented security". Data is divided into a number of different compartments. Each compartment is code-word restricted, meaning that a person must be cleared for data contained within the specific compartment which a certain code word rating which is attached to their "Top Secret" clearance will allow them access to.

As before, information is given out strictly on a need-to-know basis and one who possesses code-word clearance for a compartment of information will be given only the minimum amount from that set of information that he or she requires to do their job. Each successive compartment is more sensitive and more restricted than was the previous compartment and fewer people will ever be allowed to have knowledge of it.

Even with all these protective measures in place, however, information which deals with alien contact and alien technology falls into a category all its own. The degree of secrecy which is imposed upon those who have access to even a small amount of inside information on the subject is far beyond anything seen in the Manhattan Project. Information which deals with alien contact is far and away the most heavily-protected and highly sensitive data which has ever existed. It involves penetrating levels of secrecy so high that they do not even officially exist.

Gaining the ability to be shown information in this category involves passing investigations far more detailed than any which have come before. It requires a reputation for absolute integrity in terms of never revealing sensitive information and an unblemished service record which supports that reputation. A process of investigation and testing which literally takes years to complete and which must return pristine results in every aspect is required before code-word clearance for these rarified levels is issued.

In addition, the information which is hidden within these highly-restrictive compartments constitutes a fabric in which many pieces of intentional disinformation have been seamlessly integrated into the thread. The result is a product which provides sufficient information to allow those who see it to do their jobs efficiently.

At the same time, it ensures that no one who is given access to the information will possess the ability to form a coherent picture of the actual situation. They will be given enough facts to allow them to carry out their function, but if they try to pursue the information any farther they will be led down a blind alley.

Information regarding alien contact and technology is protected by more than just the necessity of holding code-word clearance to certain specific compartments. Before being granted such clearance and assigned to a duty station which makes use of such information, military personnel are required to sign an agreement in which they formally state that they understand that speaking of secrets to others constitutes a felony which is punishable by enormous fines and decades of imprisonment. It also states, however, that they give up their right to a trial in the event they are accused of breaking their secrecy oaths.

It goes without saying that anyone who is even considered for such high-level clearances will have first established a long record of reliability and the capacity to remain silent about any classified information to which they may be exposed.

It is no exaggeration to state that the investigative phase which is instated prior to any such clearance being issued is a process which literally takes years to complete. Interviews will be conducted with friends, family members, employers, neighbors, classmates and anyone else who is determined to be able to give an accurate account of the personal character, integrity, faults, habits and overall attitude of the subject of the investigation. No stone is left unturned and no effort is spared during this process, which is normally conducted by agents of the Federal Bureau of Investigation.

It is now the case that at highly sensitive locations such as Dulce Base, Area 51 and others, all prospective personnel must in addition formally sign documents agreeing to have their memories chemically erased each day at the end of their shift. They will be injected with drugs designed to be amnesiacs which will cause them to completely forget everything which has occurred over the past ten hours, including their own actions, before being allowed to leave the facility and go home after their shift is completed.

Additionally, it is made clear to potential recipients of code-word clearances which involve the topic of extra-terrestrials that, should they talk about the things they learn, they will be subject to termination. And that is not the worst of the threats which are made to them. Not only will they be killed, they are told, but every living member of their family is also added to the hit list. They are informed that their parents, their spouses and even their young children will be murdered and that it is quite likely that their deaths will be gruesome and cruel. Anyone who does not agree to this entire list of conditions in advance, in writing, is denied access to the special program and will never again be given the opportunity to work on such a project. They will be allowed to refuse the conditions and walk away alive...but once they do, there will be no second chances and no possibility of being involved in the government's most secret and critical operations.

In a manuscript in which I discuss a wide variety of issues which I feel are of importance, and one which I certainly hope contains many things which will surprise the reader as they make their way through it, we now come to something which may well be one of the most surprising and important pieces of information contained in the entire book. Its importance lies in the fact that, armed with this alone, the astute reader will find that they have in their possession the key which will allow them to clearly understand the degree of importance which is assigned to the topic of alien contact at the highest levels of the government. The surprise lies in the fact that, after having been made aware of this key piece of information, the reader will find that they do not know anything more about the aliens themselves than they did a few moments earlier.

It has been credibly reported that at least thirty-four and perhaps as many as thirty-eight code-word restricted compartments of information, each representing an additional level of security which is Above Top Secret, currently exist.

The most sensitive, closely-guarded information in the world is contained within the most exclusive code-word-only compartment. This level of clearance—and no other—allows those who hold it complete, unrestricted access to the entirety of the information held by all departments of the government which deal with the matter of alien contact. The documents which are protected within these virtually-inaccessible fortresses of secrecy contain the most highly-sensitive information in human history. Any unauthorized person who attempts to locate or access them will not survive the attempt.

In the world of high security and black projects, this is the absolute apex of the food chain. The few individuals who rate this security designation are members of the most exclusive club in the world. Against almost impossible odds, they are the people who have managed to have their names appear on the ultimate "short list". None but the members of this elite group are endowed with the ability to access, study and understand the full array of governmental records and data regarding alien contact. This tiny handful of individuals—and nobody else—fully understand the implications of contact with highly-advanced, non-human beings. Only they can know with certainty the degree to which these beings, for all practical purposes, already own and control our world.

It may come as a matter of considerable surprise, then, to learn that the President of the United States is not a member of that group. In fact, he is not only not a member of the group, he may not even be able to find out the names of the people who *are* members.

Learning that the President is not considered qualified to possess the highest level of security clearance may be a surprise to some readers, as I said. There will surely be others, however, who were already aware of that fact before they ever picked up this book.

In either case, it is unlikely that anyone is likely to consider that piece of information to be nearly as important as I made it sound during the build-up. Interesting, yes. Somewhat important, certainly. But the most important key to understanding the importance of alien contact? It seems there is no obvious reason to elevate it to such an exalted status, at least not on the face of it.

To better understand why I assigned such a high level of importance to it in the first place, it will be helpful to re-phrase things in a way which causes us to think about it in different terms.

The President of the United States is almost universally considered to be the most powerful man in the world. He acts as Commander-in-Chief of what is by far the most powerful, dominant, intimidating, well-funded, highly-trained, superbly-equipped military force in human history. It can project devastating power to any point on the globe in very short order. There is no other nation in the world which can assemble a military force which can even come close to matching that of America, much less have any realistic chance to defeat it in combat.

At the time this book is being written, the United States of America stands alone as the only military superpower in the world and its military budget is equal to that of the entire rest of the world's nations combined.

Although the wisdom and necessity of earmarking such an enormous sum to the military, particularly during a time of peace when no other nation is even threatening us, is a question which is open to debate. Whether one feels the military budget is a necessary evil or an example of massive overkill, one thing remains true: that's an impressive military.

No matter who you are, if you were to end up looking at it down the wrong end of a barrel there is every reason to believe that you are about to have a highly unpleasant day.

To make use of what I described as the key, to accurately assess the importance assigned to the topic of alien contact and all it entails, one must carefully consider a specific option which is available to America's chief executive.

By making a single phone call, the President of the United States can give an order which will cause thousands of American intercontinental ballistic missiles to be launched within a matter of minutes. This would result in the complete annihilation of all the world's major population centers and military complexes. It would initiate a global thermonuclear conflagration which could very possibly result in the extinction of the entire human race within a matter of a few hours.

To say that this is a tremendous amount of personal power would be an understatement of truly epic proportions. The same thing can be said regarding the level of trust and responsibility which are invested in someone who can, at any time of his choosing, destroy the world with the touch of a button.

The security clearance of the President is believed to grant him access to seventeen levels of compartmentalized, code-word protected Top Secret information. It certainly represents some of the most highly sensitive and well-guarded data the government has in its possession.

If that number is accurate, it means that there are at least seventeen and possibly as many as twenty-one levels of Top Secret, compartmentalized information secured by a code-word-only designation, which the President is forbidden to have access to. He may very well never be made aware that they exist in the first place.

Acting as Commander-in-Chief, the President of the United States can initiate global thermonuclear war—literally Armageddon—simply by making a single telephone call. But when it comes to being made aware of the whole truth regarding alien contact, the President is considered a security risk. The most critical and highly sensitive data available at the top level of the American government is beyond the reach of and forever denied to the leader of the free world.

Incoming Presidents typically do not enter office with any kind of previously-established security clearances at all. There are occasional exceptions to this. George Herbert Walker Bush, due to having previously served as Director of Central Intelligence, almost certainly possessed the highest possible level of security clearance. The same was true of President Dwight D. Eisenhower, who was formerly a five-star General and the commander of all Allied forces in World War Two. Typically, however, a new President will not have undergone the lengthy process which is necessary to be issued the highest levels of security clearance.

Due to the term of office being only four years, the time necessary to carry out such in-depth investigations as are necessary to obtain these types of clearances would consume most of that time. By the point the investigation had been concluded, a one-term President's term would be about to end and there would be little reason to bother with issuing him the clearance anyway. The result of this situation is that, despite what many people commonly assume, the President is not given access to the most secret information which is held by the government he is supposedly in charge of.

Again: the best information indicates that there are at least seventeen levels of compartmented, Top Secret, code-word secured information—each level successively more restrictive and highly-sensitive than the last—which are unavailable to the President. They are deemed to be of such critical importance that the man who has the power to bring about Armageddon and exterminate the entire human race simply by making one phone call, is not only forbidden from ever having access to them. He is not informed that these security designations--or the information they protect—even exist.

This gives us a clear indication of the extreme sensitivity the alien-related projects rate within the innermost halls of power in Washington. There is no other information possessed by the government which is given anywhere near this type of priority. We can therefore infer that this is unanimously considered to be the most critical, valuable information in the world and that it is of vital importance in terms of national security.

If that is true—as it appears to be—then I believe we can also presume that there is information about extra-terrestrial beings which describes clear and present danger to the security of the United States of America and perhaps to the entire world. If it didn't, it wouldn't be protected by layers of security which extend far beyond that required of participants in the programs which designed and developed atomic and hydrogen bombs.

In my opinion, the fact that the President himself is not allowed to have access to this critical intelligence is one of the most instructive pieces of knowledge we could hope to come across. It seems certain, from my point of view, that this is not information relating to friendly neighbors from the sky who have come to offer us assistance.

Just what can be learned at this level is beyond our ability to know or even to guess at.

When we consider the few examples of hyper-advanced technology described in earlier chapters, we must also logically presume that they represent nothing more than the tip of the iceberg in terms of the capabilities which are available to these non-human visitors. We can reasonable presume that there are even more powerful technologies which have made their way into human hands in one way or another over the years. This small group of individuals almost certainly can access and utilize all of them for whatever purposes they choose.

What we have, then, is a group of individuals who, as far as the rest of us are concerned, can be thought of as the Masters of the Universe. They can make use of technologies which would almost certainly appear to us to be magical. We cannot even begin to guess the extent of their reach and capacity.

There is, however, something we can bring into the equation even without such knowledge. The Masters of the Universe surely can make use of alien-based medical technology which can greatly extend the human lifespan. Though I have no way of knowing for certain, it has been estimated that this technology can allow a person to live for at least three hundred years and perhaps more. Combine this with the ability, when the body finally wears out, to have one's consciousness--their soul, as best I can determine--artificially removed from that body and inserted into a new, fresh synth-body which is physically still quite young, and continue. The process can be repeated over and over. What they end up having is the recipe for eternal life. In theory, people who can do this need never die. They would be able to extend their lifespans to literally thousands of years—perhaps more, barring accidents. It is the ultimate, timeless dream of all mankind…and they hold the keys to making it a reality.

If we assume for the moment that this is in fact the case, it becomes quite easy to understand the extreme sensitivity of the information and the lethality with which it is defended. If we had the keys to eternal life, would we not kill to protect our ability to make use of it? It seems to me that there is little question that most of us would, in the end, kill. I think, all things considered, we would not even hesitate to give the kill orders to our minions. If we are willing to kill to protect this secret, we can in theory live forever. If we fail to kill for some reason and the information is disclosed to the public or we lose our access for some other reason, we will be doomed to die in a few short years just like everybody else.

I'm sure that there are some gentle souls among my readers who are thinking that they would never kill to protect even this type of information. That is a very decent and highly moral attitude, one for which you are to be commended. It is, however, not shared by the people who find themselves able to make such choices.

There is not any realistic question to be raised about whether these people would kill to protect this secret of eternal life. They are men whose careers were spent in the military and intelligence services, for the most part, where killing is just an everyday part of business.

It is no easy thing to suddenly be brought face-to-face with the idea that everything you think you know is a lie. All that we are made to perceive can ultimately be described as the individual threads which make up an immense tapestry, a tapestry which is intended and used to conceal reality from those who have not been deemed worthy of being given the knowledge and concepts which are understood only by a small group of rarified and elite individuals.

Those few who have been allowed to pierce the veil and who understand the hidden realities which ultimately control and determine the course of our lives though most know it not, are the people who hold the only true power in this domain. It is their agendas the rest of humanity are unknowingly caused to serve in every waking moment of their lives. They are the puppet masters who pull the strings of the world while humanity dances in response to their will. They can live above the law while forcing all others to live in accordance with their will and dictates.

The topic of alien contact and technology contains layer upon layer upon layer of deceptions, often coming from place and in forms we would least expect to see. If the full truth were to be revealed to us, it would basically mean we would have to completely rewrite our concepts of science, medicine, history, anthropology, extrasensory perception and many other things as well.

The Masters of the Universe tolerate no outsiders in their midst and allow no third-party threats to their pre-eminence to exist. Whenever one is identified, it is swiftly and efficiently disposed of by highly skilled professionals. Under their direction, any such threats will be nullified: intimidated, assaulted, bribed, blackmailed or terminated.

These people did not rise to the top by playing fair, showing mercy or hesitating to take direct action of whatever type was necessary when it was called for. Their interests and moral compasses have absolutely nothing in common with those of the average citizen and the actions they are willing to take in service of their agenda reflect that truth in no uncertain terms.

While the average citizen would shrink in horror at the idea of committing first degree murder, the Masters of the Universe will not hesitate for an instant. They are quite willing to kill as many people as necessary, purely for the acquisition of even greater amounts of money and power or for giving them reason to believe they might someday cause that wealth and power to be shared or taken away from them.

There is no one, including Presidents, Kings and Popes, who is beyond their reach or whom they will hesitate to order the termination of if they are perceived to be any kind of threat or even a persistent nuisance.

This is the reality of the world we live in—welcome to it. Stay seated until and unless you are ordered to stand up, obey your orders immediately, ask no questions, believe what you are told to believe and do it all while working far too many hours and finding yourself still unable to meet your basic expenses.

Is this the place you wish to give your stamp of approval? Is it acceptable to you or is this the vision of something which requires and deserves your ceaseless resistance and is more than worthy of risking and perhaps sacrificing your life to change? That is something you must decide for yourselves, but it is indeed the world we are living in and as of yet we have taken no perceptible or effective actions against it.

By committing the sins of willful ignorance and blind inertia we have not only failed to rectify the situation but have encouraged it and allowed it to continue to exist and grow daily in power and menace.

Will you make the difficult and inherently dangerous decision to become an agent of change and to let nothing stand in the way of your righteous fury? Or will you continue to move along silently, keeping your head down and trying not to cause any trouble like a good little sheep? The choice is yours. The difference will ultimately be measured by the price in blood which your children and grandchildren will surely be called upon to pay.

Your country has done much for you throughout the course of your life. If you are an American citizen, you have been given the opportunity to be a part of the most wide-ranging and powerful empire in human history. You have also had the tremendous advantages that come from living in the wealthiest nation in the world, and one where the opportunity to become successful is available to almost everyone.

The combination of all this and more has resulted in a life that would be the envy of almost anyone in the entire world and one so rich it would have exceeded the dreams of kings and princes of the past. America has allowed us to be the beneficiaries of a rare and wonderful gift, one most people do not even dare to dream of.

It is now our responsibility to repay her for affording us the lives we have led and the freedoms we have known. America is under attack, from both within and without, and she desperately needs all the help we can give her if she is to survive.

Think carefully about your duty as a patriot and a human being. Choose your course of action wisely, knowing in advance that inaction will lead to certain failure…and then make your stand with all the power at your disposal. There are times in life when failure is not an option, when winning is the only acceptable outcome. This is one of those times.

CHAPTER 17: ABDUCTED!

"If you would have asked me a year ago if I believed in aliens, I'd have laughed and said no. But that was before the abduction. I don't laugh as much anymore, mainly due to severe rectal bleeding."
— Jarod Kintz

"Contact is all it takes
To change your life, to lose your place in time
Contact, asleep or awake,
You lay your sanity on the line"
--Sammy Hagar

There is much to be said about the topic of alien abductions. It is a serious issue and it deserves to be taken seriously by serious people. By this point in time the basic honesty and sanity of the overwhelming majority of individuals claiming to have been abducted by aliens has been established solidly by a wide variety of highly competent researchers and sources. The only people who believe the phenomenon of alien abduction to be simply a matter of mental instability, government deception or some type of "mass hallucination" are those who are poorly informed about the subject and therefore have no value in terms of serious consideration.

There is, by the way, no such thing as a "mass hallucination": such a thing has never been reliably documented even a single time in history. The concept is one which was invented specifically to discredit those who claimed to be alien abductees as a group—a quick and easy way to dispose of the subject without the need to investigate it in a serious manner.

Whenever you hear someone say that abductions are all a matter of mental problems or mass hallucination, you are listening to someone who has no idea what they are talking about. Disregard their opinion, which is incorrect and impossible to ever prove.

Alien abduction reports, when one gets down to the heart of the matter, are not tall tales invented by a group of wild-eyed, delirious nut cases but are instead the result of people being abducted and relating their experiences to the best of their ability.

When I was a young boy, during the time that NASA was engaged in the Gemini and Apollo programs, the thing I wanted most in life was to speak with a person from another world. I imagined that such a conversation would consist for the most part of me asking the extra-terrestrial questions, questions which were not answerable by humans, with their limited knowledge, and the extra-terrestrial answering them. I would listen carefully to everything it said and learn all I could. In this way, I imagined, I could learn the secrets which were out of reach otherwise. I would ask about its home world and its culture, I would ask about other races and civilizations among the stars which it was familiar with and of course I would ask one of the first questions which would occur to most people in such a situation: I would ask what it knew about the existence—or the non-existence--of God.

It was nothing but the dream of a naïve young boy, an impossible fantasy which had no chance of ever coming true. As I grew older I came to realize the futility of the dream of speaking to a being from another world even as I came to understand that such beings almost certainly existed.

Even if they did and even if they were here, almost nobody is ever allowed to speak to an extra-terrestrial being. Only the highest-ranking and most carefully-selected individuals within the military-intelligence community are ever given an opportunity such as that. It was something which could never come to pass for an ordinary mortal like myself. Even so, the idea was so fascinating, so intoxicating, that it never left my mind. Years later, as an adult, that fantastic and unattainable possibility retained its power over me: there was still nothing in life I wanted so much as the opportunity to speak with someone from another world.

But life is a strange an unexpected place: no matter how carefully we may plan, life will always find ways to surprise us in the end. As it turned out, against incalculable odds, something occurred in my life which no amount of careful planning or studious effort could achieve and which it is impossible for one to plan for with any realistic hope of having it actually come to pass. Eventually, I did indeed have such an opportunity. The greatest dream of my life came true: I spoke to an extra-terrestrial, a being from another world—I even had the chance to ask it a question. And it was not limited to a single opportunity--I have spoken to what appeared to be an alien at least twice.

It was nothing at all like I had imagined it would be. The result of my contact with extra-terrestrials did not leave me in an illuminated state with knowledge of their world and their ways, nor did it answer any questions I may have had about the existence of God. What it did was make me wish that I had never met one at all.

Talk about a change of perspective...

In my own personal experience, I have interviewed well over three thousand individuals who have reported alien abductions. I am quite experienced at it, I know and have known people who are considered to be the top authorities in the world on the subject, I have personal experience as an abductee to draw on and some off-the-record briefings on the subject which were provided directly to me by a high-ranking officer of the United States Air Force. I do not pretend to be perfect or to have all the answers...but it is fair to say that I am not easy to fool when it comes to determining whether someone is a legitimate abductee.

Of all those I have interviewed regarding their abduction experiences I have come across exactly one person who was in my opinion delusional, one who was lying in order to get attention and one who appeared to be a government agent trying to get information on what I was doing. Considering the number of people interviewed that gives someone who claims to be an abductee over a 99.8% chance of being the real thing.

The only serious mistake in that equation comes when people report being abducted by aliens when in fact it is the military which has abducted them. This is a very understandable mistake and it occurs with regularity for reasons which will be discussed in a moment.

It is necessary to understand that the abduction of humans is not something which began recently. It is an activity which has been taking place throughout human history. It is recorded in ancient scriptures and legends by civilizations throughout the world.

During those times, we lacked the scientific knowledge which has by now been accumulated and therefore necessarily lacked the ability to correctly understand what was taking place. There was no knowledge—or even consideration—of extra-terrestrial civilizations or any reasonable method of demonstrating how it might be possible for them to make the journey from their place of origin to our world.

Earth was universally considered to be the only home of mortal life and mankind was considered the ultimate flower of creation. We were believed to be the favored and precious children of the gods, the rightful masters of our world and the most intelligent mortal beings in the universe. The stars were believed to exist only to provide Earth with spectacular decorations for its night-time sky.

The first time that I retained a memory of being abducted, I had already interviewed literally thousands of abductees and contacted some people who worked with aliens and/or alien technology from the inside, on behalf of the United States government. I had already noticed for almost twenty years that street lights would often go out as I approached them—sometimes I would "burn out" three of them just when walking or driving down a single city block. And no matter how carefully I treated them, my computers burned out after only a year and half, like clockwork. I knew these were indicators of alien abduction, but because I had no memories of such I chose not to apply that knowledge to myself. I had been told by people who should know that I was an abductee—they somehow saw it in me, apparently—and that I should get used to the idea. I refused to believe it.

Abductions were obviously something I found highly interesting, so much so that I had taken the time to speak to a huge number of abductees personally. But speaking to abductees is one thing— BEING an abductee is something entirely different. I wanted to learn all I could about the subject…but I had no interest in BEING an abductee. That was something that happened to other people, not to me!

If I was abducted before this—and it seems almost certain, at this point, that I was—I have no memory of it. My first abduction memory was when I realized—and was forced to admit to myself—that I was an alien abductee. It was not just something that happened to other people, it had happened to me too.

Even under the best of circumstances, this is a highly shocking revelation on a personal level. It is not an overstatement to say that it shakes up one's entire life in a way that can never be undone—once a person realizes and admits to themselves that they are an alien abductee, there is no going back to the way things were before.

The first (and perhaps the most obvious) thing that happened is that I immediately and forever lost any illusion I may have once harbored about being safe when I was asleep. With doors and windows closed and locked, living in a second-floor apartment as I was at the time, we would normally consider ourselves to be reasonably safe and secure during the times that we are sleeping. There is, after all, no practical way for an intruder to enter an apartment through a second-floor window located right beside my bed. The only other way in would be to literally break down my front door, something which would almost certainly result in any intruder taking at least one 12-gauge shotgun blast directly to the face. It is not easy for the average person to have a system which offers better security than that.

Now, suddenly, I never wanted to sleep again. I never wanted to so much as close my eyes during the night-time, because I had now been forced to realize that there is really no such thing as sleeping in safety. Locked doors and windows make no difference at all to these beings—with highly advanced technologies, they can defeat these primitive measures with ease.

The top priority in my life became, without warning, to find some way of making certain that I would never again be abducted as I had been. I wanted to make sure that these strange, terrifying, remorseless...THINGS...would never again sneak up on me while I was asleep and whisk me away to their spacecraft, where God only knows what might happen.

I think it is safe to presume that virtually all of those who realize that they are abductees experience the same priority-shift in their lives. The realization that, far from being safe and secure, we are in fact highly vulnerable and completely powerless to prevent horrible, criminal abuses of our sleeping bodies is more than enough to shake up anybody's world.

Things we had once taken for granted are suddenly revealed to be nothing but naïve fantasies. Much like the bedtime stories we tell to children, they are seen to be little more than devices we use to provide a false sense of security in a world which has turned out to be far stranger—and to offer far more possibilities—than we had ever imagined it would or had ever prepared ourselves to be able to face.

But how does one go about never again sleeping at night? How does one make their home secure against intruders to which walls and doors mean nothing? How does one protect themselves from inhuman criminals who only strike after first making sure that we are completely unable to defend ourselves in any way?

Those are questions not easily answered...and they are questions which every alien abductee is forced to ask. When it turns out that the answer to each of them is "you can't", the stark realities which must then be faced are enough to give even the most courageous of people reason to pause.

Let me add here, for those who have retained no memories of being abducted and may mistakenly believe that they could find themselves in this type of situation and not be afraid: you are very wrong about that. You cannot find yourself to be a captive of these seemingly-emotionless, robot-like beings with huge, black eyes and not experience a sense of fear that will chill you all the way to your bones.

There is nothing good about alien Greys, from the point of view of their victims. People who make the claim that the Greys are their friends and have always treated them well are either lying, easily manipulated or extremely stupid. That's not how it is at all. Any rational person who has been through this experience realizes that very clearly.

Let me say, for the record, that I am 6'2" and weigh over 235 pounds—there are not many people in this world that I have reason to be physically afraid of. But those Greys, man, they are a different thing altogether. I'll tell you just how it is with those Greys: they scare the living hell out of me. If you have even the slightest bit of common sense, they will scare the living hell out of you, too, should you ever have the misfortune of meeting them.

That is not an opinion, my friends. That is a promise. If you see the Greys in the dead of the night—and that is the only time you'll ever see them, by the way, because they won't come around during the daytime-- you are about to be taught the meaning of fear. That's just how it is.

Tales of gods from the sky—always from the sky—coming down to Earth, abducting or interbreeding with humans to produce progeny endowed with unusual physical characteristics or greater than normal abilities come to us from ancient cultures across the world. Regarded as myth or fables by most, it seems to me that there is no reason to simply dismiss them wholesale before giving them additional thought and consideration. There is no reason for such stories to be invented from scratch as a method to entertain children or for some other superfluous reason. Certainly, there is no reason for these stories to be included in the holy books and to become integral parts of the history of peoples throughout the world if they did not have at least some basis in fact.

Based on what we know about the abduction and hybridization of humans on the part of extra-terrestrials in current times, it seems there is every reason to seriously consider the possibility that the same or similar things were taking place long ago as they are today. It seems that a long-term process of modification to the human genome has been underway for a very long time—all human history, in fact. Simply by changing the words "angel", "god", "demon" and "devil" to "extra-terrestrial" or "alien spacecraft" one can find a plethora of descriptions in the ancient accounts (including the Bible) which read very much like modern-day sighting and contact reports. This lends additional credence to these stories. It gives even more reason to consider them to be not just myths created out of thin air, but actual historical incidents. These accounts were passed on to their descendants. They were considered important enough to include in even their sacred texts.

We are in my opinion dealing with real events which were at the time beyond the understanding of the indigenous peoples but which were nevertheless recorded for posterity. The people of those times, though they did not have the advantages of modern-day science and research, were no less intelligent or serious than we are today. They were not fools. They had no reason to make up stories about humans being impregnated by beings from the sky and bearing children with unusual gifts if those events did not in fact occur. If we wish to gain an understanding of the realities involved with alien contact, we must consider that those ancient accounts might very well represent the truth of the matter as interpreted by our ancestors. In fact, we would be remiss in not doing just that.

I was laying on my right side on an examination table, apparently inside a spacecraft. There was an extra-terrestrial standing beside it, near my head, and another standing on the floor near where my knees were on the table. They were small of stature, had grey skin and large, completely black, almond-shaped eyes.

I was paralyzed, as though I were an immobile zombie. I was powerless to resist them or to move in any way. Some part of my brain had clearly been neutralized or somehow "switched off": it was impossible to think clearly or even to conceptualize ideas such as "I should fight them" or "I should try to escape", much less put such a plan into action had it occurred to me. No such thoughts occurred to me at all—this is the state they always keep me in when I am abducted, powerless and unable to harm or threaten them in any way, completely unable to even think of the concept of trying to escape or, for that matter, taking any actions whatsoever of my own volition.

Even so, surely because I already had so much experience speaking with abductees, I did not for one second have the problem that occurs to many who find themselves in a similar situation: I did not have to wonder where I was, who those beings were or what was happening to me. I did not have to wonder if I might be losing my mind. I knew immediately that this was an alien abduction. When I felt something cold being pressed up against my rear end by the extra-terrestrial near my knees and thighs, I knew immediately that my name was about to be added to the group of hapless individuals who have had the experience of having an anal probe unceremoniously jammed into their rectum by creepy, emotionless aliens who have no concern whatsoever about the comfort of those they abduct or the pain they inflict upon them.

It was at this point that I first spoke to an extra-terrestrial. It was extremely difficult to speak at all—I had to summon up all my concentration and all my energies just to be able to say a few words. I said them as loudly as I could...but they came out as only the tiniest whisper, barely audible: "Oh please don't do that..." I said.

They did it anyway. If you have ever wondered about alien anal probes—and there is no real reason you should have, as best I know— let me tell you that there is nothing gentle about them at all. They are pneumatic, like those old-style tire pressure gauges but bigger around. BAM! And it is all the way in. It hurt like hell, and I opened my mouth to scream from the pain. At this point the Grey standing near my head, who was holding a small device in his hand about the size of a pack of cigarettes, passed the device over the top of my left temple. It did not actually touch me, just passed over my temple at close range. As it did so, all pain—and all memory of pain—vanished instantly. I closed my mouth back up without making a sound.

The purpose of the anal probe, for those who are unaware of it, is to collect a semen sample. When the probe is shot into the body, it presses against the prostate and forces an involuntary ejaculation. The sperm is then collected. That is the one and only purpose of the anal probe. Like many other alien activities, it is related to the human reproductive system and ultimately to the process of creating hybrid beings, beings which are part human and part extra-terrestrial.

That is the only memory I retained of this abduction. The next memory I have is of being back in my bed, awakening suddenly in the dark, in my bedroom alone. I jumped out of bed and quickly flipped on the lights...nobody was in the room but me. It was over. I knew I needed to write down everything I could remember about it immediately, before the memory faded away. I did so. Although it does seem I had surely been abducted before this, I have no memories of those events occurring. But now I realized, for certain, that I had become a member of a club nobody wants to join: I, too, was an alien abductee.

People sometimes ask "What reason would an advanced race of beings have for abducting relatively primitive beings like humans?" There are several answers to that question. First, it has nothing to do with gathering information about human physiology, culture or anything else having to do with gaining knowledge of humanity. They have no reason to wonder about any of those things: they know us very well, better than we know ourselves in fact. On the other hand, even the most educated and informed among us know very little about the extra-terrestrials.

Extra-terrestrials have been coming to our world for many thousands of years—and that is an understatement. At least some of them appear to have arrived here before humans existed as a race and are almost certainly responsible for bringing us into existence in the first place. Others have been visiting this world occasionally or, in some cases, inhabiting this world throughout virtually all of human history.

From the historical records of native peoples, it seems apparent that they have sometimes gained control of entire human civilizations. There is good reason to believe that extra-terrestrials ruled over ancient Egypt as Pharaohs and that they were considered gods by the Aztecs, various peoples of the Middle East and other places as well. Though it seems clear that more extra-terrestrial races than ever are now making at least occasional visits to our world, those which were present here in ancient times certainly have no need of studying human physiology or culture. That is not the motivation behind the abduction of humans.

We must understand too that the abduction of humans is not limited to a single race of extra-terrestrials nor a single purpose. Those naïve individuals who believe that all ET contact is positive and that their motivation is always to assist us both materially and spiritually will no doubt be quite surprised to learn that there are multiple types of extra-terrestrial beings who are both willing and eager to consume human beings any chance they get.

Among those which do are both the Type I and Type II Greys. The Type II Greys do no possess a digestive tract the way humans do. They have no stomach or intestines and therefore they have no way to digest or obtain nutrition from solid foods. Food is taken in and excreted in liquid form, through the pores in their skin.

A liquid slurry which is composed of hydrogen peroxide (which acts as both a catalyst and a sterilizing agent for the rest of the ingredients in the slurry), bovine or human blood and various other enzymes and secretions which can be obtained from cattle or—preferably—directly from humans. This liquid combination of ingredients is smeared over their skin, where it is absorbed into their bodies and acts as their only source of physical calories and nutrition. It has been reported in various places that they sometimes even literally bathe themselves in this slurry, entering tubs or vats filled with it and then submersing themselves in it. Waste products are disposed of in a similar manner, by being excreted through their pores.

This is the reason that so many people who have been abducted and taken aboard spacecraft piloted by the Type II Greys report that the smell of the air on board these craft is putrid and nauseating. The Greys in the craft have been smearing this bloody combination of materials all over their body, where it dries if it is not absorbed by their pores, and excreting all their waste material through their skin. This being the case, a nauseating smell is certainly what ought to be expected of the air aboard their spacecraft.

The American government is involved in assisting the Greys to obtain a steady and sufficient food supply for themselves. If you recall the widespread stories of livestock mutilations during the 1970's and 80's, which came in from across the country, the reason they occurred was to obtain the ingredients necessary to produce this liquid slurry for the Type II Greys from bovine sources.

That is the reason that the mutilated carcasses were always found completely drained of every drop of blood. It is also the reason that various organs were cored out and removed from their bodies with surgical precision using laser beams to do the cutting. The reason that mysterious black helicopters were so often reported near the scenes of these livestock mutilations was because the military was either aware of what was going on and observing it, or was directly responsible themselves for mutilating what eventually amounted to tens of thousands of full-grown cattle over the years.

To put it another way, the military was feeding and assisting the aliens that they knew were abducting and performing medical experiments on American citizens. The same military which was formed and is paid with tax dollars to guard and protect those same American citizens.

When the bloodless, mutilated carcasses were examined by veterinarians and other scientists, the explanations they came up with always boiled down to "it must have been coyotes or something." This was said even though it was clear that lasers had been used to incise and core out various organs and that not a single drop of blood was ever anywhere to be found, either within the bodies of the cattle or nearby on the ground.

This "explanation", which is of course not really an explanation at all, represents yet one more example of highly educated professional scientists and doctors inventing, accepting and promoting ideas which are in no way consistent with the physical evidence and which are clearly not even vaguely within the realm of possibility.

Everyone knows that coyotes are not equipped to completely drain bodies of every single drop of blood, time after time after time. Hopefully we are also all aware that coyotes do not show up at the scene of a kill they make equipped with surgical lasers and containers to be used for storing and hauling away the organs of the dead animal.

If it so happens that you were not aware of those things, I can assure you with an exceptionally high degree of confidence that laser-wielding, blood collecting coyotes who remove selected organs from cattle but leave the rest of the carcass—the parts they would normally consume as food—laying on the ground do not exist. While I am unsure about many things in this world, this is not one of those things. If you take me at my word when I say that coyotes do not perform laser surgery on cattle in the dead of the night, I promise that you will never have to worry about it being debunked later.

It is also a grim fact that such mutilations were not always confined solely to livestock, but were in fact occasionally performed on humans too. Human bodies were found in many nations which had been mutilated and drained of blood in precisely the same manner as had the unlucky livestock. There were even cases where humans were physically removed from their automobiles as they were driving down the road and then, dead, bloodless and carved up by lasers, were re-inserted into their automobiles on the highway just as though no time had elapsed. The cars immediately swerved off the roadway and crashed. From the condition of the bodies it was very clear that the organs had been removed and the blood drained from their bodies while the victims were still alive and conscious. Think about that.

These incidents were of course immediately hushed up by the authorities. The families of the victims were informed that the body had been so badly burned or mutilated in a car wreck that it was no longer recognizable, and they were never allowed to view it. The bodies were secretly incinerated and weights places within the coffins for the purposes of funerals and burial. The military used all means at their disposal, including death threats which absolutely would have been carried out, to make sure that news of these mutilated humans never reached the public. The presence of highly-advanced alien beings was problem enough to worry about when the issue of disclosure was considered. Allowing the public to learn about the presence of highly-advanced alien beings who mutilated humans as they were driving to work in their cars and then bathed in their blood rather than having a sandwich for lunch was completely off the table and was to be prevented at any cost.

The Type II Greys are by no means the only non-human entities which consume humans as a food item. The other methods of consumption will be detailed in the volume which follows this one. For now, please believe me when I tell you that it could be said that among all the known alien races which are known to consume humans, the Type II Greys method of doing so—removing their organs and draining their blood while the victims were alive and awake—is the least unpleasant of all possible options. Think carefully about *that*, if you will.

Another memory from another abduction. They are coming quite frequently. Since my first abduction memory, they have been taking me sometimes up to three times in a single week. Then sometimes a week or two will go by with no apparent visitations…then it's back to every few nights for a while.

Obviously, I don't like anything about this situation. I am not, however, freaked out about it like some people become. I have an advantage over most other abductees in that I've already interviewed a rather huge number of abductees prior to this. What I heard was often the same story with slightly different details told time after time by different people.

When my memories of abductions started, I was nothing unusual or special. In fact, my experiences turned out to be very much like those of so many of the people I had spoken with. I was therefore able to identify and understand immediately what was going on. I didn't have to waste time wondering whether I was going insane, whether I already WAS insane, etc. I did not have to go through hell trying to cope with the idea of aliens coming into my home, either, because I was long aware that it happened to people sometimes. I could in large part dispense with all that and maintain my emotional balance during a time which is often—and for good reason—highly traumatizing to many abductees.

It gets so you can often tell in advance when they will be coming. It's just a feeling you get somehow. It is almost as if the air in the room becomes charged. It "feels" different in a way that is difficult to put into words but quite easy to detect if one is aware of the problem and can sense subtle energetic changes in the environment. Everything feels strange and, somewhere deep inside, you "know" that they will be showing up later that night.

They have a way of putting us to sleep whenever they want to, meaning before they come in to abduct us. I have always been a night owl anyway, so I'm often up quite late. It's not unusual for me. But a person can be going along normally, quite wide awake, and suddenly be hit with overpowering waves of tiredness. There is no way to stay awake then, even though you felt fine just seconds before. When I feel these waves of sudden, overwhelming sleepiness come over me, I've found that I will be asleep within about five minutes whether I want to be or not. Not sometimes, not usually—every single time.

After a while, you get used to it somewhat. There doesn't appear to be much way to stop it from happening, so a sort of fatalism eventually kicked in, at least in my case. They seem to be returning me home unharmed, I reasoned, and I can't stop them from taking me...so why stress myself out about something I cannot prevent and which apparently ends with me safe and no worse off at the end of the incident. It isn't a position anyone would want to find themselves in, but there don't appear to be many other options. So, though I tried the same thing all abductees surely try, meaning I attempted to stay up all night thinking that if only I could keep myself from falling asleep it might somehow keep them from coming and abducting me, I tried not to let the prospect of being abducted bother me unduly.

Trying to stay awake all night, by the way, doesn't help since they can put you to sleep when they want to. But, like many abductees I suppose, it became difficult to sleep before long. Sleeping at night soon became something I tried hard to avoid and even sleeping during the day was something I did only grudgingly.

If you ever meet someone who claims to be an abductee and they look exhausted, it's because they are—they are trying to never sleep, if possible, and sleeping only when they simply can't stay awake any more. It is a terrible way to live, believe me, and there is no point in trying to explain it to people because they really can't understand and bringing the subject up has few advantages and too many risks to make it worth doing in the great majority of cases.

I am apparently back on board an alien spacecraft. What happened to me there during this abduction is an example of the vast gap between technology of human origin and alien technology, which can certainly be described as beyond science fiction. I am being led through a room by a pair of Greys. I do not recall much about the room itself, but there is an open doorway located in the wall to my right and through it, on the other side of it, I can see a row of bodies lined up along the wall. I can see about six of them. They are standing upright, their left sides near the wall of that room, and lined up in a front-to-back manner very close together, there is not much space between them. None of them move at all, though they do not appear to be damaged in any way as best I can tell from the brief view I had of them. They appear to be completely inanimate and lifeless.

Suddenly, during the few seconds they were within my field of vision, I think I understand: they are synths, synths which have not yet been activated or imbued with consciousness. While clones begin as babies and must spend the normal amount of time growing to adulthood, synths are genetic copies which begin their lives at the same age as was the person they were copied from at the time the copy was made. If it is an adult which is used for the creation of the synth, no childhood is necessary—the synth's body will be that of an adult from the day it is created.

I do not believe that a synth is created complete with the personality and memories of the person who was used as a donor. It seems that synths are created devoid of those things, that they are basically fully functional bodies which initially possess no personality or consciousness of their own. They start out just the way they were when I observed them on board that craft: immobile and for all practical purposes "switched off". Probably it would be more accurate to describe them as not yet having been "switched on".

There is something else about these synths which seems very strange, but I can not immediately decide what that something might be. Then, just before I have walked past the doorway and they go out of the range of my sight, I am finally able to identify just what it is about them which struck me as so unusual and so strange.

They are me.

They are all copies of me, lined up along a wall front-to-back, apparently being stored there until they were needed.

Extra-terrestrial medical technology is very far ahead of anything we have in terms of its capabilities and biological science. No matter what type of medical procedures may be carried out on abductees, their technology can heal any damage which may have been caused virtually instantly. When an abductee is returned to their home, there will usually be no physical signs which indicate that anything unusual occurred to them. There will be no scars on the body and no pain, nothing which remains to be healed.

In some cases, victims will report that they wake up with scratches on their body. This is usually considered to be an indication that they were abducted by Reptilians and the scratches were caused by their claws. Other times victims will awaken with several small puncture holes in their skin, usually three of them laid out in a triangular pattern.

In addition, "screen" memories will be inserted in place of real memories. These are false memories which replace actual memory of events with scenes that the victim will assume were just part of a very strange dream. Any real memories which may remain to them will often be distorted, twisted and obscured into something which appears to make no sense. A combination of drugs, hypnosis and post-hypnotic suggestion will be used in such a way that in most cases the victim will remember nothing about the abduction at all. When they awaken in the morning they will think they had some wild, strange dreams the night before—or, in most cases, remember nothing unusual at all. A short time later even the memory of vivid, highly unusual dreams will vanish from their mind and be forgotten about.

Post-hypnotic suggestion is also used to prevent abductees from telling others about their experiences, should they happen to be able to recall some of them. As noted above, the memory erasure procedure is not always 100% efficient: in some instances, people are able to retain some degree of memory regarding what took place during their abduction. It is, however, efficient enough that even those people will have the great majority of their abduction memories erased and unavailable to conscious recall.

If they attempt to talk about their abductions to others or to discuss alien-related subjects with them, post-hypnotic suggestion will kick in. They will quickly become highly agitated, nervous, sweaty and uncomfortable. They will often begin to pace or chain smoke as they talk about—or listen to others talk about—such things. They will feel their chests tighten up and it will become difficult to breathe. Often, they will get the strong feeling that they are doing something very wrong by discussing these topics with others and that they need to stop doing so immediately.

Another thing which is often observed is that when listening to lectures or watching TV or video clips about aliens they will suddenly be hit with an overpowering wave of sleepiness and find it impossible to stay awake any longer. Many people have literally fallen asleep in their chairs in an upright position which attempting to listen to or watch information related to aliens—and the more accurate that information is, the closer to the truth it comes, the stronger the feeling of sleepiness gets. Someone who was completely awake a few moments before can find it to be impossible to stay awake for another minute, when this occurs.

I am standing in a round room on board some type of space craft. On both sides of me are other people, people who have clearly been abducted from their homes as I was. We are lined up along the wall. There are perhaps 20 or so of us altogether and lined up we probably take up about half of this round wall.

In the center of the room, directly in front of me, stands a large robot. I remember being surprised by this in a detached sort of way, since, as always, I was in a powerless and apathetic daze. A robot was something I do not recall hearing any of the many abductees I had spoken to mention. But there it was. It looked somewhat similar to the robot in the old TV series "Lost in Space". It had a bullet-shaped head, two arms of metal which ended in a pincer-type hand. It was silver, orange and black and stood around seven feet tall.

It began to select people from the group. I could not see whether it had wheels underneath it—it had no legs, just a solid canister-like appearance underneath where its waist would have been—but I do not think it did. I think it hovered somehow. It selected people one at a time from the group along the wall. And this is when I experienced what I believe to have been a Close Encounter of the Sixth Kind. A Close Encounter of the Sixth Kind means you see an animal or a human killed during an alien contact experience.

When a person was selected by this robot, it simply floated up to them, picked them up with its pincer-hands and lifted them up with what were clearly very strong arms. Some of the people, for some reason unknown to me, had been rejected for some reason. It had been decided by someone that those people were not needed or wanted, they were not people who had turned out to be worthy or of interest to the abductors for some reason.

When one of those people was selected, the robot carried the person to a small slot which was set into the wall in the back of this smallish round room. From my position, it would have been at about 11 o'clock on the wall. The slot was small, very much like a letter slot on a downtown mailbox in size. Above and below the slot there were panels mounted on the wall. They contained various colored lights and mechanical readouts of some kind, I couldn't tell what they might be for.

As the robot, with a person firmly grasped in its mechanical pincers, approached this slot in the wall, the person began to stretch lengthwise, like a cartoon. They got very thin front-to-back and this slot in the wall appeared to suck them into it. They lengthened and thinned out as their bodies were sucked into this slot from the arms of the robot. It was like watching an old Roadrunner cartoon and seeing Wile E. Coyote stretch out to ten feet long.

I do not know why, but at the time I felt quite certain that these people were being killed as they passed through the slot. I have no way of knowing for certain that this is true, but I have never found any reason to change my opinion. If you were to ask me about it, I would tell you that the people were killed and feel certain that I am giving you the correct answer. But, as with so many things when it comes to dealing with aliens, there is no way for me to prove it one way or the other.

One by one, the robot selected people from the group. It seemed to me that at least half of them were carried over near the slot in the wall and similarly stretched out like cartoon spaghetti and sucked through it. Each time that happened, I was somehow very certain that those people had been judged somehow unfit and were being killed as they passed through the slot.

Some people, however, were treated differently. The robot picked them up and carried them down a short hallway and out of our line of sight. Our eyes were all facing straight ahead, into the center of the room, and we were incapable of moving them or turning our bodies to look in any direction.

Eventually my turn came. The robot approached me, picked me up and carried me down this short hallway. At the end of it there were doorways on each side. They did not appear to have doors, just openings in the hallway wall. It turned right and took me into what appeared to be a surgical bay of some type. As I think about it now, it seems to me that all of us were wearing hospital-type gowns as we stood in that round room, the type which are open in the back.

The next thing I can remember, I am lying on my back on a table in this surgical bay which is slanted at about a 45-degree angle, with my head higher than my bare feet. I am restrained, I cannot move my arms or legs. As I look down at my feet, I can see what appears to be two Grey aliens, the same type with the big, dark, almond-shaped eyes, one standing near each of my feet. They are each holding a small device, similar in size and shape to a man's hair dryer and connected to machinery directly behind them attached to the wall by a corrugated tube which ran from the device in their hands into the machinery mounted along the wall. The tube resembled that on a commercial hair dryer. Each of these Greys was pointing the device in their hands at my feet. They each pointed their device at a different foot.

And as I watched, my feet appeared to melt like candle wax. There was no sense of pain, but I could literally see my feet, bones and all, melt like wax beginning with my toes, working its way down my feet until they had melted back almost to my ankles. I was, as always during abductions, paralyzed, in a state which I imagine is like having gone through a lobotomy. No willpower, no thoughts of trying to escape, no clear thoughts of any kind really and unable to speak. But on this occasion, one of very few I can ever recall, I was somehow able to speak. It took all my willpower and inner strength just to speak one phrase to these Greys. I tried to shout it as loudly as I could...but when it came out through my lips, it came out as the tiniest little whisper you can imagine. *"What are you doing?"* I asked them in that tiny voice which it took absolutely all my will and resolve to force out.

Their little chests seemed to puff up, like they were proud of themselves for some reason. I wasn't even aware that such a thing could happen. Is this a distorted memory rather than what really took place? Perhaps so. I wouldn't doubt it. To the best of my understanding, Greys possess only a single internal organ, sort of a combination heart and lungs, and I am not even certain that they could puff up their chests if they wanted to. But that is the way I remember it, so I am including that detail here for the sake of completeness.

One of them looked at me. When they communicate, they do not speak aloud, ever. They are pure telepaths. *"We are turning you into an alien,"* it replied in my mind. This is the only time, as far as I know, that a Grey spoke to me. It seemed somehow to think that I should be thanking them for whatever it was they were doing, as though they were doing me the biggest favor a person could ever have hoped for. I have no idea why.

I also have no idea what they meant by that enigmatic phrase, since I appear to be the same person now as I was before any of this happened. And why would it refer to...whatever it was that they were supposedly turning me into...as an *"alien"*? I have no idea.

After my feet had been melted back so far, the Greys turned their devices off, reached down and somehow—I have no idea how this is done or whether it is an entirely accurate recollection on my part or not—they began to re-shape my feet from this soft mass of melted flesh and bone which remained. They worked incredibly quickly: it seemed to take only a matter of a few moments and they had re-shaped my feet, though I do not remember them looking any different now than they ever did. But...something was wrong. One of them had gotten a result it was unhappy with for some reason. It was not acceptable—I don't know why. And that is when I came face to face with alien technology for the first time, as best I know...

Suddenly we were back in time. We had traveled into the past. Not far, just back to the point a few seconds before they had begun to operate on me. Again, they pointed their devices at my feet, again I watched as the flesh and bone appeared to melt backward over a period of just a few seconds, and again they reached down and began *to re-shape my feet. Again, they got a result they were not happy with. The same Grey as before, the one working on my right foot. And suddenly we were back in time again...*

Again, they picked up the devices, pointed them at my feet and again I watched as the flesh melted like candle wax. Again, they began to re-shape my feet somehow. Again, the Grey got a result that was somehow unsatisfactory. And once again, back in time we went...

This time we went back a little too far for some reason. I was back in the round room, facing the robot. For some reason, I decided to try to be helpful to it. I managed to stammer "They...sent me...back... here..." The robot knew immediately what the situation was. It picked me up as it had the first time, carried me down the short hallway and back into the surgical bay. I was laid on the table, the two Greys picked up their devices and once again I watched my feet melt like candle wax. It seems to me that the surgeries were re-started in this manner five or six times before the Grey—or what appeared to be a Grey—working on my right foot got a result which satisfied it and the operation was concluded.

It should by now be clear that contact with extra-terrestrials is typically not a pleasant affair and can sometimes result in harm or even death to the person involved. This does not imply, however, that most abductions will end with the abductee being permanently harmed. In fact, most do not. Most end with the abductee being returned safely to their home after having their memory wiped. It is a fact that most people who are abducted by extra-terrestrials will go through their entire lives unaware that such a thing ever occurred to them due to the memory erasure, which is probably accomplished by using a combination of drugs and hypnosis.

This memory erasure is not, however, 100% efficient. Sometimes memories are retained and abductees can remember parts or occasionally all an abduction event. These are the people who are seen to come forward and speak about their abduction experiences in public. Many, however, choose never to speak of them at all due to the very real concern of such reports causing irreparable damage to them either socially or professionally.

I do not normally recommend regressive hypnosis for those who are victims of these types of abductions. Though it is true that additional memories can be accessed by utilizing regressive hypnosis, it is also true that to do so an abductee is forced to re-live the experience in real-time as they remember those events. Many—probably most—of the memories of an abduction experience are likely to be quite unpleasant, as is demonstrated I hope by the inclusion of some of my own abduction memories in this chapter. They are nothing a person would normally wish to experience even once, let alone twice.

It seems to me that enough is known by now about the standard procedures carried out during abductions that there is not usually a great deal a person can gain by undergoing regressive hypnosis. There are, however, virtually certain to be unpleasant memories and perhaps memories of things most people would end up wishing they had never been made aware of in the first place. Unless someone has a specific and personally important reason to want to access buried abduction memories, it seems to me they may very likely be better off letting well enough alone and avoid making any such attempts. That is, of course, only my opinion about the matter. Every abductee, in the end, must consider the issue carefully from their own point of view and make their own decision about the best way to proceed.

Though it is not the sole reason for the abduction of humans by Greys, the collection and utilization of reproductive cells and DNA which meet certain criteria appear to clearly be the top priority and primary motivation for them.

The Greys have claimed that their planet is dying and that they have been forced by circumstances to attempt to create hybrid beings, half human and half Grey, so their race could survive. There is no reason to believe this is true. There is nothing which would convince me to take their word for it without a method of confirming that this is indeed the case and that their race is in fact in existential peril. These Greys are well-known to be perfectly willing to lie to us whenever it suits their need and to manipulate us any time they feel that such manipulation will give them an advantage of some kind over us. And they themselves are not the masters of their own fate. They are completely under the control of others, normally the Draco, but the military also has its own Greys that it controls. They are like worker bees. They do not make the plan themselves, they carry out the plan that someone else has made.

I am strapped to an inclined operating table, possibly on board a spacecraft or possibly inside a facility located in an underground base. There is a surgeon standing in front of me, clearly preparing to operate on me. He is a human. He is wearing surgical whites, including a white face mask and cap and he has one of those surgical spotlights attached to a headband in the center of his forehead. Curly bright-red hair is poking out from the bottom of his cap. He is wearing glasses with small round lenses, the same style worn by John Lennon and Ozzy Osbourne.

In his hand is a device which consists of two hollow half-spheres, like someone cut a tennis ball in half, which are metal and connected by a short tube which runs between them. It occurs to me in the foggy haze which serves for my consciousness at the time that the half-globes are not the same shape as my eyes...but, somehow, I instinctively know that they are precisely the same size as my eye SOCKETS and are spaced apart in a way which will allow them to cover both my eye sockets at once.

Inside each of these half-globes, ringing the open edge, is a series of blades which appear to be just like X-ACTO knife blades. There are probably eight of them in each of the half-globes and they are hanging loose, attached by their tops to the device and spaced in an equidistant manner around the interior edge. In his other hand, the surgeon holds a device which acts as a trigger and which controls the blades. He presses the trigger several times and I see that the blades are made to revolve around the inner edges of these half-spheres at a speed which varies depending on how hard he pulls on the trigger— think of the blade on a chain saw and you will get the idea. The surgeon pulls the trigger several times and I see these blades whir around in a circle, so fast they become blurred, then slower, then fast again as he varies the pressure. I understand clearly that he is about to place that device over my eye sockets and cut out my eyes with these razor-sharp X-ACTO knife blades from hell.

I summon up all the strength I have within me, it is a supreme effort but at last I force words out of my mouth. As loudly and forcefully as I possibly can I say "Oh please don't do that..." It comes out as a soft, tiny whisper, barely audible...and it is the maximum extent of the resistance I can offer as this human surgeon prepares to cut both of my eyes out of my head. It is all I can manage, to ask him to please not do it in the tiniest whisper imaginable. This was the third and last time I recall being able to speak of my own volition to one of my captors and the only time I know for sure that I was speaking to a human. There is no question that he was a doctor in the employ of the black ops community.

At that point, the memories become twisted and hazy. Obviously, a screen memory has been put in place to obscure what really happened in that operating room. I do not know for certain why they felt it necessary to cut out my eyes, though I would guess it was to insert an implant of some type behind them. I doubt I will ever know the reason for sure. But I know damned well they did it. They cut out my eyes!

And then I am back in my bed, awaking as if from a sleep. The room is empty but for me. The clock, as it almost always does when I am returned from an abduction, reads 2:58 AM. My eyes are fine, healed up as though nothing was ever done to them. But I know they did it.

Please do not ever expect me to have sympathy or goodwill toward any of these malevolent beings, whether human or alien. They do not care about me in the least. They are not in any way concerned about my pain, my terror, my comfort or my well-being other than the fact that they need to return me home unharmed so I will have no way to prove they ever took me at all and they will be free to do so again whenever they feel the need to.

I think I know how women who have been raped feel now. They have undergone something violent and terrifying, an act which is both brutal and intensely personal...and who can they tell about it safely? In many cases, I imagine, they feel just as I did then: there is no one to talk to, no one to tell about it who will believe what I say. It is something I must keep penned up inside and deal with completely on my own, without help or counseling of any kind. It is the stuff of nightmares, but it is reality.

Can you understand now why I do not ever want to fall asleep again? Can you understand why I am willing to stay awake for days and nights on end, just on the faint hope that doing so will somehow prevent them from coming back and taking me again?

It doesn't help at all. It doesn't stop them—I know this from experience. They can cause me to fall asleep whenever they need me *to. I know it well, because I have lived it. And yet still I do not want to ever sleep again. I am willing to do anything in my power to force the sleep away, to stay awake until dawn night after night, because any chance is better than no chance and I do not know what else to do or to try.*

This is no way to live. It is no way to force anyone to feel. It brings on a whole host of medical problems related to sleep deprivation before much time has passed. They don't matter to me. I will still try to stay awake anyway, all night and every night, waiting for the dawn. Only when the sun has risen will I feel safe again. They always come for me during the night and never during the light of day

It must be understood clearly that not all instances of what appears to be an alien abduction are what they seem to be. Many times, just as the source I referred to as The Colonel stated, abductions are carried out by black ops military forces rather than extra-terrestrials and that they are done in a manner which is designed to simulate an abduction by aliens.

The interview in the chapter entitled "The Colonel's Message" took place a number of years back. It was the first time I was made aware that the military performed abductions themselves. It was something I did not want to believe could be true, just as many people who read this may also not want to believe.

Because it took me so much by surprise, I made a fundamental mistake: I failed to follow the evidence, even after it had been clearly pointed out to me by an impeccable source. I didn't believe what he told me, because I was unwilling to imagine that our troops were capable of such a thing.

As was the case every time I had the poor judgment to disagree with something the Colonel said to me, as more information became available to me it turned out that he had been completely correct in what he said and I had been mistaken. Looking back on it now, it seems obvious to me that I had no business whatsoever trying to second-guess a black ops expert and who was trying to educate me about things I had no way of knowing at the time.

As is made clear by the descriptions of my abduction memories—all of which occurred years after the conversations with the Colonel that I included in the text—the military is unquestionably heavily involved in the abduction business. In fact, the great majority of my abduction memories involve military personnel, sometimes accompanied by what appeared to be Type II Greys.

Extra-terrestrials are not the only ones who are attempting to create hybrids—the military is doing it as well and has been for many years. They have other uses for abductees as well, none of which are in any way related to the well-being of the abductee and all of which are completely illegal.

After being returned home from an alien abduction, it is usually the case that the victim will display highly enhanced psychic abilities for a period of several hours. The military is able somehow to know who has been abducted by aliens and when they are returned to their homes. Often, they will then abduct the person for a second time, taking them after the aliens have returned them home and utilizing this enhanced psi ability for their own purposes. Such victims are used as remote viewers, unknown to themselves, able for a time to project their consciousness into remote places while their bodies remain seated and then reporting what they see there.

It is an advanced form of real-time spying which the public is not aware is even possible. These abductees serving as unwilling remote viewers can literally project their consciousness into a room, listen in on any conversations which are taking place there and relay the words directly to their military captors. They can eavesdrop on foreign leaders or military officials, private citizens the military is concerned about. They can be used to describe the interiors of secure installations as though they were present in those locations and looking around the room themselves.

When the period of enhanced ability ends, they are then returned to their homes for a second time the same night, their memories once again chemically and hypnotically erased. They are placed back into their beds and when they awaken no evidence will normally be found of either abduction. If they happen to recall anything at all, it is usually just presumed to have been the result of a bad dream and will be swiftly forgotten about.

It was the middle of winter. I was living on the second floor of an apartment building which had a large outdoor courtyard in the center. This time, for a reason I do not know, everyone who lived in the building was involved. We were taken from our apartments and lined up around this courtyard in front of the doorways in a large U-shaped line, facing the courtyard. There were special ops troops wearing Kevlar body armor and carrying assault rifles, accompanied by at least two of the Type II Greys, the type with large, dark, almond-shaped eyes. They stood us side by side, barefoot, wearing whatever we had worn to bed, on the grass of the courtyard which was covered with several inches of snow. It was well below freezing outside. Everyone had been rendered helpless, put into that zombie-like state I was familiar with by now which causes one to act as though they have had a lobotomy.

I saw the officer who was obviously in charge of the mission, wearing dress greens with a chest-board full of medals in place, approach one of the apartment doors on the second floor. As he stepped up to it there was a flash of light around his whole body, like a flashbulb going off...and then he vanished. He had walked right through the closed and locked door of the apartment as if it were not even there! A few seconds passed and then he opened the door from the inside of the apartment and emerged, leading the elderly couple who lived there out by the hand. They too, like all of us, were completely passive and unresisting. He led them down the stairs and lined them up beside the rest of us in the snow in their nightclothes.

Abductees sometimes speak of extra-terrestrials which come into their homes by walking right through the walls or doors. I saw it done myself, that night, by a U.S. military special forces officer who, judging by the number of medals on his chest-board, was probably a Colonel or thereabouts. I am telling you that our own military has been given this technology—they, too, can walk right through our doors and walls and into our homes while we are rendered completely unable to defend ourselves or resist in any way.

Please keep in mind that abduction is a capital crime in this country, something a person can be executed for doing. What was occurring now was a mass abduction of innocent civilians from their homes by our own military, assisted by at least two Greys.

People were sometimes moved around to a different spot in the line, I do not know why. We stood out there for a long time. It is difficult to know exactly how long because our sense of time was distorted. I would guess it was around an hour and a half.

Eventually enough time had passed that I decided—somehow— that I wanted to smoke a cigarette. I had no thought whatsoever of trying to escape—even the idea that I should try to escape never passed through my mind. I simply wanted a cigarette. For the first and only time I can ever recall, I was for some reason able to take an action on my own accord during an abduction event. The fact that the only time I took any type of action on my own volition, it was to hunt down a cigarette rather than to try to somehow escape from the situation I was in is possibly illustrative of the extreme dependency and addiction that comes hand-in-hand with a smoking habit—but that is another story for another time.

While the troops were busy tending to the other residents, I simply walked back up the stairs, down the exterior hallway to the door of my apartment and stepped inside it. I knew an open pack of cigarettes was laying just a few steps inside, on my computer desk. I walked up to it and picked up the pack.

As I did, I saw the two Greys looking at me through the slats in the blind of my large front window from the exterior hallway. One of them had pulled the slats aside so they could look inside and see me. They then entered the apartment through the open door. As they did so, I set the pack of cigarettes down, fully controlled once more, having not even removed one cigarette from the pack, and silently turned to follow them.

It did not occur to me until the next day, when I thought about this memory carefully, that to pull aside the slats of my window shade the Grey had needed to reach THROUGH the window to do it—it was an interior blind, the window did not open and the blind could not be accessed from the outside.

The two Greys led me back downstairs. I followed passively, in my lobotomized zombie-like state. When we reached the ground floor they placed me back into line, this time at a different location in the group.

The memory now becomes somewhat distorted. I cannot give a detailed description of just how this next thing occurred. All I can say is that I was force-bred right there from my position in line. Whether my partner was the girl whose apartment I was standing in front of, some other woman, or a non-human being I simply am unable to remember. I only know that it happened. I was caused to have sex with someone or someTHING right there, standing outside in the snow. I will never know who or what it was.

And then the memory of this event ends. The next thing I remember is waking up in my bed. I immediately glanced over at the big digital clock that sat at my bedside, as had become my habit. As it almost always did when I woke up directly after being returned home, it read 2:58 AM.

It was as if my captors were on a tight schedule and kept to it rigidly. Maybe their shifts ended at 3 AM, I don't know, or maybe they were due to pick up another abductee from his or her home and didn't want to be late. Once or twice they arrived later, around 5:00 AM, just as I was finally allowing myself to fall asleep. Another time, after I had managed to stay awake all night long, they came for me at seven in the morning. All the other times that I recall, I looked at the clock and it said 2:58 AM, just as it did that night.

I should add that I also made a habit of looking at the clock whenever those waves of tiredness started to come over me. When they did, the time was almost always 2:58 AM. It would seem I was sent back in time as I was being returned as a matter of regular practice rather than having it be a one-time thing. I was being returned, it seems, a few seconds before I had ever been taken and, I presume, being floated over top of my "future body" and then lowered down into it, as I described before, and then merging with it and effectively having the entire abduction event have a duration of zero seconds from the point of view of a third-party observer.

Many of those who retain memories of some of their experiences will refuse to believe those memories could be true. They will bury them, try to forget about them, write them all off as bad dreams or in some cases end up questioning their own sanity. There is no support system for abductees because the government will not allow any such system to exist. The existence of such a support group would lead to the conclusion that those who claim to be abductees are sane and speaking the truth. That would in turn lead to revelations of heinous misconduct on the part of the military and intelligence agencies, much of which would consist of the commission of capital crimes and acts of terrorism and war against their own citizens.

The only support groups which offer help to abductees are heavily infiltrated and compromised by government agents. There is no safe place for abductees to turn and the events they undergo are too traumatic to be dealt with alone. Society is doing these people a great disservice, every day.

Most of them suffer from shell shock in addition to all the other problems that come with being an abductee. That is a very serious and debilitating condition and the abductees are not offered any treatment for it. Instead, they get to live with ridicule and people making snide jokes about them behind their backs, thinking they don't know or won't notice. They *do* know and they *do* notice.

We have psychiatrists for the family dog. We spend literally trillions of dollars on wars of aggression which only hurt us in the end. But we can't find the money to help people who are our family, our friends and our neighbors who are literally being put through a living hell and then forced to deal with it on their own. It is certainly nothing for this society to be proud of. It's shameful, it's unnecessary and it is so totally beneath us that it boggles the mind to think we allow it to happen anyway. This is what we have come to as a society.

Why do some people remember being abducted while others do not? It seems to me that is partly a matter of random chance and partly because many people would not consider an alien abduction to be something which is within the realm of possibility and so dismiss any such thoughts as nothing more than foolish notions.

There can be no question that we have all been carefully and repeatedly conditioned to think of alien abductions in just such terms, despite the credibility and the demonstrable sanity of many of the victims who have chosen to come forward and speak about their experiences. That fact alone speaks volumes about our government's involvement in criminal conduct. It also leaves little question that we find ourselves in a situation in which we are in considerable danger— and that part of that danger comes from the people who are tasked with being responsible for our safety and security.

Sometimes, especially if the victim "wakes up" in their bed immediately after being returned home, memories can be retained. In such cases the victims would do well to force themselves to write down any memories they may have retained in as complete a fashion as possible and to do so as quickly as they can. If they go back to sleep rather than writing the memories down, it is most likely that by the time they wake up in the morning the memories will have vanished and will be impossible to recall.

As was related in my personal experiences, abductees are virtually always kept in a helpless catatonic state throughout the course of the abduction if the captors are of either the military or the hostile extra-terrestrial variety (and this is usually the case). Neither group wishes to deal with angry and hostile citizens who have been captured and taken out of their own bedrooms in the middle of the night, therefore they are immobilized.

They have a method which is unknown to me which allows them to force their subjects into a deep sleep before the abduction itself begins. A person can be wide awake and everything will seem fine, when suddenly they will be hit by overpowering waves of sleepiness. They will find that it is impossible to stay awake, that they suddenly feel exhausted and need to lay down and rest. Usually within about five minutes the person will be fast asleep, as will anyone else in the house who is apt to witness or interfere with the operation.

The abductors will then enter the residence either by teleporting in or by stepping through walls and doors as though they do not exist. I do not understand the technical details of how this is accomplished, but I have witnessed it being done and can attest to the fact that it does indeed happen.

Someone once explained it as a device which attaches to the belt and which is capable of somehow altering the density of either the body itself or the obstacle (wall, door, etc.) until they precisely match each other. When this is done the alien—or the military black ops member—can simply step through the barrier as if it weren't there. I do not know whether this is the correct explanation for this or not—I put it forward as a possibility only, not having the ability to accurately describe the method on my own.

The individuals who are chosen to be abducted are by no means a random group—far from it. They are selected quite carefully and have been found to meet one of several criteria which are deemed as desirable by the intruders. It is quite helpful to understand the characteristics they normally prefer and the reasons they have for doing so. Please note that the military uses a list which does not quite match the list used by extra-terrestrials, since their purposes do not match with those of the aliens either.

There is a far higher chance that a person will be abducted if they have a negative Rh factor, meaning a negative blood type, or if they have a direct ancestor such as a parent or grandparent who did. It is believed that a negative Rh factor is indicative of someone who is carrying Reptilian genetics, unknown to themselves. Those who possess this characteristic are typically followed through the generations: it is quite likely that at least one of their parents or grandparents were an abductee as well, and that at least one of their children or grandchildren will in turn become abductees as well. They follow their own, it seems. The Reptilians keep track of their own. The DNA of many generations of the same families will be collected, studied and utilized by the parties which are responsible for the abductions.

The primary attributes which seem to be valued the most highly in a victim by the extra-terrestrials appear to be high of intelligence, a high degree of creativity, a talent for thinking out of the box or of combining information in new and unique ways with the effect that new and original solutions will be arrived at. They also look for people with a family history which does not show a tendency to include genetically-transmitted diseases or medical problems. These include a family history of diabetes, cancer, heart disease, etc.

It is quite rare to find all these qualities in the same individual and all of them are not necessary for a person to be abducted. If they have one of those characteristics and a negative blood type (or an ancestor with a negative Rh factor) it will usually be all that's required. If a hybrid is created using that person's DNA it can later be crossed with another hybrid or a different person who carries another of the traits they look for. Over time, it is possible to produce someone who carries all these traits…and who is only part human.

All of the above list of desired traits are considered by the extra-terrestrials to be primary survival characteristics. If conditions suddenly change, these are the individuals it is felt will have the highest probability of being able to adapt to a changing environment or come up with useful solutions to novel problems which might arise in the future. Another way of putting it is that these people are believed to be the most likely to survive and the least likely to become extinct due to external environmental factors.

Those who are responsible for producing the human-alien hybrids clearly have done so with the long-term survivability of the hybrids uppermost in their minds. These hybrid beings are being carefully produced with the idea of creating a race which will be able to successfully survive long into the distant future rather than producing hybrids for reasons having to do with the short term. That seemingly innocuous piece of information is one which provides additional confirmation of the fact that this breeding program is in all ways a long-term project: it has taken place over a period which equates to a multitude of human generations and is aimed at a point somewhere in the faraway future.

This allows us to infer that there is an extraordinary amount of importance attached to—and priority given to—the hybrid breeding program by those in charge of it. The fact that the public is prevented from knowing that such a program even exists makes it entirely reasonable for us to presume that it is likely to be something which works against us. If it was being carried out for our benefit, after all, there would no reason to hide the fact that it exists from the public. The fact that it is strenuously denied by official sources and that so much effort has been taken to cover up its existence is sufficient reason for us to conclude that, over both the short and long term, this program is intended to achieve something which will result in lasting harm to humanity.

Another memory. I am traveling in a bus, part of a group of people who are all clearly abductees and all clearly as helplessly immobilized as I am. It is night time. At some point the road we are traveling on slants downward and we enter what appears to be a tunnel. It is not actually a tunnel. We have been transported to a secret underground base.

The next part of this event that I recall takes place in what appears to be a small auditorium or gymnasium. There are bleachers in place. It appears that the rest of the people who were aboard the bus have been seated in them. I am not.

For reasons unknown to me, I am standing down in front of the bleachers, behind a lectern on a podium. I can hear myself delivering an orientation speech to them. I tell them that they will not be harmed, that the best thing they can do for themselves is to try to remain calm and simply follow any orders they are given. If they will do, I tell them, they will be returned safely to their homes afterward and will retain no memories of ever having been here.

I have no idea why I was chosen to be the one to give this orientation lecture to these people. I seemed to be observing it as a third party, as if I was seeing myself standing there through someone else's eyes rather than looking out through my own. I certainly did not appear to have any control over the words that I was speaking, nor did I have any conscious intention of speaking such words.

It is possible that an alien consciousness was controlling my actions at this point and that my consciousness perhaps really WAS observing it from a third-party perspective. I have no way be certain. But this is certainly a situation I would never have expected to find myself in as an abductee—give an orientation lecture in which I encouraged people to follow their orders and not make trouble. To be clear, this was a military abduction, not an alien abduction.

There are too many unknowns here for us to be certain about the true agenda and purposes behind alien abductions. It seems clear that genetics, DNA and creating alien/human hybrids are a top priority, but the reason for this could be one of several things or a combination of them. We cannot rely on their explanations because it is known that they are more than willing to deceive and manipulate us to suit their own purposes whenever they find it to be necessary.

There are virtually no scenarios I am aware of which would indicate that what is occurring is anything other than uninvited genetic tampering, most probably including a long-term re-ordering of the human genome itself. It also seems likely that these hybrids are being created at least partially with the idea of eventually replacing the native human population of Earth with a population of hybrids. If that is indeed the case, we must consider that a de facto invasion of this planet is now underway and has been ongoing for quite some time.

Whatever the ultimate purposes may be for this genetic tampering, there are no scenarios which lead to the long-term benefit of humanity and none which appear to be concerned at all with our safety or preferences for any reason other than as a source of food and resources. In other words, livestock. It seems clear that some of the extra-terrestrials concerned are treating humans as a resource, a crop to be experimented on, manipulated at will and then harvested in the end. We are given no choice in the matter nor do we appear to be able to defend ourselves against it in any meaningful way.

The aliens can silently manipulate the lives of abductees in way which are beneficial to the aliens but not the abductees. A typical abductee will be a person of high intelligence, someone who might normally have been expected to become a successful doctor or scientist, perhaps. But such success has not been their fate. Instead they are living alone, either due to a contentious divorce or through the inability for one reason or another to find a mate. They will probably be living in either a small town or in an isolated rural location. Rather than having the income they might normally be expected to have, they are instead living in poverty or close to it.

Overall, they are isolated, vulnerable targets who do not have the means to defend themselves. They often live in an area where there are potentially only a small number of possible witnesses should an alien or military spacecraft appear to abduct them from their homes. They have been purposefully turned into victims, intentionally made powerless and unable to change their own situation due to poverty and lack of support.

Another memory. This time I am apparently being trained for warfare as a soldier. I am crawling on my belly through deep mud, part of a line of men who are doing the same thing. There are trenches and foxholes behind us and in front of us. We are armed with submachine guns and under heavy fire. I have no idea who we were fighting, but the weapons being used against us certainly appear to be very real. Suddenly an object comes flying from somewhere ahead of me and lands on the ground a couple feet to my right. It looks like a Contac cold capsule, but it's about 12-18 inches long. One half of it is glowing bright green, lit up. The other half is glowing red and flashing. The red light, which comprises half of this capsule-shaped object, is blinking on and off with a steady rhythm.

I have no idea what it could be. It occurs to me that it might well be some type of hand grenade and that the red blinking could be a countdown timer. If that is true, we are only seconds from death. I grab the object as quickly as I can and hurl it forward, back the direction it came from, with all my power. I see it arc through the air. When it hits the ground, there is a tremendous explosion upon impact. It WAS a grenade! I appear to have just risked my life to save the lives of the other people crawling through the mud with me.

The next thing I remember was standing outside a small building, surrounded by a group of extremely tall beings in military uniforms. I am facing a man who appears to be a non-com, like a gunny sergeant perhaps. He is covered in sweat and his uniform is torn. He grins widely and slaps me on the back. "They told me you were a good one and I see they weren't kidding!" he says, grinning again. "Great job out there! Here, drink this!" He hands me what seems to me to be a mug half-full of beer. I gratefully swallow the whole thing down.

I step inside the building, which appears to be a small house or office building of some kind. There is a desk in one of the rooms I walk through. It has paperwork on it. I walk over and glance at the paperwork. All I can remember seeing of it was a name: Spyder something. The surname has been lost to time and I can't recall what it was.

I walk slowly into the next room, where I see a girl seated on a couch. She is young, late teens or early 20's. Skinny, good looking, dressed only in panties and a bra. Somehow—I have no idea how—I know she is this Spyder person whose name I had seen on the paperwork. I am, as always, little more than a mindless zombie. I look at her, hard. "I...just saw..." I start to say, intending to tell her I had just seen her name on a paper. I don't know why I wanted to tell her that. I had never seen her before.

Suddenly I am grabbed and dragged back outside the building by several of those very tall soldiers. Were they Tall Whites? I don't know. Perhaps. I am 6'2" and they were much taller than me. They had to be around seven feet tall. I am thrown onto the ground and they begin to brutally kick me with their Army boots. I am powerless to resist, immobile and apathetic as they always keep us. "This will teach you never to tell secrets, you son of a bitch!" they hiss at me, kicking me until I am unconscious.

Abductees often develop a strong aversion to doctors and hospitals. They will often neglect their own health, refusing even to see a doctor for a physical examination. They would rather not be checked than be in the same room with a doctor. I am certainly this way myself and I am far from the only one.

Once one knows they are an alien abductee they will always try the same things to hopefully prevent it from recurring. They will start to sleep as little as possible and whenever they can they will limit their sleeping period to daylight hours only. They will often take to leaving the lights on all night if they must sleep at night. Whenever possible, they will stay awake until dawn, with the idea that if they can somehow just keep themselves from falling asleep, the aliens won't return and abduct them again.

We have all tried it. It doesn't work at all. They can cause us to go to sleep whenever they want us to, no matter how determined we may be not to sleep. We will of course never again sleep with a door unlocked or a window open…but this does no good either, because they can simply bypass those things by walking through the walls into our rooms. Even if we are atheists, we will eventually get down on our knees and beg Jesus to help us, to make it stop. This also helps nothing, despite what some people want to believe or claim. It does not prevent abductions from taking place. Those who claim otherwise are either delusional or are intentionally lying to give Jesus some credit he didn't earn. When they want us…they will have us. And we can't stop them from taking us.

I am in a line of people, all of us males. We are led into what appears to be a theater from what seems to be the sidewalk of a city I do not recognize. We are seated in the darkened theater, facing the stage as if we were about to watch a play.

The next thing I remember, we are all deep underground and I am certain we have been somehow transported to the future. How far, I have no way of knowing. We are underground in the tunnels of a copper mine. We are given mining picks and used as mining slaves by human supervisors. We are almost never allowed any rest at all and we are never fed a thing.

Day after day, for weeks it seems, perhaps even for months, we toil underground in this copper mine. Our bodies waste away, eventually leaving us bone-thin and gaunt, like the photos you see of starving

- 249 -

people who are being released from Nazi prison camps at the end of the Second World War.

We are starving to death. We are being worked to death. Nobody cares at all about our condition. Their only concern is that we continue to ceaselessly chip away at the rock walls of this mine in search of copper.

Finally, when we are only one short step from death...suddenly I wake up in my bed, back home again. My body is no longer bone-thin, it is just as it has always been. It is as though the event never even took place.

They have come backward in time from the future, kidnaped us and used us as slaves until we were nothing more than walking corpses...and then sent us back to where we were before any of that began. Presumably we were replaced by a fresh crop of humans from our own time, who would in their turn be abused and starved down to nothing as they were forced to live as slaves in that copper mine.

How many other mines, in other place, may be staffed by others who are utilized in the same fashion, treated as slaves and worked ceaselessly as they are slowly starved almost to death, is anybody's guess. Certainly, it stands to reason that there are more of them— perhaps many more. The fact that this is being done to us by what we would normally think of as "our own people" is, of course, highly disturbing.

It makes me wonder if our captors are not part of some so-called "breakaway civilization"—something which will be discussed in the second book of this series—and no longer have any direct interest in the safety or well-being of either us or the society to which we belong. It certainly seems possible that this is the case.

Another memory of being used as a slave, this one also from what I feel sure was the future. Again, there are a group of us. We are in what appears to be a multi-level building, perhaps a storage facility for munitions. There are futuristic artillery weapons set up around the perimeter of the floor I am on, perhaps the third floor up. The outside of this level has half-walls of concrete with the top half open— similar to the way many parking garages are built today.

The artillery is not sitting idle. They are engaged in combat. They are firing constantly at some unseen enemy. We are used again as slaves, to take artillery shells which come up on freight elevators on pallets, over to where the artillery is. The shells are then fired at the unseen enemy as we return to the elevator for another load of shells. The pallets are stacked on wheeled carts, which we pull.

If it was ever possible to stop the Greys, it is my opinion that such an opportunity has already passed us by. They appear to already control our power structure and leadership, our media and military and our food and energy resources. We are, in other words, at their mercy and powerless to prevent them from abducting us, stealing and tampering with our reproductive tissues and DNA and ultimately disposing of us in any way they wish.

There is no reason I am aware of to see the Greys, the Reptilians and their associates as anything other than unwelcome intruders, a direct threat to our world and our species. It stands to reason that if there were a way to force them to stop or to make them go away, it would have been implemented long ago. No such thing has happened. This leads me to believe that one of two things are true: either we are unable to do it or our leadership is being controlled by an alien intelligence and no such efforts will be undertaken on our behalf.

It is the very last conclusion I would wish to come to, the very last answer I would choose to find if I had my way. But my personal preferences have nothing to do with the situation which exists and it is not my intention to attempt to sugar-coat reality attempting to make it seem more palatable and less harsh than it really is.

At the beginning of this manuscript I stated in no uncertain terms that the truth is what we seek, not a substitute for it which we find to be more comforting. We seek to understand the situation as it exists, not to close our eyes to it if it turns out to be unpleasant nor to hide from it if it is revealed to be threatening. If we do indeed seek the truth then we must be willing to state clearly that we appear to be in danger, we appear to be controlled by agents of a hostile non-earth-based intelligence and it seems quite likely that we cannot change those things no matter how much we may wish to. Humanity is revealed to be not the flower of all creation and the master of his world, but rather a creature of feeble capacity and low intelligence which is controlled by extra-terrestrial powers and in danger of being forever at their mercy.

The reality of alien contact does not get much more uncomfortable or threatening than that. The idea that the destruction of one's entire race is completely dependent upon the sufferance of aliens who are by no means our friends and who could--at any time, completely without warning--easily bring our existence to a fast and brutal end is something no researcher ever hopes to discover along the way.

Now the question must be considered very seriously: was the Colonel correct when he said that the military is responsible for all the abductions and that none are performed by the aliens he always referred to as "the visitors"?

This is a difficult idea to accept, when one has had numerous personal contacts with being which certainly appeared to be Type II Greys. It is quite tempting to think that he was wrong about what he said and that abductions are performed by both black ops military forces *and* alien beings.

There is one major problem with doing so, at least from my point of view. There were several things the Colonel said to me at various times that did not match up with something I believed to be true. Several times I made bold to contradict him.

This was a mistake, as it turned out. With the passage of time— my conversations with the Colonel occurred years ago—I have had the opportunity to either obtain addition information about those things from other solid sources or to learn about them the hard way, through personal experience. In every single instance that I have been able to eventually check and be sure about what the correct answer was, the Colonel has been right every single time, and I have been wrong.

He knew precisely what he was talking about—a position which would represent a dream scenario to any ufologist, due to the level of his access and the quality of his information, to say nothing of the literally decades of personal experience in these things that he brought to the table. I was attempting to argue about details with a man who had done this for a living during all of his adult life and who lived in a world where secrets passed across his desk every single day that would merit a death sentence to any unauthorized person who happened to get ahold of them.

The bottom line is this: when you get a source of that quality, which I would think is something that probably only happens to a person once every several lifetimes, you do not presume to argue with that source or to tell it its business. You shut up, listen as carefully as you can and learn as much as possible from someone who can to know infinitely more about the topic from an insider's perspective than anyone else you will ever come across in your life. When he speaks, you shut up and you listen. What you never do it argue with him.

So, then, we return to the question: is it possible that all the abductions are being carried out at the behest of an unsupervised, out-of-control, covert military force?

It is a difficult question, even under the best of circumstances. Clearly, I am hesitant to disagree with the Colonel about this, since every other time I ever did so he turned out to know exactly what he was talking about. Let's consider this carefully for a moment.

Speaking for myself, I am quite certain that I saw and interacted with legitimate Type II Grey aliens on at least one occasion. But that was the incident where all the residents of my apartment complex were brought out of their homes and gathered outside, standing barefoot in several inches of snow in sub-freezing cold. The military was obviously in charge of that event. There is no question about that. A couple of Greys were there with them, but they were carrying out the orders of others, as they always do. In that case, those "others" were the men in charge of the military abduction that was taking place. So, in the end, those Greys don't count for the purposes of this question, other than to confirm that the military does indeed have access to its own Greys and can control them just as if they were worker bees or robotic servitors.

I must believe what the Colonel said about the military having the ability to make their own units appear to be Greys during abduction events. He never lied to me and had no reason to do so. The truth is, he risked his career at the very least simply by talking with me about the topic at all.

I have, since that time, also had the opportunity to confirm this from other sources. They unanimously agree that the military has technologies that effectively prevent abductees from being able to tell whether the being they were looking at was really a Grey or was a cleverly-disguised black ops unit. The most common reaction, just as the Colonel stated, would be for abductees to make the natural assumption that they were dealing with Greys, without ever considering the possibility that it could be special forces in disguise.

All things considered, this makes arriving at an answer we can have a reasonably high degree of confidence in quite a difficult proposition, at best. And it's important that we find the correct answer to this, too, because if it is indeed the military which is carrying out all—or virtually all—of the abductions which are reported, it changes the implications of the situation considerably. In theory, it could change our entire perception of both the Greys and the military in terms of their agenda and intentions, both over the short term and the long term.

So, then—an important question, and one we need to get right if we possibly can. If it turns out that aliens are not actually responsible for abducting *anyone*, which is literally what was asserted by the Colonel, then we would have to consider the possibility that we have spent a lot of years pushing the blame on a group which doesn't deserve it. We might then, in theory, also have incorrectly identified our primary enemy.

Based on my own abduction memories, I must say that it is indeed possible that the military could have been responsible for virtually all of them, if they had utilized alien technology and been disguised as Type II Greys. Though I am quite certain Greys are among the beings I encountered, I do not have a definitive reason to state that they were necessarily in command of any of those abduction events.

Could they have all been planned and supervised by our very own black ops military forces? Yes. It is possible. *Was* the military responsible for all of them? I do not know.

On the other hand, there is no question whatsoever that non-human beings of various descriptions have abducted humans throughout history—the records our ancestors left to us makes this very clear. It is, in my opinion, not something which is even open to debate by a serious person.

A friend of mine named James Bartley, who is a civilian researcher with a background in Naval Intelligence, has stated that anyone who is abducted by the military has previously been abducted by aliens. I consider James to be the most well-informed and experienced person in the world when it comes to the topic of military abductions. I will therefore defer to him on this matter. I am in no position to present evidence which would serve to disprove his statement, and I furthermore know that he would never have made such a statement unless he had good reason to believe it was true.

Also, with all respect to the Colonel—and taking the chance of one more time being someday proven wrong when I disagreed with him about something—it is my personal feeling that alien beings can and do abduct humans. How often this occurs in comparison to military abductions, I have no meaningful way to estimate. I am quite certain, however, that many of the abductions which people believe were the work of Type II Greys were carried out by disguised black ops personnel. I do not think the victims would have any accurate means of telling the difference and naturally believed what their eyes told them. Which, as it turns out, is not always accurate.

What is worse: being repeatedly abducted from the presumed safety of one's own bedroom and then undergoing surgeries performed by emotionless extra-terrestrial beings, or having the same thing done to us by members of our own military special forces units—and, in addition, being starved and worked almost to death as slaves in some dark, rocky mine from the future?

I don't know. Try as I might, I can find no way to justify either of these things in terms of what we think of as ordinary human morality. I can find no way to excuse them or to make them right. I do not know how to forgive those involved, or why anyone should expect to me to. These are beyond being even capital crimes. They are clearly war crimes and there is no reason to believe that they are not being committed every day in a systematic manner which has been ongoing for decades at the very least.

Where does light end and darkness begin? At what point does self-interest trump all the other things that we hold dear? When does the survival of our physical shells begin to outweigh the values and morality which make us human and separate us from the animals? What does it take to cause us to be willing to force enslavement upon our brothers and sisters, to brutally work them without pause even as we cause their bodies to wither away and starve?

I don't know. To think in these terms is something for which I find I am completely unprepared.

Even the act of typing these words on the page is something I am unwilling to do. It requires an act of sheer willpower. It is something I force myself to do, despite the instinctive revulsion that falls around me like a heavy shroud and envelopes my soul even as I attempt to find the words.

At what point do we give ourselves permission to become less than human for the sake of our own survival?

I just don't know. I am not equipped to answer questions such as these. I do not want to even consider them. But there they are.

CHAPTER 18: GENETIC WARFARE

We all know interspecies romance is weird.
-- Tim Burton

"Through these fields of destruction
Baptisms of fire
I've witnessed your suffering
As the battle raged high
And though they did hurt me so bad
In the fear and alarm
You did not desert me, my brothers in arms"
-- Dire Straits

Let us launch our minds out of the box and consider something I like to call Genetic Warfare. To do this, we will need to step back, far back from the personal point of view with which we normally view the world. We are going to step out of the box and consider a form of warfare which is eternal, unavoidable, utterly ruthless, unceasing and always to the death. To do so efficiently, we will imagine watching this war over a grand scale of time, with years and millennia sliding rapidly past.

We all like to think our lives are important—and they are! They are important not only to ourselves but also to our families, friends and associates and in many other ways we need not list here. But stepping back and watching the sweep of history pass by on a grand scale, we can see that any individual life is extremely unlikely to matter much on a scale of ten million or a hundred million years. Not that it can't happen—it can and occasionally does, individuals do sometimes come along who change the world forever...but lives like those on a scale like this are very rare indeed. If you're Genghis Khan, you'll make the list. If you're a dentist or an interior designer (or an author like me) well, it's just not going to happen. A million years from now nobody will know we ever existed at all...and nobody will care, either. That, I suppose, is how it should be and how it must be. It is in any case an inevitable and unavoidable fact—so let's deal with it on its own terms. And so out of the box we go...

On a scale of a million years the value and importance of the individual life rapidly fades away. Over tens and hundreds of millions of years, it is virtually nothing in the big scale of things.

If the individual life is indistinguishable from a billion other lives as the uncounted ages pass, what then is important over the vast stretches of evolutionary time scales?

The only thing which really matters on time scales like these is DNA. Genetics. Reproduction. Because your DNA is at war with every other set of DNA in the known universe and it always will be. What that means in practical terms is this: the only important thing we will ever do in our lives on this time scale is reproduce. The most successful DNA is always in the long run the DNA which produces the highest number of viable offspring and sends them forth into the world to copy the genetic information by producing yet more healthy offspring. If you don't have children—for any reason—your unique individual genetic code, your DNA, will be lost forever when you die. Your DNA will vanish from the genetic pool and will have failed to perform its one over-riding purpose. It was not successful and it won't be seen again.

Consider the Black Widow spider. The only purpose it has in the entire world is to attempt to cover the surface of planet Earth with black widow spiders. Nothing else it does matters, so long as it continues to reproduce all it possibly can. With luck, maybe it can end up making a million copies of itself, a million Black Widows which could in theory each go out and produce a million more copies of the DNA, each of which would in turn bring forth a million more in a cycle which is theoretically infinite and which, if not interrupted, would in short order cover the face of the Earth with Black Widow spiders.

Fortunately, they don't all have a million each and some get stepped on before they can lay any eggs at all. But the point is the same as far as the spider is concerned. Its only job is to either fertilize as many females as possible (usually that number is "one", for these males—they're not called Black Widows for nothing!) or to lay as many eggs as possible during its lifetime.

If the genetic information is copied and spread to new generations of spiders, it has fulfilled its only truly important function. Sending its own DNA forward in time helps its kind survive and prosper over the long term in a way nothing else ever could. It is, in a very real sense, the only form of immortality or eternal life available to a flesh-and-blood organism.

It is the same way--always and forever--with every living organism on the planet. A rabbit's primary evolutionary duty is to have as many baby rabbits as it can, attempting in its own way to cover the entire world with rabbits and sending its own unique genetic markers into the future, another generation of itself which will continue to do battle with all competing DNA types and attempt to once again successfully reproduce and carry on the genetic line. The hawk which catches it will try to cover the world with hawks. A flea will try to cover it with fleas. And so on.

This eternal struggle for life and dominance and the continuation of a species is by no means limited to just animals. Plants, too, do battle in a never-ending war of domination and conquest waged against every other plant they encounter. They will compete for sunshine, soil and water. They will wrap themselves around their competitor's trunk as they grow and attempt to choke the life out of it and so gain all that precious sunshine and topsoil for their own exclusive use. They will try to grow taller than the plants around them, to be able to utilize the maximum amount of sunlight possible (while at the same time denying it to the competition). They will each produce a multitude of seeds, attempting to cover the world with their offspring.

If dandelions can find a way to take over your yard, they will. If cedar can find a way to push Douglas fir off a hillside or out of an area and take it over, it surely and inevitably will do so. Such is the nature of unceasing genetic warfare and of the eternal dominance dance of heredity, succession and DNA.

In modern society, medical technology and living conditions are such that most people can be expected to successfully reproduce at some point. This has the effect over the long term of weakening the gene pool because we make a practice of feeding those who cannot feed themselves, providing shelter and food to those who do not have it, giving them free medical care when necessary, etc. Survival of the fittest does not really apply in that sense because for the most part everybody can have kids regardless of their fitness, intelligence or physical prowess.

How, then, do various genetic lines compete in a world where the weak are artificially protected and even encouraged to reproduce?

Money, power and influence. Opportunities afforded to your genetic line which are denied to others. The wealthy attend the finest schools and universities, live in the finest homes on the best land, know all the right people, grease all the right palms and provide their offspring with virtual assurance of success, prosperity and eventual wealth themselves while a night clerk at a mini-mart struggles just to pay her power bill and keep a little gas in her car. When we look beyond the superficial and step backward, we can see that this is nothing but another form of genetic warfare taking place—just as it always has and always will.

If you want to fulfill your one and only primary duty to the eons, then, and if you want to succeed in the only thing which will matter a thousand years from now...get rich, very rich. And have as many children as possible.

The most successful human DNA in history, by the way, belonged to Genghis Khan. By conquering and raping his way across most of the known world at the time, it is estimated that 8% of the male population across a huge part of Eurasia carries his DNA and that one in every two hundred men worldwide are by now descended in some way from him! His methods, though brutal and socially repugnant, were nevertheless tremendously effective in terms of carrying out his hereditary duty to his unique genetic footprint—in fact, nobody else in human history even comes close to this level of effectiveness.

Now we will step backward even further, to the point where Earth itself is too small to even be seen and our sun is just a tiny point of light in a sky filled with hundreds of billions of suns. Across this galaxy, on every one of the surely billions of worlds which support some form of life, this dance of death and succession proceeds apace and without end. Predators, prey, empires and forest fires, it continues always across each of those other worlds just as it does on our own.

It is nothing less than an eternal interstellar genetic war. There are intelligent beings on many of those worlds who have developed the means to travel rapidly and efficiently between the stars. They have been expanding outward, spreading their genetics and their racial DNA imprint to other worlds and other realities. Just like the Black Widow spider, their over-riding and imperative racial duty when considered in terms of the vast scope of passing eons, is to try to cover not just one world this time, but every habitable world in the entire galaxy with copies of themselves and thus be crowned King of the Hill and the ultimate victor in a genetic war which due to the nature of DNA itself can never be avoided or settled by any type of negotiations.

Now let's step back into the box for a minute and think about all that. The first thing which had better occur to us is this: extra-terrestrials of many dozens of races and types are already known to either visit this world occasionally or to inhabit it permanently even as we speak. And what is their goal? The same goal any other DNA receptacle would have, the same one you or I would have if we were in their place. It's to try to cover the entire face of the planet with copies of themselves and to do eternal battle with any other forms of DNA which resist their onslaught or present a danger to them in some way by eliminating, enslaving or consuming it. Think about THAT for a minute, if you will!

Among such a vast and diverse group of interstellar races as we already know exists—and there are without question many more intelligent races scattered throughout this galaxy of which we are still unaware, surely many times more than our scant knowledge at present allows us to have come across at this earliest stage of human space travel—all races and groups will not always get along. They will have disagreements, they will engage in competition for resources and for dominance and control of desirable uninhabited worlds by their own kind, their own genetic lines.

It is an established fact that interstellar warfare has and does take place between various factions of our ET visitors. There have been multiple historical reports of large numbers of people witnessing wars in the sky, chariots of fire blasting each other apart in our own atmosphere. Such violence, when it occurs, is by no means limited to our own little world—it takes place in all areas of conflict just as it does here. It is even said that there are two ET groups which have been waging constant war against each other for over a billion years.

When the proximate causes and intrigues of such interstellar conflicts are stripped away and we step back once again and view the situation through the span of eons, it becomes quite clear that what we are looking at is one more example of genetic warfare in action, this time on an interplanetary and interstellar scale. Everybody out there is, in their own way and using their own methods, instinctively attempting to conquer not just single worlds but the whole galaxy by covering it with copies of its own DNA. The harsh reality of the bottom line is this: if somebody else beats them to it, they will lose the genetic sweepstakes by being the second-to-the-last race left standing. Clearly that is a position nobody would wish to occupy and one which nobody would allow to occur if they had the power to stop it from happening.

Now we are constantly told about friendly extra-terrestrial races, visitors who have come here only to aid and assist us in our development as a people. I do not doubt that friendly and helpful extra-terrestrials exist—there are too many reliable witnesses to think otherwise. But we must keep in mind that for all their friendliness they, too, have their limitations.

Apparently, some among us believe that all of this assistance they want to give us will be undertaken at their own expense utilizing their people, resources, time and energy in a purely philanthropic mission to aid a human race which freely admits it is violent, brutal, dishonest, manipulative, scheming, cruel, warlike, bigoted, greedy, selfish, vain and untrustworthy. Ask yourself: would you spend your money, time and energy to help a race which fits that profile?

Would you send your sons and daughters forth into the galaxy to a faraway world to assist a race of killer apes who would surely declare war on your own civilization and conquer it if they had the ability to do so? What would motivate you to decide like that? If you chose to assist them, would you not have an ulterior motive for doing so, some reason that assisting them would in some way be profitable or helpful to you rather than be nothing but a large drain of your resources and manpower?

Why should we presume that the so-called "friendly" ET's do not have motives for helping us that we know nothing about and which do not involve benefiting humanity but instead are intended to benefit the ET races in question? I would never make such a presumption and you probably shouldn't either.

Going by our own history, the odds that they are spending their resources purely for our benefit without intending to somehow be reimbursed or emerge with a profit or advantage of some kind are very small indeed. That alone is in my opinion reason enough to bet against it being the case.

In the long term, they will ultimately be engaging in genetic warfare no matter where they go or what they do, as will we. There is no way to avoid it. Without the fact of genetic warfare, it could easily be said that life itself has no objective purpose and no long-term value or worth.

No sane and rational race or group would ever sacrifice its own genetic code for the benefit of the genetic code possessed by a race from another world. To do so would amount to racial suicide, voluntary consignment to oblivion. Such a thing is unthinkable. It is also out of the question, because the over-riding instinct of any life form must be reproduction of its own DNA—even if an alien race should consciously make the decision to do such a thing, the DNA itself would ultimately override that choice and ensure that breeding and reproduction continued one way or another.

Whether we realize that we are engaged in eternal genetic warfare against not only our own kind but all other DNA in existence, our DNA at a cellular level realizes it very well indeed.

It has no intention of losing that war and will do anything within its power to make sure it does not, regardless of what our own personal intentions might be.

I often make the point that for all the extra-terrestrials who claim to be our friends and who say they want only to assist us, such assistance to this point has not resulted in anything we can actually notice or identify. The alleged assistance we have been given could easily be thought to be nothing but a series of high-minded diatribes written by humans themselves with no outside assistance of any kind.

In practical terms, if one were to take the position that they have so far not helped us in any way that matters, it would be quite difficult to argue against that statement. If one were to say that as best we can tell they have in fact not helped us in any way at all up to this point, there is no rebuttal argument which can be made because there is no way to identify what that help may have been and therefore there is no reason to think any help was really given.

There will surely be many who would point out that such a viewpoint is jaded and I will not disagree with them. I do, however, think it is fair to say that the viewpoint—jaded though it may be—is also accurate. I would also mention that I have never yet met anyone who could demonstrate that it is incorrect other than by presenting an argument which consists entirely of wishful thinking and personal hopes being projected onto a reality which does not support them.

What if helping us would result in an attack by the Reptilian/Grey consortium against their own home world and possibly result in its destruction? If that is the case, no help will be forthcoming no matter how much they might wish to assist us. They can be expected to do the same thing we would do under such conditions: withhold assistance and thereby protect our own interests, which is another way of saying that our top priority would be to ensure the safety of our own DNA and all other considerations would be secondary to that one.

Even if that is not the case, even if they can safely help us progress and choose to do so, the eternal drumbeat of genetic warfare will never cease and dominance will always be its only purpose. If at some point in the future we find ourselves in a situation of disagreement or conflict with even the friendliest of extra-terrestrial races, if it comes down to the choice of them or us...they will most assuredly not choose "us". Their DNA itself will make very sure of that.

This long-term perspective and the fact that it is inevitable, unceasing and impossible to avoid should give us ample reason to keep our guard up always and never intentionally allow ourselves to be placed in a position where our existence is in the hands of extra-terrestrials rather than ourselves. It may well be impossible to avoid ending up in such a position—in fact we may very well occupy it at this very moment. If so, it gives us even more reason to be aware that if the race or races which hold our fate in their hands ever decides it must choose between its own interests and our survival...that will be the day we lose the genetic war for good.

CHAPTER 19: QUESTIONS AND ANSWERS

"I can assure you that flying saucers, given that they exist, are not constructed by any power on earth."
--U.S. President Harry Truman, 1950

Oh, hear me cryin' 'cause the people like me,
That long to be free, are not actually.
Please everybody won't you hear this song,
Help a country that's wrong, to someday be strong."
-- Grand Funk Railroad

As we approach the end of this first volume, I thought it might be helpful to take a preliminary look at some of the questions which needed to be asked, as well as provide the answers to as many as I can. Though my research has been far too exhaustive and extended over too long a period of years to allow me to include anything resembling a complete bibliography as far as listing the sources of my information goes, I have not drawn any conclusions based on information which I do not feel have been either confirmed by multiple credible sources or are otherwise known by me to be true.

This is far from a complete list of the questions we would like to be able to answer in a perfect world, but it is enough to cover the aspects of alien contact we have dealt with so far. More questions and answers will be provided in the second volume, some of them dealing with highly complex topics we have yet to come to in our investigation.

Q: Does intelligent alien life exist? If so, is it present on and around Earth right now?

A: Absolutely. It exists and it is present on and around Earth.

Q: How do we know that the whole thing is not part of a carefully-planned, intricate, long-term psychological warfare operation which includes the use of exotic aircraft, aimed at convincing people that aliens exist to cover up a different covert operation which is in progress?

A: This is a possibility which has been raised by many serious people and I think it is a reasonable and logical objection, on the surface. I do not agree that this is the case, however. There have been too many people of high rank, whose credibility is beyond question, who have spoken out about alien contact for us to be able to write the whole thing off as an intricate psy op. There have also been too many witnesses who have reported seeing alien beings to reasonably presume that all of them have been victimized by even the most large-scale covert deception program, and these witnesses span the globe. There are many NASA mission photos and films in existence which clearly show evidence of vehicles and facilities which cannot be of human manufacture. Many military pilots have reported pursuing them at high speeds and many military personnel have reported interacting with alien beings while involved in clandestine programs. The weight of the evidence must be judged to conclusively demonstrate that alien contact is indeed a fact.

Q: Is the U.S. government aware that aliens exist?

A: Absolutely. This is beyond question.

Q: Does the U.S. government consider at least some of these visitors to be dangerous?

A: Yes. Again, this is beyond question.

Q: Is the U.S. government involved in a conspiracy of silence regarding the alien presence? Will it kill to protect those secrets?

A: Yes, and yes. Both these things have been demonstrated repeatedly and are established beyond any reasonable doubt.

Q: Has the United States signed one or more treaty agreements with alien powers or nations?

A: Yes, we have. We signed at least one with the Draco co-op in the late 1950's. This is established as true by the reports of multiple witnesses, all of whom describe the same conditions for the treaty and circumstances under which it was signed. I have heard that we are involved in at least two other treaty arrangements with other groups, though I cannot say with certainty which groups those may have been.

Q: Are some of these non-human races friendly toward humanity?

A: It appears that they are non-hostile—for now. Whether they are friendly, I consider a question which has yet to be resolved to my satisfaction. They appear to have carried out some friendly and helpful actions on behalf of a small number of individuals whom they have contacted. They have not provided any help of a substantial nature that has benefited the population, nor is there any evidence that they have acted to defend us against those races and groups with are hostile to us. Personally, I classify these alien races and groups as being in a neutral, non-interventionist position at present. It is possible that some of them might wish to genuinely assist us, but they are prevented from doing so due to agreements they have with other spacefaring civilizations (including, presumably, the Draco).

Q: Can we ever trust NASA?

A: No. NASA has been definitively proven over time to be dishonest and deceptive. They have intentionally tricked the American public and have acted for the most part as a propaganda and diversion tactic to take public attention off the projects which the government deemed more important and wished to conceal from the public.

Q: Are the grey aliens really humans from the future who have had genetic problems and come backward in time, hoping to find a solution for them?

A: No. This is a lie. There is absolutely no reason to believe that we evolved into the Greys, or even that we would evolve into such a form naturally in any case. The fact that the Greys are an artificially-created race has been established and must be considered a fact.

Q: Is Bigfoot really an alien?

A: There has never been a credible report which involves a Bigfoot utilizing technology of any kind or interacting with an alien race. There has never been a legitimate inside source who has come forward and reported that Bigfoot is an intelligent alien being or that they are in any way associated with such beings. I consider reports which speak of things like this to be fraudulent and anyone who claims to have seen such a thing personally I consider to be lying. Aliens come in many different shapes, sizes and configurations...but Bigfoot is not one of them.

Q: Are the Space Brothers really going to help us solve our problems and rid ourselves of any hostile elements?

A: No. We are on our own. If they were going to help, they would surely have done so long before now. The best information indicates that they have previously made agreements with other cosmic races or groups which prevent them from becoming directly involved in our affairs on a global basis. They may occasionally assist humans individually, but that is the extent of the assistance we should expect or that they will provide.

Q: Are the Roswell-type Greys considered to be hostile?

A: In my opinion, anything which has a habit of consuming humans must be considered hostile and unwanted on this planet. I have never seen anyone give a reason to consider them as being anything other than an invasive alien race. They are generally believed to be in a cooperative relationship with the Draco and others. In my opinion they should be considered hostile, highly dangerous and unwelcome on Earth.

Q: What is the deal with those big, black almond-shaped eyes the Type II Greys have?

A: The best information available to me states that these are not actually their eyes, but are instead dark, artificial covers which are attached over their eyes. "Eye caps" is how they were described to me. They serve to protect their natural eyes, which are extremely sensitive, from bright lights. This is also one reason Greys are almost never spotted during the daytime—they prefer to operate during the hours of darkness.

These eye caps might also serve additional purposes, for all I know. It is possible that they contain technology which enhances the natural psi abilities of the Greys or serves some other purpose. But all I know for certain is that they are used to protect their natural eyes, which are apparently much smaller and round, from bright lights.

I would note that it makes sense that these would be some type of artificial coverings rather than their natural eyes because the large, dark "eyes" we think we are looking at do not contain pupils, irises, coronas or any means of moving the eyes or changing the degree of focus to compensate for changes in distance.

Q: I once saw a video online which claimed to show an attack on a NASA facility located in Fort Worth, Texas by aliens. Is that film legitimate? Was that facility really attacked by aliens?

A: The film is legitimate and yes, that facility was really attacked by aliens. I know several people who live in Fort Worth and who saw the attack take place. They all agree that the film clip shows a real event. In addition, I have several sources within NASA and the military who have confirmed that this is the case.

Our military forces found and took possession of an ancient artifact which was located deep within a cave in Iraq (or Afghanistan, according to some reports) and which was of alien origin. The artifact was transported to the United States and stored at that facility, which is attached to airport in Fort Worth, Texas.

It was reportedly an example of a craft known in India as a "Vimana". Ancient Indian texts, written thousands of years ago, describe the Vimana in detail as well as including drawings of them made by the people who had seen them.

Per those texts, there were several types of Vimana, some of which were made available to certain Indian mystics or kings for purposes of rapid transportation and enlightenment. The records of the time also describe these vehicles of being up to seven stories tall and of taking part in ancient wars in the sky which were witnessed by the people of the time. The Vimana are described as having the ability to become invisible to sight (a cloaking device of some kind), to travel through the air at very high rates of speed, to be capable of utilizing weapons which fit the description of laser beam weapons, and even to make use of nuclear or thermonuclear weapons as well. There is a description contained in these texts of an ancient city which was destroyed "by the gods" and the description is virtually a perfect match for the description of a city which has been attacked by an atomic bomb. The residents who were not incinerated had their skin burned, their hair and fingernails fell out a short time afterward and they fell ill and died of what was surely radiation poisoning.

The Vimana which was in the cave was reportedly around 5000 years old. It has been said that it was the Vimana which was made available to Zarathustra, also known as Zoroaster, for his personal use. Whether that is true or not is unknown to me.

The Vimana which was located by the American troops was reportedly protected within something known as a "time well", an artificially-generated field which kept the Vimana within it in a perfect state of preservation and in full working condition despite the passage of long periods of time. Gaining entry to this time well reportedly cost the lives of eight soldiers.

This ancient Vimana was a craft of such power that the aliens did not want us to possess it and potentially make use of it. To prevent such use from occurring, they launched an attack on the facility which apparently involved lasers and plasma beam weapons fired from several alien spacecraft, some of which can be seen moving through the air above the facility in the film clip. The attack lasted for almost a half hour and resulted in the death of at least five hundred soldiers and employees of the facility.

At least five different people filmed the event as it was taking place, each of them capturing it from a different location near the facility and with a different angle of view. All the film clips are, as best I can determine, legitimate.

Q: How can I be certain that some or all my abduction memories are not simply screen memories rather than the real thing?

A: I cannot be certain of that. Memories which I personally believe to have been likely screen memories, I did not include in my testimony. It is possible that some of the memories I included are screen memories, but if so I doubt it is the case with more than a couple of them. I should add that there are still some things which remain to be discussed about alien abductions that will be covered in the second volume of this series.

Q: Are the reports of the military having time travel capability true?

A: They are indeed. This is a difficult thing to accept as the truth. I fully understand that because it was the same way for me when I was first exposed to it. But, having been exposed to it, I can say without question that this technology does in fact exist and has probably been in the hands of the military for at least the past half century.

Q: I have found your book to be a big disappointment. I feel it was a waste of money. How can I punish you?

A: Log on to the website of the store or distributor you purchased the book from. Look up the title of this book and add a Customer Review. Give it a rating of only a single star and in the comments section tell people why you didn't like it. This will let others know that the book is no good and will discourage them from purchasing it. Thank you for your honest feedback, I appreciate it very much.

Q: I have found your book to be quite interesting and would like to encourage others to read it. How can I do this?

A: Log on to the website of the store or distributor you purchased the book from. Look up the title of this book and add a Customer Review. Give it a five-star rating and in the comments section tell people what you liked about it and why they should purchase a copy.

This will encourage them to order a copy. Thank you for your honest feedback, I appreciate it very much.

Q: Why should we believe any of the things you are telling us about alien contact?

A: If the situation today was what it was a couple of decades ago, my answer would probably be as follows: "You shouldn't. You should go out and do the research yourself, if you're able to. If you are not, or if you should choose to believe that the things I have told you here represent the actual truth, you will have saved yourself an enormous amount of time which would have otherwise been spent doing research that I have already done."

Unfortunately, the situation today is far different than the situation was in the past. The pace of events is rapidly accelerating and the technological capabilities which can be turned against the civilian population have become so incredibly versatile and effective that the plain truth is that if you are new to the study of ufology, you simply no longer have enough time available to do the necessary research on your own. Long before you would be able to finish doing the research, events will almost certainly unfold which will result in making that type of research redundant and pointless. The reasons for this and the events we can expect to take place over the next several years will be covered in the forthcoming book "Alien Contact: Paradigm Shift". I recommend that those who read this book also make it a point to read that one as well.

To be clear, I do not mean to imply that the government is going to disclose the truth any time soon. I intend rather to observe that the world around us is going downhill at an ever-increasing pace and the United States of America is headed straight down the path toward a fascist dictatorship, a police state which is run for the benefit of the bankers and corporate tycoons and where everybody else will be considered useless and worthless. It is not going to do anybody a whole lot of good to learn about aliens when they are struggling to survive in a prison camp located in a police state that used to be the world's great beacon of liberty and hope.

I do not, nor have I ever, made the statement that anyone should necessarily believe anything I say on my word alone. In the end, anything I say falls into the category of being the testimony of a single person. As such, it is open to reasonable doubt about its veracity and subject to being checked against the statements of other witnesses for consistency and accuracy. That is standard procedure and due diligence and I encourage anyone who wishes to compare my statements with the statements of others to do so freely and then form their own opinion about the things I have said here.

At the same time, I would humbly suggest that it will be to your advantage if you choose to accept me as a well-informed source who has studied the topic intensely and who has sufficient personal experience and connections to be able to make credible statements on the subject. I hope you will agree that I have demonstrated both tough-minded skepticism and hard-headed logic throughout the course of this manuscript, as well as being careful to point out that there are many things I do *not* know.

It is far better to have a correct understanding of the situation and some warning of the things which have been planned for us than it is to be caught unaware and by surprise when everything is on the line. This is what I have tried my best to provide here.

Choose as you will. I simply offer the information. What you decide to do with it, and whether you decide to believe it at all, is completely up to you.

Q: Each of us have our own truths. Why can't you concentrate on your individual truth and have the decency to leave mine alone?

A: Because I don't care what your "personal truth" is. Whatever it may be, it has absolutely no effect on me and it never will. I am interested only in objective truths.

I am far more interested, for example, in learning about the true extent of alien influence within our political and military organizations—something which affects us all—than I am in hearing about your belief that you have several extra strands of DNA which, though invisible, are simply awaiting your spiritual enlightenment to be activated and allow you to advance to the fourth density and take your place among a galactic order of friendly aliens. I am far more concerned about attempting to find ways to stop people from being abducted by aliens than I am about learning that it is your individual truth that all aliens are our brothers and have come here to assist us.

Please listen to the following words as closely as you can, because I have chosen them with great care, and have done so only after spending most of my adult life researching these matters. The idea that all extra-terrestrials have come here to assist humanity is demonstrably untrue. It is nothing short of ridiculous. All the people who live within a hundred yards of me don't even want to assist me, much less be my friends. To imagine that all the aliens in the galaxy do is nothing but ignorant, uninformed nonsense. If you are ever to have any realistic hope of penetrating the shield of lies and getting to the truth, you're going to have to drastically improve the level of your game. That's just how it is.

As for the notion that humans have twelve strands of DNA, ten of which can only be observed from a fourth-density perspective, there is absolutely no evidence anywhere that such a thing is true, nor is there any reason that I am aware of to spend any time at all seriously considering such an idea. Time is swiftly running out and we do not have any to waste on foolishness or wishful thinking.

Convincing people to spend their time on those things is one of the major objectives of the psychological warfare campaign that is being waged against us. The fact that there are people who seriously believe that we have extra fourth-density strands of DNA just because someone claims to have channeled that information is an indication of just how successful that campaign has been.

So, as I said, I am not at all interested in what your "personal truth" about these things might happen to be. While you are trying to convince people that you have some spare strands of invisible DNA, I am trying to do something which might be constructive and helpful. That's a big difference, and I'm not going to change my course or do you the discourtesy of pretending that it's okay to be ignorant or that foolishness is something we can afford to live with.

It's not. We can't. Life is short. Nobody can afford to waste their time believing in fairy tales.

I am not here to hold anybody's hand or to comfort them with words of peace and love when my home planet is being controlled by an alien race whose technology which is millions of years ahead of our own. I am working on the cutting edge. It's a dangerous and stressful place to be, but somebody must step up and take that responsibility.

People who believe in invisible strands of DNA are not anywhere close to the cutting edge. They are, so to speak, dog paddling around in the shallows. Sadly, most of them will probably remain there for the rest of their lives because they are committed to defending their preferred point of view rather than coming to terms with truths they are unwilling to accept.

I learned long ago that it is pointless waste of time to attempt to argue with people who refuse to listen, and I have no intention of doing so here. Virtually none of those people will ever read this book, much less take it seriously, so there is nothing I can do for them.

Truth is not to be found lurking in the shallows. If it is truth we seek, we must abandon the safe harbors. We must brave the perils of black water—deep, uncharted seas far from the safety of home and the shore. It is not a place for the faint of heart…and that is where we are bound. We will break free of our chains and look to the far horizon, knowing as we do that all men can and must be brothers…and that all of us will ultimately share the same fate.

CHAPTER 20: A GIFT OF LIGHT

"When I reach for the edge of the universe, I do so knowing that along some lines of cosmic inquiry there are times when, at least for now, one must be content to love the questions themselves."
-- Neil deGrasse Tyson

"School's out for summer!"
-- Alice Cooper

As we near the end of this book, much has been discussed but much remains to be learned. If we are to eventually arrive at a clear, balanced and reasonably accurate picture of reality as it exists, it is going to require a lot of effort on our part. There are no shortcuts to be found here, nor are there any answers which will satisfy everyone.

Nobody can truthfully claim to have all the answers when it comes to this subject, nor can we ever reasonably hope to arrive at a place where we have them ourselves. The questions are too numerous, the answers too difficult to ascertain and the number of disciplines which are ultimately involved are far too great for any one person to be able to master. Try as we might, we have no choice but to accept the fact that such absolute knowledge is beyond our grasp.

This is not necessarily a bad thing. The fact that we will never have all the answers is in fact one of the aspects of this subject which can be of the most value to us. It provides us with a field of research which is, for all practical purposes, limitless in nature and there is never an end to the learning. I have found this truth to be something which serves to keep me motivated and interested in continuing to expand my knowledge: no matter how much I may manage to learn, there will always be more which is unknown than which is known.

If you happen to be a person with an insatiable curiosity, as I am, the subject of alien contact provides an arena of limitless opportunity and unending potential for the expansion of our personal awareness and understanding of reality and our place within it. I can think of few things which are more worthy of a sustained and dedicated effort than seeking knowledge of such a profound, mysterious and intimate nature than this.

For that reason, I find the subject of alien contact to be endlessly fascinating in a way nothing else I am aware of even remotely approaches. Regardless of what your personal beliefs about it may be, the reality of the situation is that alien contact affects each of us in a multitude of ways every single day of our lives. The effects are concealed with great care and cleverness. Nevertheless, it is a fact that everything from the things we are taught in school to the taxes we pay to our eventual fate as individuals and as a human society are affected by the fact that extra-terrestrials are present on and around our world.

Those who hold the true power in this world have gone to great lengths to instill certain beliefs in us and to manipulate our view of many things. These beliefs do not necessarily have anything at all to do with reality, nor should we assume they do.

We understand human nature well enough to understand that it is virtually beyond question that these powerful individuals and groups are primarily interested in serving their own purposes and looking after their own welfare. The best interests of the rest of us do not appear to matter at all to them. That is the reality of the situation and it serves no useful purposes to pretend otherwise.

If you happen to feel this book contains too little alien content, I ask you to accept it as it is and trust that the alien content you are looking for will be coming in the second volume. When it does, you will be able to maximize your ability to understand it and put it to use immediately. The groundwork must first be put into place—that's just how it is, it's the nature of the terrain.

To the best of my ability, what I have done with this first volume is to present the curriculum I feel would be necessary if one were to enroll at a major university in a program which would lead to a postgraduate degree in the field of Ufology. The volume which follows this one will contain what will effectively be the equivalent of a second year of instruction on the topic by a qualified and motivated instructor.

When you finish reading these books, if I have my way, you are going to be competent and well-informed to a degree that most people will find both shocking and a little bit scary.

It is my firm belief that if the student—and we are *all* students here, always—consistently utilizes the principles I laid out during their investigations, they will be well served. They will be difficult to fool and the answers which they eventually find will have a high probability of being accurate.

Considering the amount of effort and the degree of difficulty involved in finding such answers, the ability to have high confidence in their accuracy is something which is literally beyond price. If I have accomplished nothing else here, I hope I have at least managed to pass this along to those who read this book.

I also hope that I have been able to share some of the things I have learned throughout a lifetime of research with people who will appreciate them and utilize them in a way which both increases their knowledge and assists them during future investigations they choose to undertake. There seems to be little purpose in dedicating so much time and hard work to attaining knowledge of something, only to keep it to oneself. Sharing what I have learned with my brothers and sisters is one of the greatest joys of my life, as well as something I consider to be my responsibility to those of my kind, and this has always been my primary motivation throughout the course of writing this book.

Though it will of course be up to others to decide how successfully I have done so, I am satisfied that I have cut no corners, pulled no punches and given it my best effort. A great deal of time and care has gone into the preparation of both this volume and the one which will soon follow it and I will never be cursed with the thought that, if I had only been more careful or taken more time in their preparation, I could have done a better job. For better or worse, these combined manuscripts represent my best work and I will have no regrets about it regardless of what the verdict of the public may eventually turn out to be. If I could have done more, I certainly would have. What I could do I have done to the best of my ability and with all the skills at my disposal.

As I prepare to send this creation of mine out into the world to await its judgment, my greatest hope is that those who read it will find it to be worth their time and that it will help them in some way to understand certain aspects of alien contact in a deeper and more complete way than they did before. If this turns out to be the case, I will be satisfied that I have done my job regardless of how many copies it may or may not ultimately sell.

As the reader is surely aware, we have at this point barely scratched the surface of this multifaceted, endlessly mysterious subject. There is much that remains to be discussed and many things of importance that I have yet to share with you. As information-dense as this manuscript has turned out to be, the volumes which are to follow it are likely to be even more so. They will discuss topics of greater complexity and will touch upon many things related to alien contact which are completely foreign to us in terms of the way we have been taught to see the universe and the limits we have been told are placed upon reality, when it often turns out that no such limits actually exist.

It is no exaggeration to note that if we are to have any hope of understanding our alien visitors in more than a superficial way, it requires us to discard and dispense with many of the ideas we have been brought up to believe in. As has been the case with every generation which came before us, many of the things they were taught in school have turned out to be incorrect. As has also been the case with every generation which came before us, the scientists themselves were among the last to notice that fact and accept it.

Without first laying the groundwork as I have done in this first volume, it would not be possible for the reader to effectively absorb and properly understand the material which will be made available to them in the second volume. To build a strong and lasting structure, one must begin by constructing a broad and sturdy framework which will support it. That is what I have attempted to do here.

No matter who you are, no matter how hard you may have studied and how much knowledge you may have attained, I hope I have successfully shared information here which is new to you and that you feel both your time and your money were well spent. Surely one cannot hope for or expect more than that.

Most books on the topic ultimately turn out to add little to our knowledge, and many are written for purely mercenary purposes. These books are unlike that in every possible way. They are intended to inform the reader to the maximum extent possible, to do so at an affordable price and to leave the reader in a position where they will almost always find that they possess a more thorough and detailed knowledge of the subject than anybody else in the room, no matter what room they might happen to find themselves in.

They are not intended for beginners, although beginners will find much here that can be of use to them. I have long felt that there is a need for more discussion of these topics at an advanced level and that this type of discussion, while it can occasionally be found, is not contained in the great majority of books which are available to the public.

It could be said that a superficial knowledge is better than none. I have found it to be true, however, that a superficial knowledge can often result in a misperception of the underlying realities. It can prevent people from gaining a level of understanding which is necessary to be well-informed. It is my intention here to provide a remedy for this situation, to the best of my ability.

I will never claim to be the world's top authority on this or any other subject. I will never imagine that I have all the answers and, like anyone, I am perfectly capable of making mistakes.

Even so, it is within my power to know *some* of the answers. By reading these books you can share in that knowledge in a way which is far easier and carries less risk than does coming by them the hard way, as I did.

Incomplete as my understanding may be, I offer it to you with all the sincerity and honesty I am capable of. As weak and insufficient as they may be, I offer you my shoulders to stand on as you continue your search for truth and I commend you for having the courage to make the attempt.

We are all in this together, brothers and sisters, whether we agree about certain things or not. We will ultimately succeed together or be destroyed together. The stakes cannot possibly be higher…and our time is swiftly running out.

With that said, have a nice summer and I'll hopefully see you here when classes resume for another round of discussion and shared knowledge. We still have far to go, but I am confident that the information we have covered so far will serve you well when we take on subjects and issues which will challenge our minds and reveal many more strange and wondrous things which lie hidden behind the veil of illusion.

Class dismissed.

THE END

44361377R00174

Made in the USA
Middletown, DE
04 June 2017